Internet Privacy For Dummies®

Sensible Steps for Avoiding Online Disasters

- Use a password to limit access to your computer and important files.
- And, for goodness' sake, use hard-to-guess passwords and change them often!
- Keep your operating system and important software updated with current security patches.
- Install a good antivirus program and update it regularly (once a month and whenever you hear news about a new virus).
- Back up your data regularly, and keep the backups someplace safe.
- E-mail never goes away because any recipient can keep copies of it, so think twice before you write. If you don't want something you write coming back to haunt you, learn to use encryption.
- When someone sends you files by e-mail, think twice before opening them and always run your virus-scanning program.
- If anybody unknown to you asks for your password or credit card number, tell that person to buzz off.
- Before giving any personal information to a Web site, always check the Web site's privacy policy first.
- At least once a month, clear out cookies from your browser and scan for spyware with a program like Ad-Aware, from Lavasoft.

Safe Banking, Stock Trading, and Shopping Online

- Use a browser with 128-bit encryption.
- Make sure that your bank, broker, or store uses a secure server.
- Make sure that your broker is a member of the Securities Investor Protection Corporation (SIPC).
- Always read the privacy policy to determine how your private information will be used and with whom it might be shared.
- Learn from the mistakes of others: Check out consumer rating services to see how your vendors rate.
- Online escrow services can help prevent rip-offs when you're buying goods on auction sites.
- Once a month, check your credit card and phone bills for unauthorized charges.
- Check your credit report every six months.
- Identity thieves love your trash, so buy a shredder!
- Be suspicious of any e-mail or instant message that asks (or sends you to a Web page that asks) for your password, account number, or credit card information.

Tracking Down Spammers

Follow these steps to track down spammers in your e-mail:

1. Look at the e-mail headers in the message.
2. Follow the flow of Received headers backward from your ISP.
3. Identify the owner of the last verifiable e-mail-handling server.
4. Look for URLs and e-mail addresses in the contents of the spam.
5. Track down the correct addresses for every one who should receive the complaint.
6. Send a firm but politely worded complaint.
7. Await responses.
8. If complaints bounce back, continue complaining upstream.
9. If your complaints are ignored, report the spammer to a blocking list.
10. If all else fails, complain to your ISP.

For Dummies: Bestselling Book Series for Beginners

Telemarketing-Call Logging Form and Script

Ask each question as written. Be courteous but serious. Your call may be recorded, so speak clearly. If the telemarketer refuses to answer your questions or is confused, ask to speak with that person's supervisor. Write down each response on the blank line following the question or circle Yes or No.

Today's date: _____   Time: _____ : _____ a.m. / p.m.

"Can you please give me your full name?" Write caller's name:

_____

If you're speaking with a supervisor, ask for her full name:

_____

"You're calling on behalf of?" Write caller's organization:

_____

"Do you work for that organization, or did they just hire your company to do the telemarketing?"

If the person works for a telemarketer, ask: "Can you tell me your company's name and mailing address?" Write name and address:

_____

"In case we get disconnected, can I also get your company's phone number, area code first?" Write number:

_____

"Does your organization keep a list of phone numbers that it has been asked not to call?" Circle: Yes / No

"I want you to put my number on your do-not-call list. Can you do that now?" Circle: Yes / No

"Does your company make telemarketing calls for any other organizations?" Circle: Yes / No

If the answer is Yes, ask "Can you make sure that your company won't call me for any other organization?" Circle: Yes / No

"Will your company keep my number on its do-not-call list for at least ten years?" Circle: Yes / No

"Does your company have a written policy saying that?" Circle: Yes / No

"Will you please mail me a copy of that written policy?" Circle: Yes / No

"Have I made it clear to you that I do not want telemarketing calls from anyone — ever?" Circle: Yes / No

If it's appropriate, add "Thank you for your cooperation. Good-bye."

For Dummies: Bestselling Book Series for Beginners

Internet Privacy

FOR

DUMMIES®

Internet Privacy FOR DUMMIES®

by John R. Levine, Ray Everett-Church, and Gregg Stebben

Foreword by David Lawrence

Wiley Publishing, Inc.

Best-Selling Books • Digital Downloads • e-Books • Answer Networks • e-Newsletters • Branded Web Sites • e-Learning

Internet Privacy For Dummies®

Published by
Wiley Publishing, Inc.
909 Third Avenue
New York, NY 10022
www.wiley.com

About the Authors

John R. Levine was a member of a computer club in high school — before high school students, or even high schools, had computers — where he met Theodor H. Nelson, the author of *Computer Lib/Dream Machines* and the inventor of hypertext, who reminded us that computers should not be taken seriously and that everyone can and should understand and use computers.

John wrote his first program in 1967 on an IBM 1130 (a computer somewhat less powerful than your typical modern digital wristwatch, only more difficult to use). He became an official system administrator of a networked computer at Yale in 1975. He began working part-time — for a computer company, of course — in 1977 and has been in and out of the computer and network biz ever since. Since he's been on the Internet for a long time, he started getting spammed early and often, leading to his joining the board of the Coalition Against Unsolicited Commercial E-mail (CAUCE) and starting the Network Abuse Clearinghouse (www.abuse.net).

Although John used to spend most of his time writing software, now he mostly writes books (including *The Internet For Dummies* and *Internet Secrets,* both published by Wiley Publishing, Inc.) because it's more fun and he can do so at home in the tiny village of Trumansburg, New York, where he is the sewer commissioner (Guided tours! Free samples!) and play with his small daughter when he's supposed to be writing. John also does a fair amount of public speaking. (See www.iecc.com/johnl, to see where he'll be.) He holds a B.A. and a Ph.D. in computer science from Yale University, but please don't hold that against him.

Ray Everett-Church published his first article about computers — and about the mischief a person could cause with them — in a community newspaper in Nashville, Tennessee, back in 1983. Nobody has been able to shut him up since.

In 1999, Ray became the world's first corporate chief privacy officer, creating the position at the Internet advertising company AllAdvantage.com. He has spent much of his career since then evangelizing to the global business community about the importance of respecting consumer privacy. Now more than half the Fortune 100 firms have a senior-level privacy executive, many of whom Ray helped to train at the dozen or more training seminars, conferences, and lectures he gives every year.

After receiving a degree from George Mason University and spending several years working as a political campaign consultant, Ray settled into the respectable profession of lobbying (the local used-car dealership wasn't hiring). But even as he walked the halls of Capitol Hill in the mid-1990s, technology was always on his mind: Using his self-taught technical expertise, he built online lobbying and issue advocacy networks for two trade associations in Washington, D.C.

Ray supported himself through law school by working as a consultant for an upstart online service named America Online, helping it to devise some of the world's first antispam policies. Even before receiving his Juris Doctor in 1997 from George Washington University's National Law Center, Ray began making his mark on the field of Internet privacy when he was asked to testify before the Federal Trade Commission at one of its first public workshops on the issue of junk e-mail and online marketing.

Ray now works as the chief privacy officer and senior consultant for the international privacy consulting firm ePrivacy Group (www.eprivacygroup.com). He lives a stone's throw from Silicon Valley in always-lovely northern California, with his very patient partner, Justin, and two rather strange-looking cats. You can learn more about Ray at www.everett.org.

Although you probably wouldn't recognize **Gregg Stebben**'s face, you have surely heard his voice because he is interviewed almost every day by radio stations all over the country about the Internet, Internet privacy, and lots of other interesting stuff. Privately, he confides to friends that he has been heard by millions of radio listeners nationwide as a veteran of more than 1,500 live radio interviews since 1998. He also knows his way around a television studio, and he has been seen on CNN, "Entertainment Tonight," The Learning Channel, The Discovery Channel, and many regional television newscasts. Motormouth that he is, he is a proud member of the National Speakers Association.

If Gregg isn't on the radio talking about the Internet, he's probably on the air talking about all kinds of "men's stuff" as the spokesman for *Men's Health* magazine, where he has been a contributing editor for eight years. His writing has also appeared in magazines like *Bon Appétit, Esquire,* and *TV Guide.* He is the author of nine other books on a variety of seemingly unrelated topics ranging from physics to cowboy wisdom and lore.

In his spare time, Gregg enjoys hiking and backpacking and running with his wife, Jody. He describes his ideal weekend as a series of exhausting athletic endeavors by day followed by substantial quantities of pepperoni pizza and mint chocolate chip ice cream by night.

You can find out more about Gregg at www.radioguru.com.

Dedication

John dedicates his part of the book to Tonia and Sarah, again and forever.

Ray dedicates his part of the book to Nancy and Richard Everett (also known as Mom and Dad) for their boundless love and support; Scott Everett, for his brotherly harassment; and most especially to Justin, who gives meaning to life.

Gregg dedicates his part of the book to his wife, the ever-smiling and ever-loving Jody Stebben, and to Zucker-Bob Stebben, who valued privacy like no other being on Earth.

Authors' Acknowledgments

John thanks Matt Wagner, for his invaluable help in shepherding this book through a formative process that took about two more years than anyone dreamed it would; Trumansburg Elementary School; and particularly Sarah's teacher, Taina Heptig, for keeping Sarah well-occupied while he wrote and returning her better educated each day.

Ray thanks Carol Church and the late Charles Church (the world's best in-laws, even if the law doesn't recognize it yet), for their constant love and for the use of Chuck's study, where a substantial part of this book was written; Jim, Johannes, Carl, Oliver, and the whole AllAdvantage family (some of whom Gregg thanks next), for giving him the chance to "go Hollywood" with privacy; Robb Watters and Luke Rose, the best unindicted co-conspirators any guy could hope for; Vince Schiavone, Michael Miora, and the rest of the incredible team at ePrivacy Group, for their friendship and their professional prowess in privacy and security; and Jonathan Turley, for whetting his appetite to fight the good fight. A special thanks to all those clients who have paid Ray to help them practice what he preaches.

Gregg thanks Denis Boyles, Kelly Rodriques, and Kim Garretson, for giving him his first paid Internet gig way back when. He thanks his radio friends, like Sheri Tobin of KZLA/LA; Katie Pruett of KRLD/Dallas; Austin Hill of KFYI/Phoenix; Sterling Schiessler and Laura Smailes of WTVN/Columbus; Dave Wingert of "Dave 'til Dawn"; David Lawrence and Lili VonSchrupp of "Online Tonight"; Gary Nolan of "Nolan At Night"; Gary Allen of WOOD/Grand Rapids; and his two great Florida pals, Bill Mick, of WMEL, and Joe Scott, of 96-KROCK. Gregg also thanks his Internet friends, like Alex Gourevitch and the entire Wyoming state press corps, Jim Jorgensen, Bill Kritzberg, John Weil, Noel Wood, Patty Herrera, Nancy Booth, Julie Prunier, Bill Trento, Mark Anderson, Quinn Daly, Michael Moore, Jennifer Laird, the other Jim Jorgenson, Marty Stebben, Bill Armstrong, Ted Hoffman (of Alliance Ventures), and, finally, Jeff Holder, for the amazing talents he displayed as the technical editor of this book.

Publisher's Acknowledgments

We're proud of this book; please send us your comments through our online registration form located at www.dummies.com/register/.

Some of the people who helped bring this book to market include the following:

Acquisitions, Editorial, and Media Development

Project Editor: Rebecca Whitney

Acquisitions Editor: Steve Hayes

Technical Editor: Jeffrey Holder

Editorial Manager: Constance Carlisle

Editorial Assistant: Amanda M. Foxworth

Production

Project Coordinator: Regina Snyder

Layout and Graphics: Scott M. Bristol, Brian Drumm, Kristin McMullan, Jeremey Unger, Mary J. Virgin

Proofreaders: Laura Albert, John Greenough, Susan Moritz, TECHBOOKS Production Services

Indexer: TECHBOOKS Production Services

General and Administrative

Wiley Technology Publishing Group: Richard Swadley, Vice President and Executive Group Publisher; Bob Ipsen, Vice President and Group Publisher; Joseph Wikert, Vice President and Publisher; Barry Pruett, Vice President and Publisher; Mary Bednarek, Editorial Director; Mary C. Corder, Editorial Director; Andy Cummings, Editorial Director

Wiley Manufacturing: Ivor Parker, Vice President, Manufacturing

Wiley Marketing: John Helmus, Assistant Vice President, Director of Marketing

Wiley Composition Services for Branded Press: Debbie Stailey, Composition Services Director

Wiley Sales: Michael Violano, Vice President, International Sales and Sub Rights

Contents at a Glance

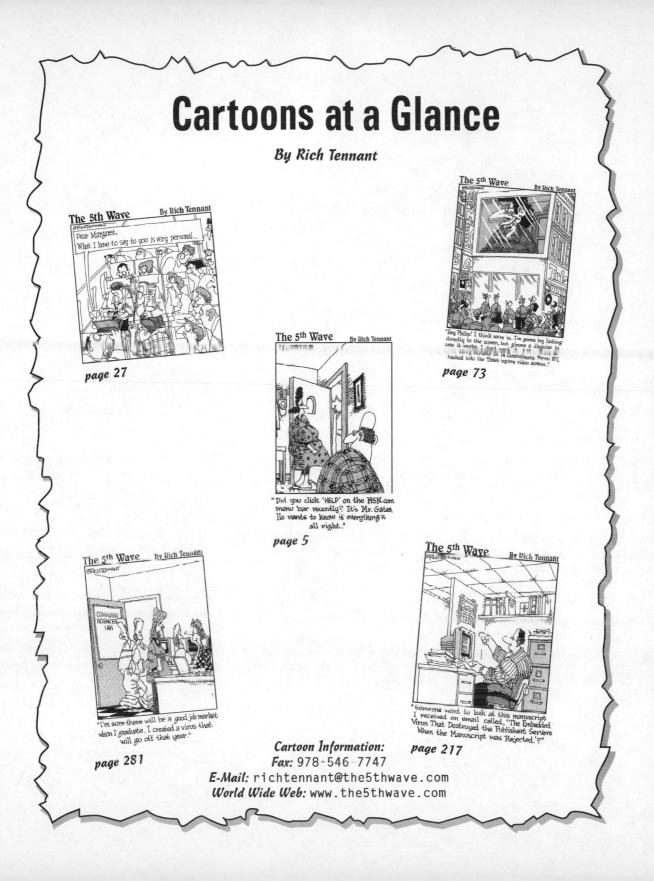

Table of Contents

Foreword

1f I know who you are, where you live, and what you do, I could ruin your life.

How? Imagine that I'm the clerk at the grocery store that you just handed that clipboard back to. You filled out a simple little form that told me everything I needed to know to make your life miserable. I handed you a chainwide discount card that's going to be my weapon of choice.

Oh, sure, I'm going to give you 35 cents off that next pack of generic cigarettes you buy. But just knowing who you are and where you live means that if I'm resourceful enough, I could do some simple investigations on the Web, tie you in with your workplace, call your company pretending to be a job-seeker looking for benefits info, and see who provides your insurance.

And then I could hold over your head the fact that you never told them you smoked. Or then I could hold over your head that you buy condoms from time to time; from 9 a.m. to noon on Wednesdays and Thursdays, to be precise — when you should be working.

And all for a few cents off on products you were going to buy anyway.

This scenario probably won't ever happen to you. But it could, and if you aren't at least interested in the state of your privacy, you should be. You could be like me: I've already thrown my hands in the air and given up.

I'm of the opinion that privacy and anonymity are two different things: Privacy is a God- (and Constitution-) given right that is sacrosanct, while anonymity is a shield we tend to hide behind so we don't get caught doing stuff we shouldn't be doing, and I think that anonymity is what people are often talking about when they say the word *privacy*. I've long since lost any hope that I have any privacy left. But I'm a public figure, and you're probably not. Maybe you'll have better luck. If you read this book, luck won't stand a chance: You'll have knowledge and power.

John, Ray, and Gregg have been on the front lines, not only making sure that the companies they work for don't invade your privacy (and, as you'll find out, it doesn't mean that they don't think companies should have information on you — they just want to make sure that the information isn't misused), but also that you are forewarned and forearmed in the fight to maintain your privacy. Situations like the ones I've described are a little far-fetched. But others are not. Read and learn from someone who has your best interests at heart.

David Lawrence
Host of the nationally syndicated radio show *Online Tonight*
Washington, D.C.
May 2002

Introduction

Two problems crop up when you're talking about — or trying to write a book about — privacy. First, just mention the word *privacy* in a crowded room, and everyone starts looking at you like you're some kind of a kook; a paranoid, whining, blathering idiot with no life and nothing better to do than to complain about shadowy figures of the underworld who are following you around, wiretapping your phone, reading your mail, intercepting your e-mail, and pointing lasers at your head to tap in to your innermost personal thoughts. On the other hand, everyone has his own little privacy pet peeve. As a rule, you're not a whining, blathering idiot and you don't go through life worried that forces larger than yourself are out to get you. And you know that you're being followed on the Internet, but so what? You know that you should be furious with spammers, but you can't be bothered. And you know that every time you subscribe to a magazine, they cash in by selling you out, but who cares?

Still, you do have that one little pet peeve: Let's say it's telemarketers. Darn them! It's a complete invasion of privacy when they call, and they should all be punished! Tortured! Forced to sleep in dark wet caves, where, deprived of food, they're subjected to the sound of ringing telephones 24 hours a day. They should be — well, let's just say that your friends all know not to get you started on that subject.

This illustrates the problem with talking about — or writing about — privacy. Looked at in a larger context, the topic makes a person sound absolutely paranoid and nuts. If you look at all the little individual pieces one by one — as seen by whoever happens to be cursed with that particular little pet peeve — it's clear that privacy is a gigantic snowball of a problem that will only get worse. And we're not even talking about the stuff that everyone agrees is real and serious stuff, like identity theft and hacking and viruses and fraud.

Here's our promise to you: At the risk of sounding like utter paranoid geeks, we tackle the topic of Internet and electronic privacy in its entirety. At the risk of facing great personal and professional humiliation, we leave no stone unturned, we stop at nothing, and we tear back the layers on all the privacy stuff that has everyone really worried as well as on your own, personal pet privacy peeve and the personal pet privacy peeves of everyone else who has ever busted a gasket after feeling that their privacy has been invaded.

In return, we ask just one thing: As you read on, please keep in mind that although we may be the chroniclers of all these peeves, it doesn't mean that we take 'em all to heart. We're writers, after all, so it's our job to call 'em as we see 'em, even when it's someone else's personal pet privacy peeve we're reporting on.

About This Book

We don't flatter ourselves that you're interested enough in privacy issues to sit down and read the entire book (although it should be a fine book for the bathroom). When you run into a problem using the Internet ("Hmm, I *thought* that I knew how to keep bad guys off my home network, but I don't seem to remember . . . ."), just dip in to this book long enough to solve your problem.

How to Use This Book

To begin, please read the first chapter. It gives you an overview of the online privacy landscape.

Because privacy issues change every day, we have a Web site to help keep the book up-to-date. Check for more up-to-the-minute information available on our Web site, at

net.gurus.com

When you have to follow a complicated procedure, we spell it out step by step wherever possible. We then tell you what happens in response and what your options are. When you have to type something, it appears in the book in **boldface.** Type it just as it appears. Use the same capitalization we do — a few systems care deeply about CAPITAL and small letters. Then press the Enter key. The book tells you what should happen when you give each command and what your options are.

When you have to choose commands from menus, we write File⇨Exit whenever we want you to choose the File command from the menu bar and then choose the Exit command from the menu that appears.

Who Are You?

In writing this book, we assumed that you

- Are a reasonably intelligent person (all *Dummies* readers are) who wants to know more about privacy issues, but you don't want to be a full-time privacy geek.

- Have a computer with access to the Internet, or at least can use one when you need to.

- Want to learn how to improve your privacy and that of your kids (if you have any).

How This Book Is Organized

This book has five parts. The parts stand on their own — although you can begin reading wherever you like, you should at least skim Part I first to get acquainted with the big online-privacy picture.

Here are the parts of the book and what they contain:

Part I, "Electronic Privacy Overview" gives you the big picture of what privacy is and isn't and how computers and the Internet have changed the rules of the privacy game.

Part II, "PCs and Privacy," looks at the privacy features and problems (more problems than features, unfortunately) of individual PCs, PCs connected to home and office networks, and portable and handheld computers

In Part III, "Privacy on the Internet" looks beyond your home or office computer at Internet Service Providers, viruses, Web browsers, e-mail privacy, and spam. This part also covers online banking and concludes with two chapters about the particular privacy issues that affect children.

All sorts of organizations use computerized systems where privacy problems arise. Part IV, "Beyond the PC: Offline Electronic Privacy," covers money and credit, telephone privacy (and telemarketers), privacy at work, and how the government is and isn't improving our privacy.

A compendium of ready references and useful facts is in Part V, "The Part of Tens" (which, we suppose, suggests that the rest of the book is full of useless facts).

Icons Used in This Book

Lets you know that some particularly nerdy, technoid information is coming up so that you can skip it if you want. (On the other hand, you may want to read it.)

Indicates that a nifty little shortcut or time-saver is explained.

Oh, drat — another good idea gone awry.

"Say it ain't so!" Sorry, it's so.

Points out a resource on the World Wide Web that you can use with Netscape, Internet Explorer, or other Web software.

Each of the three authors steps forward for a moment to tell you what we think about a privacy question or issue.

When you spend lots of time thinking about privacy issues, you can start to feel really, really paranoid. (We speak from experience.) So pause for a moment, take a breath, and reflect.

What Now?

That's all you need to know to get started. Whenever you have a particular question, just look up the topic in the table of contents or index in this book.

Feedback, Please

We love to hear from our readers. If you want to contact us, please feel free to do so, in care of

Dummies Press
10475 Crosspoint Blvd.
Indianapolis, IN 46256

Better yet, send us Internet electronic mail at privacy@gurus.com (our friendly robot answers immediately; the human authors read all the mail and answer as much as we can), or visit this book's Web home page, at net.gurus.com. These electronic addresses put you in contact with the authors of this book; to contact the publisher or authors of other *For Dummies* books, visit the publisher's Web site, at www.dummies.com, send e-mail to info@hungryminds.com, or send paper mail to the address just listed.

Part I
Electronic Privacy Overview

The 5th Wave
By Rich Tennant

"Did you click 'HELP' on the MSN.com menu bar recently? It's Mr. Gates. He wants to know if everything's all right."

In this part . . .

How big of a deal is electronic privacy? It's pretty darned big. In this part, we look at the big picture of your privacy, the threats from business and government, and how the Internet fits into all of it. If you're like us, you'll be astonished and not a little outraged, so read on.

Chapter 1

How Private Are You Right Now?

In This Chapter

▶ What privacy really is

▶ The new privacy rules of the Web

▶ New online threats

There you are, quietly sitting in your chair, reading this book about electronic privacy. You're a long way from the nearest electronic device. You have no computer, no Web browser, no e-mail appliance, no telephone, no cell phone, no Palm, and no pager within easy reach. It's reasonable to expect — isn't it? — that for this moment, at least, all's quiet on your personal privacy front.

Protecting Privacy Begins at Home

If you read this entire book, you'll discover that your relationship with your own electronic privacy is much like your relationship with the family of mice that has been living in your attic. For years and years, you've gone about the daily business of your life, completely unaware that the mice are there. They've been quite successful at darting through the shadowy recesses of your home, keeping their presence hidden from you as they scramble about, searching for any food morsel they can find.

Over time, the mice have gotten bolder and bolder, pushing the envelope of safety and inching closer and closer toward revealing themselves to you in their quest for food. At times, they have even done damage to the infrastructure of your home and your life as they have chewed away on your home's wiring and even photos and books and clothing

One day, as you're cleaning the garage or the kitchen pantry or some other deep corner where you rarely go, you discover the trail of these little mice, and the damage they have caused becomes apparent to you — in much the same way as you will discover the trail and the damage of many little "mice" chewing away at your privacy.

A Day in the Life of the Privacy Cyberpests

Here you are, still sitting quietly in a chair and reading this book about electronic privacy. Can you begin to hear the faint scratches of the privacy pests as they claw away at the walls of your electronic security?

No? Then it's time to start looking in some of the mustier corners of your daily activities to see whether you can see any telltale signs. As an example, look at an everyday action, like buying a book (this book!) about Internet and electronic privacy. Did you buy this book:

✔ **Over the Internet?** Did the Web site ask you for any personally identifiable information — your mailing address perhaps, or an e-mail address? By buying the book over the Internet, you revealed some information about yourself to the bookseller. As you continue to read this book, someone at the site may be adding that information to all the other personal data that has already been collected about you, based on all the other things you have purchased — or even just looked at — while on that Web site.

✔ **While browsing the Web at home?** If so, you may have revealed to your Internet Service Provider some information about yourself, including your interests and purchasing habits. As you continue reading, someone may be adding that information to all the other personal data that has already been collected about you based on all the places you've surfed and the things you've bought online.

✔ **While browsing the Web at work?** If so, you may have revealed to your employer some information about yourself. Luckily, you weren't looking for job-hunting books. Oops! You *were* looking for those, too? Whatever the case, someone may be adding that information to your personnel file now, along with all the other personal data that has already been collected about you because your employer has the legal right to monitor you and record every move you make on the Internet while you're at work.

✔ **Using an insecure Internet browser?** If so, you may have revealed some information about yourself to a hacker in a faraway place who may have already targeted you as the one whose credit card number will buy him a new video game player — or maybe even a wardrobe or new car. As you're reading now, he may be busy collecting additional information and building an intimate profile of you that he can use to fraudulently spend your money, online and offline.

✔ **At a bookstore where you have a frequent buyer's card?** If so, you may have contributed to a growing profile the bookstore is compiling about you and your interests. The bookstore could now be adding information about this purchase to all the other personal data it has already collected about you based on books and other purchases you've made at any of its stores.

✔ **With a credit card?** If so, you revealed to the credit card company some information about your purchasing patterns and purchasing tastes. The company could add that information to all the other personal data it has already collected about you based on all the other places you have shopped — both online and offline — and all the other things you have purchased with your credit card.

My, How Your Garden Grows

Like a garden sprinkler, round and round you go, shooting dribs and drabs of your private information across the landscape even as you do something as innocent as buy a book.

Sometimes, you give up this information and someone does good things with it. Your information may be used to personalize a Web site for you or to make book and other product recommendations or to alert you to good deals on the kinds of merchandise you've shopped for in the past. Or, the information may simply be used to serve up the latest baseball scores for your favorite teams if you're a baseball fan or the latest stock prices for stocks you have in your portfolio if you're an investor — or both.

Sometimes, the information sits unused in a computer server log. At other times, the information is compiled with telemarketing lists to make sure that you get a call at dinnertime to sell you subscriptions to sports magazines or to sell you the (wink, wink) hottest new stocks. Or, maybe you have renewed a prescription through your drugstore's Web site, only to end up on a mailing list of coupons for thousands of products you would never want in a million years.

The most important thing to understand is that nothing about your purchase of this book is unique because these invasions of privacy occur all the time, whether you're shopping online or at the mall or talking to a friend on the phone or out in your real-life garden or simply sitting in a chair and reading a good book.

Does History Repeat Itself?

Thanks to the Internet, privacy has become front-page news. But the little mice who are there chewing away at your privacy were there chewing long before you ever heard of the World Wide Web.

Two who can't sell your personal information

Your public library: Most states have laws protecting library lending records — and potentially your surfing activity from terminals in the library — from being revealed publicly. These laws are not universal, however, so you should check with the American Library Association (www.ala.org) to make sure of your rights in your state.

Your local video store: Thanks to Robert Bork, who was almost appointed to the Supreme Court, your local video store cannot release information about the videos you rent. This law was enacted in 1988 after a newspaper published a list of 146 videos rented by Bork and his family during Bork's Supreme Court confirmation hearings. You can read more about the Bork bill, also known as the Video Privacy Protection Act of 1988, at www4.law.cornell.edu/uscode/18/2710.html.

In fact, you don't have to think very hard to recall two of these pests' most common pre-Internet privacy invasions:

- ✔ **Junk mail:** The route by which junk mail ends up in your mailbox is long and invasive. You buy something from a catalog, and it sells your name and address to someone else. You subscribe to a magazine, and it sells your name and address to someone else. Donate to charity, and it sells your name and address to someone else. Open a bank account, and it sells your name and address to someone else. Open an airline frequent flyer account, and it sells your name and address to someone else. Fill out the little registration cards that come with new products, and those companies sell your name and address to someone else. In some states, registering to vote or getting a driver's license or marriage license may result in your name and address being sold to someone else. Or buy a house, and the whole world (it seems) rushes down to your county courthouse to buy your name and address so that they can send you a few hundred pounds of junk mail.

- ✔ **Telemarketer phone calls:** Much like junk mail, your name and phone number have been bought and sold and traded for years. The result: Telemarketers call you during the family dinner hour every night.

From Mice to Rats!

In the good old days (before 1995 and before most people had ever heard of the Internet), the amount of information that could be gathered about you without putting a wiretap on your telephone or physically following you around was fairly limited. Your credit card company knew where you shopped and what you bought — only when you used that credit card. Your bank knew where you spent your money — only when you paid by check. Each store you shopped at knew what you bought only when you made your purchases at that store.

Thanks to the Internet and other advances in technology, the most intimate and minute details of your life are now being gathered and catalogued and stored — and even data-mined (inferring personal information from your access patterns) by others with or without your knowledge or permission. To misappropriate the lyrics from a Jerry Reed tune, when it comes to data-mining, "they get the gold mine (and you get the shaft)."

Why the Web Breaks All the Rules, Part 1

When most people think of the Web, they think of their Web browser and the Web sites and pages they visit. If I want to buy a book, I use my browser to go to BuyTheBook.com to search for the title and make my purchase.

What most people don't think about are all the databases behind the scenes of the Internet that make it possible for you to go to BuyTheBook, find the page for the book you want to buy, give BuyTheBook.com your credit card number, and have BuyTheBook.com send your purchase information to some computer terminal at some warehouse so that someone can get the right book and ship it to you at the right address.

Why Are These Databases Such a Threat to Your Privacy?

Because the millions of little pieces of data spread all over the databases of the Internet show the details of your life, they're a day-by-day chronicle of your interests, your likes, your dislikes, your momentary lapses of common sense or good judgment, your whims, your health, your financial condition, your employment prospects, your membership in organizations, and maybe even your refrigerator contents. (After all, you're one of the millions of people who order their groceries over the Internet — that is, if your refrigerator doesn't already have its own Internet connection.)

Think back over all the places you've been and everything you have looked at on the Internet. If someone were to collect all that data and analyze it, she may know more about you than you even know about yourself. And maybe that person would draw correct conclusions about you — and maybe not.

The reason that the Internet breaks all the rules is that it's not there just to serve up Web pages for you at your command. It also sneaks away with a tremendous amount of personal and intimate data about you and stores it in a database for later use.

You are where you surf. Think of it this way: Almost every Web server keeps a record of every Web page it serves, and it records the unique address of the computer to which it serves things. Every Web site you've ever visited may be recorded somewhere. Who knows who may be willing to pay for access to that information about you? Consider these possibilities:

- **Have you ever bought anything online?** Online booksellers would love to know what books you have been buying from other online booksellers so that they can send you advertisements for other books you may enjoy. You can apply this same principle to all other goods and services you've shopped for on the Web: That you have browsed for or bought widgets and whatchamacallits and wakadoos on the Web is valuable information to other companies in the same or related fields.

- **Have you ever researched an illness on the Internet?** If the illness was serious enough, your insurance company may like to know about it. So would the insurance company you're thinking about switching to. But what if you were doing the research for a family member or friend? For example, the day may come when your health or life insurance is suddenly canceled — just days after you've helped your child do some research on the Web for a fourth-grade book report about cancer. When a relative has a heart attack, you may use the Web to learn more about the condition — only to find your insurance premiums skyrocketing because your insurance company now believes that your family has a history of heart attacks.

- **Have you ever used the Web to read about political viewpoints that are new or different from your own?** Some people fear that using the Web to satisfy this sort of curiosity or as a tool for self-education could lead to political persecution.

- **Have you ever used the Web to manage your finances?** We can think of several thousand fast-talking, stock-trading telemarketers in boiler rooms in Florida who would love to have your phone number and be able to call you and sell you some jim-dandy new stocks just minutes after you have made a big pile of money selling some other securities online. Online banking and financial services sites, like Quicken.com, provide consumers with excellent control and useful information for controlling personal finances along with strong privacy protections.

Why the Web Breaks All the Rules, Part II

Before the Web existed, companies gathered whatever information they could get about you. The amount of information each company could gather was extremely small, though, and the sum of all information gathered about you by all sources was limited and scattered all over the globe in piecemeal fashion.

That's no longer the case. The Internet makes it possible for entities (a fancy word for companies and organizations and even governments) to collect lots of information about you, and all that information is being stored in one central network of databases: the Internet.

Chapter 2

The Law, the Privacy Industry, and You

At various times, the U.S. government has found it necessary to regulate how information about you is gathered and used. For instance, the Telephone Consumer Protection Act of 1991 set down strict guidelines that telemarketers must follow when contacting you by phone. (You can read more about the 1991 act — and how you can sue telemarketers when they don't play by the rules — in Chapter 15.)

The Internet is a new technology, and we have yet to see — or even understand — the full strength of its power as a tool for gathering and manipulating personal data. Many consumer advocates fully believe that the time is at hand for the government to step in and regulate how the Internet is used to collect this personal information about individuals. Others — particularly those in the business of buying, selling, mining, or otherwise profiting from personal data — believe that online industries can be self-policing or self-regulating in order to protect consumers' privacy without the need for government regulation.

The Current Face of Internet Industry Self-Regulation

Many Web sites ask you for personal information. Many other Web sites gather information about your visit, but don't bother to tell you that they're doing so.

We talk in depth later in this book about *how* Web sites gather information about you. For now, the more obvious question that you're probably asking yourself is "Why do they want all this information, and what are they doing with it?"

As it turns out, you're not alone. Lots of people — other consumers, consumer advocates, and lawmakers included — want to know what companies are doing with all the online personal information they gather. To answer those questions, starting around 1996, increasing numbers of high-profile Web sites began telling the world in easy-to-find statements posted on its sites about their data practices, what information they collect, what they do with it, and whether you-the-consumer have any say in the matter. These statements are known as *privacy policies.*

To understand more about what a privacy policy is, you may think that reading a few would be useful. Go ahead and try it. But grab a cup of coffee and some aspirin first because after just a few moments, you will realize that most privacy policies are not written to be read by the average human being. More often than not, they're dozens of pages long and read like they were written by a committee of lawyers (which, in most cases, they were).

Privacy policies, on the whole, are not meant to be informative. Instead, they're written with the knowledge that if a legal dispute ever arises, the privacy policy will become Exhibit A in the lawsuit. That's why the lawyers got put in charge of writing the policies in the first place. We know that you will be shocked to learn that adding lawyers to the process certainly hasn't helped.

Ray-the-lawyer's privacy policy checklist

Ray says:

Hey! Lay off the lawyer jokes! I'm a lawyer, and I really am here to help. In fact, just to prove it to you, in this section I let you in on what lawyers are thinking as they write privacy policies. Then I tell you what you should look for when you read them.

Take it from me: When a lawyer sits down to write a privacy policy, he has to make sure that the policy covers a great deal of territory — with as much detail, as few specifics, and as few words as possible — yet with every last possibility covered.

If you think that this discussion already sounds like a bunch of vague lawyer-speak, you're learning fast.

When it comes to privacy policies, I know what I'm talking about. I've been on a few of those privacy-policy-writing committees, and I know that a good privacy policy must

✔ Describe every bit of information a Web site gathers and explain why it is gathered, exactly what is done with it, who has access to it, and under what circumstances — and describe precisely any control that you as a visitor have over the process.

✔ Be brief enough that it can be read and understood by the average Internet user whose eyes glaze over after half a page or 6.2 seconds, whichever comes first.

✔ Be precisely worded so that if a dispute ever arises, the company can defend itself in court.

✔ Be worded loosely enough that if the lawyers have missed anything, no liability is created for the company.

✔ Be stated in friendly advertising-speak so that it doesn't sound like the site is rifling through your wallet when you're not looking.

Ray-the-Web-surfer's privacy policy checklist

Ray has more to say:

Have you ever seen the magicians Penn & Teller vow never to show you how their magic tricks are done — and then play the old shell game with a small ball hidden under one of three clear plastic cups so that you can see exactly how the trick is performed?

I am about to perform the privacy lawyer's equivalent of that trick by showing you what you should look for in a privacy statement as though you were reading it through the clear plastic lenses of the sneakiest, most cynical lawyer in town. Ask yourself whether a Web site's privacy policy tells you

✔ **Explicitly what information the Web site is collecting.** Is the site getting your name and address? Your e-mail address? The IP address of your computer? Your credit card number? The combination to your gym locker or to the hidden safe in the den? If the site doesn't say exactly what information it's collecting, you should assume the worst.

✔ **How and from where the site is collecting your information.** Does the site use an order form to collect data? Is it buying databases from other advertisers? Is it searching public records down at the county courthouse? Is it paying some nasty-looking guy to tail you? You should know from where the site is getting information about you because the amount of information it's gathering should be appropriate to the service you're getting. A Web site that's selling you a new flamingo for your front lawn doesn't need to know as much about you as an online mortgage banker needs to know when you're shopping for a home loan.

✔ **How your information will be used.** Here's where the worst advertising-speak action usually happens. You have to read carefully and be deeply skeptical to figure out what it's saying because everything it says emphasizes how exciting and wonderful the site's services are and how thrilled you will be with all the benefits it provides because you're so willing to share your personal information. Will the site customize or personalize its content for you the next time you visit? Will it drive you crazy by sending you catalogs by snail mail and e-mailing you ads by the dozens? Will it sell your personal information to other advertisers? Will it call you at home every week during the last five minutes of "The Simpsons"? If you're already sick of all the junk mail and spam and phone calls you receive, you need to know this information to decide whether you want to have anything more to do with these sites.

✔ **Whether and how you can make the site stop collecting information about you.** If you don't want a company to collect information about you, either it can give you a chance to object, or you can take your business elsewhere. Some places would rather annoy you and drive you to their competition than give you a chance to make your feelings known. If a site's policy doesn't tell you how to stop the data collection, take that as an invitation to visit the competition.

✔ **How to see what information about you it already has on file and how to delete it or correct it if it's wrong.** On an episode of the TV show "Friends," Chandler Bing receives *TV Guide* addressed to a "Miss Chanandler Bong." If Chandler knew how to get his information corrected, you wouldn't have plot points from a sitcom inflicted on you in a book about Internet privacy.

✔ **How the site protects your information.** Does the site use encryption to keep bad guys from snatching your personal information as it passes between your computer and its own? Does it have security measures in place to keep people from stealing your information from its databases? Sites are sometimes vague about specific security measures, and that's a good thing. Providing too many specifics gives crooks an edge, and the unknown keeps them guessing. If the site's policy fails to mention security or doesn't assert that it's using "industry best practices" or some other silver-tongued phrase to reassure you that it's protecting your data, your privacy and security may be the last thing on its list.

✔ **Who is responsible for making sure that the site lives up to its promises.** Many e-commerce firms have appointed chief privacy officers and other dedicated personnel to manage their consumer information practices and to be the point person in ensuring that all promises made in a privacy policy are honored. If a site's policy doesn't say who has responsibility for overseeing the privacy of your data, you're better off assuming that the answer is "nobody."

Three E-Commerce Watchdogs

Unless you have the time, commitment, and deviousness (sorry, Ray!) to try to make sense of all the lawyer-speak in every privacy policy on every Web site you visit, you have to find an easier way to know which Web sites you can trust and which ones you can't.

At first glance, you may think that privacy seal programs, like TRUSTe and BBBOnline and WebTrust, are the answer to your privacy-policy dreams, as shown in Figure 2-1.

Figure 2-1:
Three high-profile trust marks.

You see the TRUSTe seal everywhere — or at least it seems that it's always visible as you're surfing around the Web. In fact, in an August 1999 study, 69 percent of Internet users said that they recognize the TRUSTe seal, and 5 percent said that seeing the seal truly increases their confidence in Web sites that display it.

Can these watchdogs be trusted?

What do privacy seals like TRUSTe really stand for? Are these trust marks really the equivalent of a *Good Housekeeping* seal that you can, well, trust?

We let you be the judge.

You have the right to remain silent

If a company posts a privacy policy and then violates the policy, the Federal Trade Commission (FTC) has the legal authority to prosecute the company for fraud and deceptive trade practices. Ironically, if a company *doesn't* post a privacy policy, it has made no public promises to which it can be held, and the FTC can't really touch it.

Privacy loopholes in cyberspace

A company that displays a privacy seal on its Web site has a choice to make:

✔ Maintain the right to continue displaying a privacy seal by adhering to the promises it has made in its own Web site privacy policies.

✔ Ignore its own privacy policies and have high-powered lawyers start looking for loopholes when someone catches it violating that privacy policy red-handed.

Here's how a few well-known companies have used loopholes rather than simply play by the rules:

Real Networks: When the Real Networks RealAudio Jukebox software was discovered to be capable of capturing and communicating your online musical tastes (in direct violation of the company's posted privacy policy), it avoided enforcement by claiming that the seal program covered only its Web site privacy policy — not the software distributed via that Web site.

Microsoft, Part 1: After experiencing several security breaches in its online services, Microsoft was required to have a third party audit its compliance. However, under the terms of the TRUSTe license, Microsoft could (and did) refuse to disclose the findings of the auditor, and even refused to release the identity of the auditor! Not surprisingly, many people were less than impressed with vague assertions of compliance from a privacy auditor who wasn't even willing to step out from behind his own cloak of privacy.

Microsoft, Part 2: In 1999, someone found that files produced by several popular Microsoft applications, including Word, generate something that's generically called a Globally Unique Identifier (GUID). As it turns out, if your computer is connected to the Internet through a high-speed Ethernet connection (such as an office network, a cable modem, or DSL line), the Microsoft GUID (naturally, they call it the *MS*ID) adds the unique serial number of your Ethernet card to the MSID, which then gets passed along to Microsoft in the form of a cookie every time you visit the Microsoft.com Web site. Microsoft announced that it would eventually distribute a software patch that would address this issue, but you would have to go to its Web site and register with your personal information to get a copy of the patch. Gee, that sure dispels all concerns, doesn't it? Luckily, if your computer doesn't have an Ethernet network card, the software just makes up a random number, and although it still uses the number as a cookie, at least it's not coded to your PC and doesn't threaten your privacy as much.

ToySmart: When the online retailer ToySmart went bankrupt in 2000, the bankruptcy receiver (the person appointed by the court who takes over and manages the closure) began tallying all the company's assets to be sold off to pay the debts of the company. One of the biggest assets he found? The ToySmart database of customer information, including lots of information about lots of kids. But when the bankruptcy receiver put the ToySmart database up for sale, lots of people complained, including TRUSTe and the Federal Trade Commission. Why? Because ToySmart had promised in its privacy policy to never give its customer data to any third party — ever. Suddenly, a standoff took place; in one corner, the bankruptcy court had a legal mandate to sell as many assets as it could to cover debts; in the other corner, the FTC had a mandate to make sure that ToySmart honored to the bitter end the promises it made in its privacy policy. So who solved the problem? Who's the leader — of the club — that fights for pri-va-cy? M-I-C-K-E-Y M-O-U-S-E. Disney agreed to buy some of the Toysmart assets, including the customer list, which it promised to promptly destroy as a condition of the sale. Disaster averted — until the next online retailer goes belly up.

You should understand that seal programs merely verify that a Web site's privacy policy discusses certain privacy topics (like the use of cookies and sharing data with third-party marketers). The seals don't set any specific quality standards or benchmarks or practices. A site could, theoretically, earn a seal for making the required disclosures, even if in the course of the disclosure it reserves the right to scrawl your Social Security number and mother's maiden name on the walls of public restrooms all over town.

These seal programs have been criticized for failing to crack down on companies that violate the provisions of their own privacy policies. For instance, until recently the best-known seal program, TRUSTe, had not taken action to revoke a single seal — except against companies that failed to pay their TRUSTe licensing fees. This situation occurred despite hundreds of complaints and more than a dozen formal inquiries about member companies. In several high profile incidents (see the sidebar "Privacy loopholes in cyberspace," earlier in this chapter), TRUSTe licensees have been found violating provisions of their own Web site privacy policies. They avoided enforcement actions by TRUSTe, however, by weaving escape routes through a variety of contractual technicalities.

These seal programs have been criticized for their failure to reach beyond the top few percent of Web sites and for failing to require any particular privacy standards or benchmarks or practices. Although most top 25 Web sites have some form of privacy-policy certification, many thousands of e-commerce sites haven't had their policies certified, according to a series of studies conducted by Georgetown University. Also, only a fraction of those sites surveyed have privacy policies that provide any formal notice about data practices, allow consumers to exercise an informed choice, make specific statements about their data security practices, or allow consumers to access and correct data stored about themselves.

Seal programs have been criticized for being dependent almost completely on the licensing fees of the same companies they're charged with policing. Some of the biggest TRUSTe corporate sponsors are firms who have had numerous complaints brought against them, and not one has had its seal license seriously threatened.

The Big Three privacy seals

The world of privacy seals has three main players:

TRUSTe: With nearly 2,000 members, TRUSTe is the grand-daddy of privacy seals. But don't let the presence of the TRUSTe seal at the bottom of a page necessarily overwhelm you with confidence. One of the main criticisms that privacy advocates have levied against TRUSTe is that it verifies only that a company has a privacy statement and follows it. TRUSTe does not offer any opinion about whether the privacy policy is any good.

So whom can I trust?

John: A cynical viewpoint says "Anyone without a TrustE seal." My answer is "Anyone you would trust in the real world." If an organization behaves decently in its offline dealings, it's probably okay online. If it's sleazy offline, why expect anything different?

Ray: The presence of a privacy seal means that the site cares enough about privacy policies to have gone through the (sometimes long and drawn-out) rigmarole to get their privacy policies certified. Seeing a seal, however, is absolutely no substitute for reading the privacy policy. I have seen the TRUSTe and BBBOnline privacy seals on documents that have no business having the word *privacy* associated with them. A seal means that the company can be counted on to do what it says it will do, even if its so-called privacy policy is a road map for invading yours. Ignore the seals and read the policy. If you can't make sense of the policy, e-mail the company and state that you won't do business with it until it has a policy that you *can* understand. But you had better e-mail the company from a disposable e-mail account from Hotmail because there's no telling what it will do with your e-mail address!

Gregg: I'm with Ray. If you can't make head or tails of a company's privacy policy, let someone there know. State that you won't do business with the company until it gets it right. Let's face it: Only when enough of us take the time to let e-commerce sites know that we demand better treatment and more respect will they take us seriously and provide it.

BBBONLINE: As with TRUSTe, BBBONLINE verifies only that a Web site has a privacy policy, and it doesn't comment on whether the privacy policy provides any legitimate protection for consumers.

WebTrust: WebTrust is the least known and the most protective privacy seal. Only a few dozen companies and organizations have passed the WebTrust audit (not a verification, mind you, but rather a full-blown audit) by a licensed CPA or chartered accountant.

Convergence

This section could have been named "Why That Wireless-Cell-Phone-Pager-PDA-E-Mail-TV-Gameboy-Walkman May Not Be Such A Good Idea After All. A new buzzword is sweeping the technology scene: *convergence.* That's a 25-cent word for the merging of many different technologies into one doodad that does it all.

A good example of convergence in action is the new generation of wireless phones that also have personal digital assistants (PDAs), pagers, and Web browsing capabilities all built-in. Convergence is also occurring in the way voice, data, and video can be delivered, such as cable television systems that now provide interactive TV, telephone, and Internet service through the same set of wires, and probably through the same device sometime soon.

The combination of these technologies makes for some amazing new toys and services, all of which have an incredible "wow factor." You know: It's what makes you spend hundreds of dollars for some new gizmo that you never knew existed the day before but now you suddenly can't live without, such as these items:

- **Blackberry:** This pager-like device has PDA features and the ability to "do" e-mail wirelessly on a screen that's big enough to actually read an e-mail (as opposed to your cell phone screen) and with a thumb-size keyboard that can be used to write e-mail (as opposed to your cell phone's keypad or your Palm's graffiti pad).

- **Palm VII:** This Palm PDA has a built-in wireless modem that allows you to check e-mail and surf the Internet.

- **Iridium:** This satellite-based cell phone is from the now-defunct company that was going to let you make calls from anywhere on the planet, even where no cellular tower was nearby. (Its network of satellites was bought for pennies on the dollar, and the new owner relaunched the service in 2002).

- **XM Radio and Sirius:** Satellite-based radio lets you drive across the country listening to your hometown radio station without ever disrupting its CD-quality sound.

- **Internet Telephony:** Encoding your voice into the kind of data packets that travel over the Internet provides dozens or hundreds of telephone lines over one Internet connection.

- **Broadband over cable:** With this service, vast amounts of Internet data are pumped at high speed through the cable TV wires that already serve your home.

- **Wireless broadband:** This method provides high-speed Internet and phone service to rural areas where cable and phone-based broadband can't reach.

- **TiVo:** This service continuously records television programs to a hard disk, letting you treat live television like it's videotape (pausing and rewinding). Its use of interactive television schedules lets you record an entire season's shows with one click.

- **"Smart" refrigerators:** Scan your food as you put it in, and the fridge not only warns you when the milk is about to go bad but also makes a shopping list for you, which you can access from work via the Web.

- **OnStar:** Using global positioning units and cellular phones, this service calls an ambulance when your airbag deploys, helps you find your way when you're lost, and can unlock your car if you lock your keys inside.

If you're noticing a theme here, you're right: Most of these technologies are about finding newer and faster ways to move information (including entertainment content) from one place to another and delivering them to users in any number of formats, with tremendous control, on many kinds of devices.

In addition to showing the latest episode of *Monday Night Football* or an e-mailed grocery list, these devices are increasingly sharing loads of information about your life with people and companies (and maybe even agencies) that you've never even heard of! Many of these technologies use Internet technology and in too many cases have the same security problems and privacy concerns that you face with your not-so-trusty desktop PC. But, unlike with your PC, these new devices may be storing — and using — more information than you realize.

Will That Be Cash, Check, or Information?

The world has so many cool new gadgets and gizmos, all internetworked and transmitting gobs of data all over creation. But that data doesn't ride for free; somebody has to build and run the networks. A key part of how our modern communications infrastructures operate — or, more precisely, how you get billed for them — is the necessity of obsessively tabulating every moment of usage, to meter every second of dial-tone or scrap of bandwidth you consume. As a by-product, those same technologies can also catalogue and cross-reference every aspect of the content you consume and be used to build a revealing and valuable profile about you.

This situation has its ups and downs. In Chapter 9, we talk about the ways in which Web sites and companies called ad networks and even your ISP can keep tabs on you. Sometimes the data is collected for billing purposes, but frequently it's kept to help companies learn more about your needs and interests so that they can market things to you themselves and sell the data to other companies that want to market things to you.

Throughout much of this book, we talk about the ways in which data is collected through various activities, both online and offline, and how to take control over it. But, until recently, where you bought your lunch today didn't have much bearing on what e-mail would arrive in your e-mail inbox or what telephone solicitor would be calling to annoy you this afternoon.

In fact, convergence is enabling some amazing new ideas:

✔ Push a button on your pager to pay for a soda from a wireless-enabled vending machine.

✔ Hear your cell phone ring to tell you that the shop you're walking past has a sale on the items on the grocery list stored on your PDA.

✔ See billboards flash personalized advertisements that have been chosen especially for you as you drive by.

✔ Watch television commercials that appeal to your particular interests appear on every channel, no matter how hard you try to flip the channel and get away.

Take a moment to think about it. To make every one of these modern conveniences possible, a great deal of personal information is required — and much more personal information is created; for example:

✔ When you push that button on your pager to buy a soda, you have revealed where you go, when you go there, and what you like to drink.

✔ Before your cell phone can ring to tell you that you're walking past a sale, the phone has to know where you are and what it is that you're interested in buying.

✔ Billboards that flash personalized messages must be able to track your movements as well as your interests and then zap that information all over the countryside.

✔ Interactive television lets advertisers know exactly when you watch, what you watch — and judging by your response to ads, they can also begin to profile your interests.

Begin to think about the costs that are incurred with every new wrinkle in technology. For some, the benefits far outweigh the costs. For others, the costs far outweigh the benefits. For most, a delicate balance exists.

Exercising Your Privacy Muscles

Learning about how to protect your privacy is much like working out at the gym:

✔ You can stretch, pump iron, and race to nowhere on the exercise bike and treadmill and stair-stepper machine during every free minute of every single day of your life.

✔ You can choose to do no exercise and suffer the consequences.

✔ You can devote just enough of your time to exercise that you stay in shape, but not so much that fitness becomes an obsession.

As you read other chapters in this book, you will discover that you *could* obsess over your privacy and worry about it every minute of the day. Or you can hide your head in the sand and pretend that absolutely no threats to your privacy are out there. Or you can do what you can to stay informed and protect yourself while keeping your privacy concerns balanced with all the other important things in your life.

Although this chapter gives you a taste of the many issues we cover in the rest of the book, you must remember that only certain issues pertain to you and your personal circumstances.

Much as runners and bikers and swimmers have different needs and tailor different types of workout programs for themselves, as you read on you'll want to plan a privacy program that works best for you. At the same time, don't fret over stuff that isn't relevant to you or over which you have no control. No one — not even your three faithful authors — can claim to follow every piece of advice offered in this book.

As you raise your awareness about different privacy issues, you will suddenly find that you have developed new muscles for protecting yourself. Guarding your privacy will come more easily, even naturally, for you. And just as you hold your future fitness in your hands when you pick up a barbell at the gym, the solutions to many of your privacy concerns are right here in your hands, starting with this book.

Part II
PCs and Privacy

In this part . . .

We say "Enough already!" to obsessing over the Internet and all the privacy hazards it presents. Instead, now is the time for a little introspection, for a look within, for some gentle probing to discover how many privacy leaks you can find and repair right there inside your very own computer.

Chapter 3

Safety Check: Looking under the Hood of Your Computer

• •

• •

*B*eing a privacy fighter sometimes makes you feel a bit like Don Quixote — as you climb into your knight's shining armor and ride off into the distance to slay demons and dragons and hackers over the Internet — even when it's sometimes hard to prove that the bad guys are really there.

Yet, to mix metaphors, just as the cobbler's children often have no shoes, it's also true that privacy fighters' kids often have no current antivirus software or other essential protective gear on their computers. Why? Let's face it: It's much more fun to fight heroic battles and windmills out in cyberspace than it is to tackle mundane domestic chores.

In Cyberspace, No One Cares If You Scream

Crash goes the hard drive, freeze goes the CPU, corrupted go the files and documents, destroyed goes your data from hackers and viruses. If it ever happens to you, you will either laugh because you heeded our advice and took the proper precautions or scream because you thought that it would never happen to you.

"Free" Patches and Updates

Given the way the software industry operates — release the product way too early and then repair problems by distributing free updates and patches via the Internet — we say a silent prayer every time we get on an airplane and cross our fingers in the hope that all those Seattle-based software companies haven't been sharing their quality-control secrets with that other Seattle-based giant, Boeing Aircraft.

From a privacy and security perspective, Internet patches and updates *are* a blessing because after a security problem is discovered, users can easily download the patch and get it fixed. But these same patches can also be a curse because downloading them is time-consuming and sometimes the patches themselves are so buggy, unstable, or riddled with privacy or security problems that they too are in need of a patch.

Don't think that we're kidding about a patch needing a patch needing a patch. The perfect example is the way the Office 97 suite was patched by Microsoft. The first set of patches, known as Service Release 1, or SR-1, contained its own little bug that prevented users from saving the changes they were making to documents. Following that fiasco, Office 97 Service Release 2 was recalled because it often caused computers to crash. It took Microsoft another month to patch the patch and rerelease it. After Windows XP came out, with proud claims that it was the most secure version of Windows ever (which, sadly, is probably true), nine security patches were issued within a year. You can see some of the Microsoft patches in Figure 3-1.

To patch or not to patch

That is the question. If you're like most of us, zillions of different pieces of software are running on your machine. How do you know when patches are available and which ones you really need?

We like to think of it as computer triage, with a little Hippocratic oath thrown in for good measure. In case you haven't been watching "ER" or reruns of "M*A*S*H," *triage* is a way of classifying the wounded in order to help those who have the best chance of recovery given the number of resources available. The Hippocratic oath is a pledge that new doctors take in which they promise to practice medicine in such a way as to "do no harm." We think it's smart to apply the same two principles to software patches.

Triage rules to patch by

Because we don't expect you to spend your life installing updates, here are some rules of thumb to figure out what updates you really need.

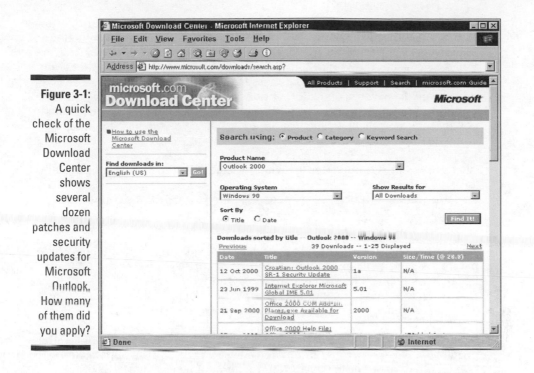

Figure 3-1:
A quick
check of the
Microsoft
Download
Center
shows
several
dozen
patches and
security
updates for
Microsoft
Outlook.
How many
of them did
you apply?

Must-do patch #1 — antivirus software: To continue with our clever medical analogy in this section, think of antivirus software as an empty syringe — it's absolutely essential for applying antidotes, antibodies, and inoculations, but is useless on its own. The same thing applies with your antivirus software: It's useful for applying the medicine that keeps your computer safe, but without updated antivirus definitions that fight against current viruses (which are being written and released almost every day), your antivirus software doesn't do you much good. Antivirus software manufacturers are continually updating these definitions, and you *must* get their updates from the Web at least once a month — and every time you hear about a new virus that's storming the computer world like a plague.

Here's how to get to the update sites for two of the most popular antivirus programs:

✔ **Norton AntiVirus:** www.symantec.com/avcenter/download.html

✔ **McAfee Anti-Virus:** download.mcafee.com/updates

More recent antivirus software packages automatically update their own definitions from the Internet, so you don't have to. If you're absentminded, like one or two of us, you should invest in one of these auto-updating antivirus software programs even if an antivirus program is already installed on your computer.

Must-do patch #2 — privacy or security patches: Privacy and security problems are most likely to show up in operating system software (like Windows 3.1, Windows 95, Windows 98, Windows 2000, Windows XP, Windows Me, Windows NT, and the Mac OS), e-mail and browser software, and other communications software, like instant messenger programs. The good news is that the media is very good about turning stories about privacy holes in software into front-page news — so you can be sure that if one of the programs you use has a problem, you'll hear about it. When you do, high-tail it to the Web and download the security fix.

Check these sites for updates for Windows and Macintosh operating systems:

- ✔ **Mac users:** www.info.apple.com/support/downloads.html
- ✔ **Windows users:** windowsupdate.microsoft.com

The Hippocratic update (or, don't patch for the sake of patching): Lots of patches are available in addition to critical, security-related ones. But just because a site offers a patch doesn't mean that you have to take it — or even that you need it. If your computer is humming along as expected and all software is performing fine, don't mess with those other patches.

On the other hand, If your hardware isn't performing up to expectations, the problem may be a corrupt or outdated *driver,* a little software application that lets hardware (for instance, your monitor, mouse, scanner, or printer) communicate with your computer. To download the latest driver for your underperforming hardware, visit the hardware manufacturer's site and look for a link labeled Drivers or Downloads or Software or Support.

If one particular piece of software seems to be slowing you down, surf over to the software manufacturer's site and see whether it's offering a patch that fixes the problem. For example, a popular graphics-editing program, Photoshop, was released in a new Version 6. The new version worked well enough, but a few months later the manufacturer quietly released a 6.0.1 patch that made the program start up and process images about 50 percent faster.

When bad patches happen to good people: When it comes to patches, our theory is that it's best to treat yourself like royalty — in other words, let someone else go first and take the poison for you. Unless you're in dire need and *must* have that patch today, why not let everyone else download it and suffer the possible consequences? If their computers crash or hang, you can sit back and wait for the "updated" patch.

Take the proper precautions: Obviously, some patches — like those for your operating system — have a far greater impact than, for example, a patch for your Solitaire program. But the prospect of a crash or lost data is horrific in any case. That's why you may want to consider taking these precautions:

✔ Read the release notes before downloading a patch to make sure that it really will cure what ails you.

✔ Before downloading, back up your files. (We talk about backing up data *extensively* later in this chapter.)

✔ Have a start-up disk ready, just in case your computer refuses to boot up. To make a start-up disk, choose Start⇨Settings ⇨Control Panel⇨ Add/Remove Programs. From there, select the Startup Disk tab and follow the instructions.

Updates: There must be an easier way, right?

Right!

We live in the age of information and automation, so it only makes sense that the whole update "thing" should be automated, too. Here's where to go to get it done automatically:

✔ **McAfee Oil Change Online:** It does exactly what you would expect — and a little more. First, this program scans your computer for installed software. Next, it scans the Web for patches for your installed software. Then it tells you what patches are available, and you choose which one you want to install. As a bonus, the program analyzes how you use your computer and makes recommendations about which patches you should install. Oil Change Online is available as part of a suite of online McAfee products that includes auto-updating antivirus software, an uninstaller package, and performance optimization software. As you may expect, you pay for this suite of online services.

✔ **C|Net Catch-Up:** If you strip away the McAfee antivirus, uninstaller, and performance optimization software and its recommendations about which patches you should download (and the price tag), you get the C|Net freebie package Catch-Up. Like McAfee Oil Change Online, Catch-Up scans your computer and keeps you up-to-date on which patches are available for your software. But Catch-Up also does something that the McAfee suite does not: It runs a security scan of your computer and identifies security holes in your software applications and operating system and then points you toward the patches that will fix those security leaks. How does C|Net do all that for free? Like so many other services on the Web, this one is supported by advertising.

✔ **For McAfee:** www.mcafee.com/myapps/clinic

✔ **For C|Net Catch-Up:** catchup.cnet.com

AUTHOR SURVEY SEZ

Should you use an online update service?

John: I would just as soon know what software is running on my computer, so I do my updates manually, checking weekly. C|Net Catch-Up is a fine way to keep track of what you may want to update and then do the updates yourself.

Ray: I'm a little leery of giving a Web site the power to start fiddling with my software, so I'd suggest using those services that give you the latest news and then make the judgments (and updates) for yourself.

Gregg: As with many things, privacy risks are associated with these services, and you have to decide whether they are risks you're comfort-

able taking. How big of a risk are they? It's hard to say because services like this one are relatively new. Although C|Net and McAfee are both well-respected and trusted names, when you use a service like this one, you're exposing your computer to a third party — and maybe to hackers and other intruders. I think that it's premature to sign up for a service like this one. However, if I were going to sign up for one, I would probably go with the McAfee offering and pay the annual fee. After all, you usually get what you pay for, and in this case the stakes are so high that it's not worth cutting corners to try to save a few bucks.

Updater programs and the breaches of privacy they create

You *must* obtain updater programs directly from the manufacturer or Web sites (sometimes known as *mirrors*) that the manufacturer has authorized to offer patches. (Two reliable mirrors are `www.tucows.com` and `download.cnet.com`.) After all, what sweeter revenge for a virus author than to trick people into running an infected "virus patch" program!

TIP

You should never run files or programs sent to you that claim to be a security patch — instead, make sure that you download them yourself from a reliable source.

Back Up Your Data — Please!

Trust us when we say that if a virus or a hacker ever destroys your hard drive — or the little bugger just goes dead all on its own — you'll be mighty glad that you listened to us: Backing up your files is as essential to good computer health as brushing your teeth is to good dental health.

We recommend that you back up your data at least once a day. That's a good minimum number to live by when it comes to brushing your teeth, too, by the way.

Do you back up? How often? And how do you do it?

John: I decided to solve the problem once and for all, so I bought myself a DLT tape drive, like the one Internet providers use, and back up all the changeable data on all my servers every night. I have a set of seven tapes, one per day, plus an extra Monday tape that I swap every week into a safe deposit box.

Ray: I have many computers with many different backup regimes. My Web and mail servers use *RAID,* which means that the computer has at least two hard drives that constantly duplicate each other in order to keep an exact mirror image of each other at all times. If one goes bad, the system switches to the other without a hiccup. In addition, a copy of the system is backed up to another computer on the other side of the country, and CDs are burned periodically. I save files from my desktop and laptop to a central file server and run tape backups regularly.

Gregg: I back up every day to an Iomega Zip drive. When the Zip disk gets full, I compress the files and copy them to a CD and then keep the CDs in a fireproof box.

Welcome to Squirrel World: How and where to store your backed-up data

For a squirrel, securing long-term storage is a 3-step process:

1. Gather nuts.
2. Stuff them inside your cheeks.
3. Find the nearest tree with a hole in it.

Luckily for you, you have lots more options when it comes to collecting and storing your backed-up files:

- ✔ **Iomega Jaz and Zip drive:** These products are two of our favorite ways to back up data (the slower Zip drive is perfect for casual users, and the speedier Jaz drive with increased storage capacity is necessary for heavy users) because they're easy to install and easy to use. But, wait — there's more! All Iomega drives come with software that automatically backs up data for you, and you can set the drive to copy files on a timed basis periodically during the day so that you're constantly backing up as you work. You can also use the software to do an initial backup of all the work files on your hard drive. *The downside:* Whoo-ee! At a starting price of about $15 for a Zip disk and $89 for a Jaz disk, this form of storage can be expensive.

- ✔ **Personal CD Writer:** This product is another one of our favorites because the hardware and disks are cheap (less than a buck a disk, and they hold as much as 650MB), they're fast, the hardware is easy to install, and it doubles as a CD burner for all those MP3s you've been downloading. If you decide to get a CD writer, get one that says "CD-RW" or "rewriteable" so that you can reuse the CD several times to save money. *The downside:* The drive probably doesn't come with nifty backup software, like the Iomega drives do.

- ✔ **Online storage:** What a great idea! Rather than store your backup files at home, you send them into cyberspace to be stored on someone else's servers. *The downside:* It's a great idea until the company storing your files goes out of business and you lose access to your data. Or, the company's servers could go down — right when you most need access to your files. Or, someone at the company may decide to open your files to see what kind of interesting stuff you've been storing there.

To find out more about online storage, visit xDrive), iBackup (`www.ibackup.com`), or iDrive (`www.anuvio.com`).

- ✔ **Your network server:** If you're sitting at work and wondering how to best back up the files on your company computer, consider using Windows Explorer to copy them into a backup folder on the company server. Then, periodically, have your backup files burned on a CD to avoid bloating the company's storage resources. *The downside:* We can think of two. If the company servers go down, you lose your backup data, and if you're worried about privacy in the workplace, you've just made it easier for someone else to read all your files.

When you "need your space"

No matter how big your backup drive may be, at some point it will reach its limit. Then you can either run out, buy another disk, and pop it into your drive — or you can use one of several easy-to-use compression software programs to shrink the size of the data already on your backup disk so that you can squeeze on even more. The two best compression software programs for Windows are WinZip (`www.winzip.com`) and NetZip (`www.netzip.com`); the best program for Macs is StuffIt (`www.stuffit.com`).

The two main reasons people don't back up their data

The good news about backing up your hard drive is that it's much easier than backing up a 1960 Cadillac. The bad news is that most people have never tried parallel parking a 1960 Cadillac, so they don't appreciate in comparison just how easy it is to back up their files.

Here are the two main reasons that people don't back up their data:

- ✔ They think it's too complicated.
- ✔ They forget.

Microsoft Windows comes with its own backup utility, but it's lacking in features and can be cumbersome to use. Choose Start⇨Programs⇨ Accessories⇨System Tools⇨Backup. You may have to use your Windows CD to get it if it wasn't installed when your system was set up.

If you want a backup system that 's more user friendly and offers more features (like a reminder), go to www.tucows.com or www.cnet.com to find lots of freeware and shareware backup and reminder systems that will help you avoid becoming another "lost-all-my-data" statistic. (As always with freeware and shareware, the principle of *caveat emptor* and other privacy rules apply: Choose software that is highly rated by others, and use the Web to do a little investigation into the programmer and the company that offers it.)

But will your backups be there when you need them?

Here's the funny thing about backup files: If you don't take care of them, they may not be there when you need them most. Here are some hints for protecting your backups.

- ✔ **Put them to the test:** Gregg has a friend who backed up all the most important and sensitive data from his business, every day, for many years. Then, after all that time, a virus destroyed everything on his hard drive — and he found out that none of the files on his backup disks could be deciphered. The moral of the story: You can't just back up your files — you also have to periodically test the files and disks to make sure that you can read them when you need them.

Computers and software may come, and they may go, but some backup disks stay with you forever. Keep this statement in mind as you upgrade your hardware and software and your backup system, and make sure that you have the right disk drive and software to read those old backup disks when you need them.

- ✔ **Put them where they're safe:** If someone steals your computer — and your backup disk is still inside the drive — it doesn't do you much good, does it? Ditto if your house burns down, which brings us to our next two points.

- ✔ **Make multiple copies:** Make copies of your backup disks regularly, and keep one copy in the safest place you can find. Depending on the value and sensitivity of the data in your files, that may be a fireproof box or safe you keep at home or even a safe-deposit box down at the local bank.

This advice may sound extreme — until you lose all your data; only then will you think back on this as the best advice you've ever heard.

✔ **Treat them with care:** Considering how valuable your backup disks are if you ever need them, you may want to take a little better care of them now. We suggest putting them back in the case after each use, and storing them in a drawer or other safe haven that's away from the dog, the cat, spilt coffee, and direct sunlight.

Just to reinforce the need to back up your files and to store them securely, please remember these actual screams heard outside a smoky office building that was being evacuated by the fire department: "You've *got* to let me go back in there! My doctoral thesis is on one of those computers!" (No, we *won't* tell you whether it was one of us who was doing the screaming.)

Don't pull a Monica Lewinsky!

As you may recall, Monica thought that she deleted all the tell-all files from her computer — but what she didn't know was that the files she thought she got rid of could still be recovered from her hard drive. Don't pull a Monica: If you have secrets to hide and you *really* want to delete them from your hard drive, use disk-wiping software, such as BCWipe (`www.jetico.com/bcwipe.htm`), as shown in Figure 3-2, or Spytech Eradicator (`www.spytech-web.com/eradicator.shtml`).

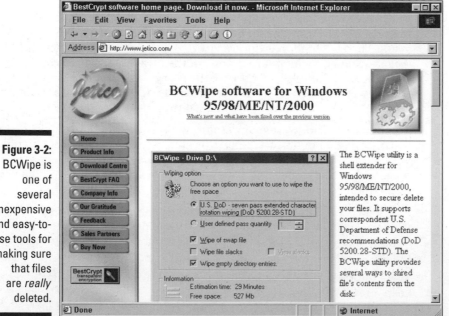

Figure 3-2: BCWipe is one of several inexpensive and easy-to-use tools for making sure that files are *really* deleted.

Using Passwords and Encryption

For the most part, when we think of passwords and encryption, we think of e-mail and e-commerce and other accounts we have opened or used over the Internet. But what about using the same tools to protect the data that's sitting right there in the computer on your desk?

Passwords: Like windows to your soul — and to your data

As more and more of everyday life is managed — lived, really — through a computer, passwords become increasingly prevalent — and important.

Are the passwords you use really protecting you? Is all the data on your computer getting the protection it needs?

What's a 4-letter word for "I forgot my password"?

For those who don't have *enough* passwords to remember, let us suggest a few more places to introduce them into your life:

- **Password-protect your operating system:** Ever since Windows 95, a user has been able to set up her computer to require a password before it boots up. But, depending on the operating system and your particular installation, this password can be overridden, or even bypassed, by a skillful snoop or your company's system administrator. Still, the password provides a good first line of defense. To set a password in Windows XP, click the Start button and choose Control Panel⇨User Accounts to give yourself access to set and change your Windows system password. In Windows 98, click the Start button and choose Settings⇨Control Panel and then double-click on Passwords to give yourself access to set and change your Windows system password. In Windows 2000, click the Start button and choose Settings⇨Control Panel. Then double-click on Users and Passwords, where you see buttons for setting and changing passwords and for creating new user accounts. If you want more information about setting up multiple users and passwords, check out Chapter 4.

- **Password-protect your files:** Many software packages come with built-in password-protection features. For example, you can save documents in Microsoft Word 2000 with a password so that you always need the password to open them again: Save the document by choosing File⇨Save As from the menu bar. From the Tools menu in the Save As dialog box, click on General Options (as shown in Figure 3-3) and enter a password.

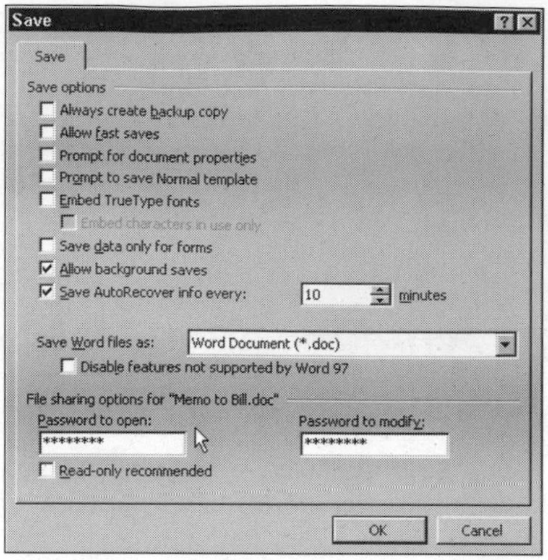

Figure 3-3:
Word lets
you set two
passwords:
one to open
the file and
another to
make any
changes
to it.

Save

Save options
- ☐ Always create backup copy
- ☐ Allow fast saves
- ☐ Prompt for document properties
- ☐ Prompt to save Normal template
- ☐ Embed TrueType fonts
  - ☐ Embed characters in use only
- ☐ Save data only for forms
- ☑ Allow background saves
- ☑ Save AutoRecover info every: 10 minutes

Save Word files as: Word Document (*.doc)
- ☐ Disable features not supported by Word 97

File sharing options for "Memo to Bill.doc"

Password to open: ********   Password to modify: ********
- ☐ Read-only recommended

OK   Cancel

You can also save documents in Word 2000 so that they can't be modified without a password. To do this, enter the password you want in the Password to modify box and click OK. The program asks you to re-enter your password as a safety precaution. Reenter the password as requested and click OK again. Finally, finish by clicking on Save and closing the dialog box. To find the password features in other software programs, choose Help from the menu bar and search for *password*.

✔ **Password-protect your access to the Internet:** In Windows 95 and later, you can password-protect your Internet dial-up connection so that no one else can use your ISP account. Most ISPs require you to have a password for your Internet account; to make the process more convenient, however, most dial-up software programs allow you to store your password so that you don't have to type it every time you connect to the Internet. If you're concerned about the unauthorized use of your dial-up connection, you can remove the password from your dial-up settings, which then requires you to enter it every time you connect. Again, it's privacy versus convenience, and you get to make the call.

✔ **Password-protecting the whole enchilada:** If you want to password-protect your software and everything else on your computer, browse to Download.com (www.download.com) at CINet and use that Web site search to look for *Password* entries. We found more than 500 freeware and shareware applications that enable you to generate random passwords, remember your passwords, and lock up your machine with a password.

As always with freeware and shareware, the principle of *caveat emptor* and other common-sense privacy rules apply: Choose software that is highly rated by others, and use the Web to do a little investigation into the company that offers it. Be sure to read the user's license to make sure that by installing the software, you're not agreeing to give away your first-born child.

Should you password-protect files?

John: I don't bother, but then most of my files are on Unix machines with password-protected user accounts already. If I kept important data on Windows machines, I would take care of at least the important stuff, like my bank account info.

Ray: The password protections offered by most files, such as Word or Excel documents, aren't sophisticated and can be cracked by those who are determined to get at your data. However, those protections can be useful for making sure that changes aren't made to documents without authorization and for generally putting a crimp in the style of anyone who's just a little nosy.

Gregg: I confess. I have been lax in this department, and I foolishly carry all my files around with me on a laptop! But, I promise, the minute we finish this chapter, I'll download one of the shareware programs from the Web.

How to choose a password

Do the math, and you may suddenly feel very confident. After all, 10,000 possible combinations exist for a 4-digit password (for you math majors, that's 10x10x10x10 = 10,000). How long would it take a hacker to try out all 10,000 of those combinations? With a good password-cracking software — available for free from the Web, of course — all it takes is about a minute.

Now that we have your attention, here are some rules for choosing passwords:

- ✔ **Don't pick obvious passwords:** Don't use your first name or last name or your dog's name or your spouse's name or your birthday or your birthday backward or common words in English or any other common language. Someone who *really* wants to get access to your computer already knows to try this kind of personal information first. If you aren't feeling creative or otherwise up to the task of inventing random passwords, you can find freeware and shareware password-generating applications by visiting Download.com (www.download.com) at CNet and searching for *Password*.

- ✔ **The longer the password, the better:** As we say a little earlier in this section, 10,000 combinations are possible with a 4-digit password. The number of possible combinations for a 5-digit password is 100,000 (or 10x10x10x10x10). For a 6-digit password, the number is 1 million combinations.

- ✔ **Use both numbers *and* letters:** Throw a few letters into the password, and you really make things complicated. A 4-character password consisting of both letters and numbers has 1,679,616 possible combinations. (That's 10+26x10+26x10+26x10+26, for you math fans.) For a 5-character password, 60,466,176 combinations are possible.

✔ **Throw in a few symbols, like $, %, & and *, just to make guessing your password even harder.** The reason, we think, is obvious. Sometimes a software program or your operating system doesn't let you use non-alphanumeric characters, but if your system lets you, you certainly should! (This advice applies to your ISP and other online passwords as well.)

A good password looks something like this: kl5K8$d.

✔ **Don't write down your password:** In particular, don't tape it to your monitor or jot it down on the bottom of your coffee cup.

How can you remember kl5K8$d and all your other passwords if you can't write them down?

Encryption, by golly, encryption! We explain this subject next.

Encryption: Thank Goodness for Glorious Gobbledygook

Encrypt a piece of data and suddenly it doesn't mean anything to anyone any more — except for you and anyone else who has your password or key. So the fear of data being stolen or intercepted is gone because your data in the wrong hands is just gibberish.

If you use your encryption software to encrypt your list of passwords for safekeeping, you have to remember only one password: the one for your encryption software!

Goody-goody gobbledygook!

If the benefits of glorious gobbledygook sound good to you, here's how to put encryption to work on your own data:

✔ **Encrypt passwords:** Use a password encryption program, like RoboForm. You can find out more about these programs in Chapter 12.

✔ **Encrypt files on your hard drive:** They're your files, darn it, and you don't want anyone else reading them. The trick then, is to encrypt them so that if someone without the password does open your files, all they see is something like this:

```
dfjklsdfjkl;sdfjkl;fsdjkl;sdfjkl;sdfawertsdfjkl;sdfjkl;sd
        fajkl;dfgweruioerwjio or sdfjkl;werouiweruion-
        jklsdflnjku90wer or xcvnm$9ke*sd893
```

Lots of freeware and shareware programs are available that enable you to encrypt your files. To find them, browse to Download.com (`www.download.com`) and search for *Encryption*.

For more information on encryption, including how to encrypt e-mail, see Chapter 10.

Before you give that computer to charity or to Grandma or a friend

Do you really want Grandma checking out your old love letters and e-mails, your friends checking out your old tax returns, or your favorite charity, as a way to make money at its next fund-raiser, auctioning off pictures of you at *that* bachelor or bachelorette party?

Take it from us: You'll be much happier if you just remove all that stuff from the hard drive before giving the machine away.

Depending on your time, patience, and level of paranoia, you can

- Go into Explorer and manually delete the sensitive files (see Chapter 9).
- Use one of the disk-wiping software packages discussed earlier in this chapter, in the section "Don't pull a Monica Lewinsky!"
- Remove your hard drive from the computer and carefully place it into a wood chipper (like the folks at the CIA do).

The Dummies for-free, do-it-yourself, at-home computer security tests

Okay, we admit it: It's not really ours — but we did test it out for you.

This free service, at `www.symantec.com/securitycheck`, tells you whether your machine is revealing any personal information about you that may arouse the interest of a hacker. It also checks for any open ports that may make your machine vulnerable to hackers, tests your susceptibility to Trojan horse viruses, and scans your computer for other security issues.

One catch is involved, of course: The provider of this service, Symantec, is in the business of selling security software — so you may want to get a second opinion on any security risks it finds before rushing out to buy the software it recommends as the solution. Still, we have to say that we're impressed with the value of the security check itself as well as with the other useful security information and tutorials available at the site.

Just to reinforce the need to get a second opinion, when Ray used this service to scan one of his computers, it said that he was "at risk" with respect to antivirus protection because he has a competitor's antivirus software loaded on the machine and it couldn't vouch for how current the version was. (Ironically, the antivirus software had been updated just a day earlier.)

For a quick check of your computer's security profile, visit Symantec Security Check, at www.symantec.com/securitycheck.

Chapter 4

Privacy for Computers and Networks with Multiple Users

In This Chapter

▶ If your computer has more than one user

▶ If your network has more than one user

Back in the 1950s, only one or two homes on a block may have had a television set. By the early 1980s, everybody had a television in every room of the house, and by the mid-1990s, each of those televisions had cable and maybe a VCR. Think it will be any different with computers? Think again!

Many households still have only one computer, with kids and parents competing for time on it. Recognizing this situation, companies like Microsoft have made it possible to have multiple users registered on one computer, allowing them each to customize settings and features to suit their own preferences. The first part of this chapter discusses ways of keeping your own information to yourself — even when you share your computer with others.

In a growing number of households, the computer scene is very different. Mom and Dad may each have a computer, and each school-age kid has one. Whereas parents once vied with their gossipy teenagers for use of the phone, everyone in the house is fighting over the modem line. One benefit of the new high-speed broadband services, such as the phone company's DSL service or the cable company's modem service, is that with so much bandwidth, everyone in the house can establish and share a home network. With that capability, however, comes the challenge of keeping out outsiders (from the neighbors next-door to hackers halfway around the world), so the second half of this chapter talks about ways to keep your home network safe from intruders.

One Computer/Multiple Users

At home, at work, at the library, at the local cyber-café — whenever you share a computer, privacy issues (not to mention some convenience issues) are sure to be involved.

Everybody likes the computer set up differently. One child may love the desk-top wallpaper with the Powerpuff Girls and neon scroll bars, and another may immediately dispense with the Powerpuffs and need the screen resolution set specially for a space-age shoot-'em-up game. Later, one parent may have to adjust everything again because a soccer Web site has somehow replaced the stock market report as the Web browser home page (the page it shows when it starts up). Then the other parent may have to fiddle with the settings again to be able to read the latest project from Martha Stewart's Web site.

Those clever folks at Microsoft had exactly this scenario in mind when they added a new feature to Windows that allows you to create a different user profile for each user on a computer. Each profile for each user then gets its own configuration settings. The second edition of Windows 98 makes it easy to create multiple users, set passwords, and more. Let's take a look at how it's done.

We use Windows 98 in many of the examples in this chapter, but the same general procedures also apply to Windows Me. The appearance of the set-tings menus may vary a little among versions of Windows, but the overall procedure for creating and managing multiple user accounts is the same.

You may run across two other versions of the Windows operating system: Windows 2000 and Windows XP. Both these versions are geared toward busi-ness and professional users, and each one has slightly different — and in many ways much more complex — systems for managing multiple users. We mention some of those differences along the way. Configuring Windows 2000 and XP for multiple users isn't extraordinarily difficult, but because of their slightly more complex security features, be warned: You can lock yourself out of parts of your own computer if you're not careful! See the sidebar "Why Windows 2000 and Windows XP create users differently," later in this chapter, for more info on setting up user accounts in Windows XP.

Prepping your system

Two steps are involved in setting up multiple users in Windows 98. Both are accessed through the Control Panel. Click the Start button and choose Menu⇨Settings⇨Control Panel. Your first stop is Passwords, as shown in Figure 4-1.

Click on Passwords in the Control Panel to call up the Password Properties dialog box, which has several tabs. The first tab, Change Passwords, allows you to set and change your Windows password (the password you use to log in to Windows when you first start the computer).

In Windows 2000, the control panel for Users and Passwords is combined. Similarly, in Windows XP the unified control panel is labeled User Accounts. By default, both operating systems automatically permit users to maintain their own settings, so this step isn't necessary.

TIP

A bucketful of tips for setting passwords

If you don't have a password set, you should add one unless you're certain that no one else will ever have access to your computer.

Although you can access your computer without knowing your password, having one at least keeps casual snoops from getting in. Also, you should change your passwords from time to time, just to keep snoops on their toes.

Having just advised you of how wise you are to have a password set, if you would rather not have to type one every time you log on, you can cut out that inconvenience by setting a new password, but leaving the new password field blank. This method will gives the appearance of having a password, but all you really have to do is press Enter and you're logged in. Of course, if pressing Enter is still too much trouble, you can do away with multiple users altogether and

reset your system to not require any login. But then, why you are reading this section of the book?

Windows 2000 and Windows XP already have a user named Administrator. To create users and manage passwords for accounts other than yours, you first log in as Administrator or on another account with Administrator privileges.

Given the ease with which someone can make off with your laptop computer, having a login password makes sense, even if you're the only one who uses it. For people in the business of stealing laptops, some technical tricks allow them to get past a login password, but you can at least make the thief work a little harder to be able to read your files. (It doesn't make much difference if the thief decides to just wipe the hard drive, though.)

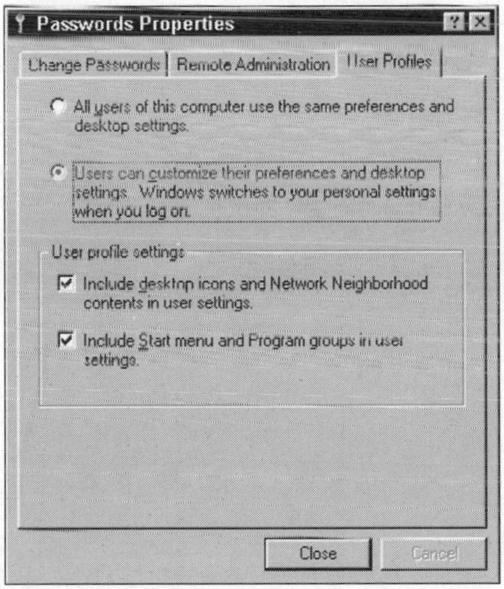

Figure 4-1:
Manage
passwords
and let
multiple
users
maintain
their own,
unique
system
settings.

Passwords Properties

Change Passwords | Remote Administration | User Profiles

○ All users of this computer use the same preferences and desktop settings.

● Users can customize their preferences and desktop settings. Windows switches to your personal settings when you log on.

User profile settings

☑ Include desktop icons and Network Neighborhood contents in user settings.

☑ Include Start menu and Program groups in user settings.

Close   Cancel

Setting a password

The default setting for most Windows 98 installations is to have just one user. When you first set up your computer, it may have asked you for a login name and password, and it may even ask you for this information again every time you start your computer. It's there, under the Password Properties Control Panel, that you can add or change your password.

Enabling multiple user profiles

After you've set a password for yourself, click to select the User Profiles tab. Click the button that allows users to customize their own preferences. Click OK and then close the Password Properties box. The computer needs to restart before you continue.

Creating new users

After you've enabled users to set their own preferences, it's time to tell Windows who these new users are! Click the Start button and choose Settings⇨Control Panel⇨Users to display the panel shown in Figure 4-2.

From the Users Control Panel, you see a list of users (hopefully, including you). Click the New User button, and a series of dialog boxes leads you through the steps to creating a new user. You're asked to specify a username and password.

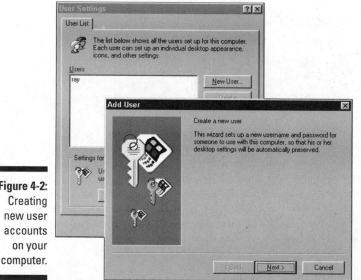

Figure 4-2:
Creating
new user
accounts
on your
computer.

TIP

Usernames can be as long as 128 characters, but do you really want to have to type that many characters every time you log on? We suggest using a password of 8 characters.

Why Windows 2000 and Windows XP create users differently

The creation of new users in Windows 2000 and Windows XP is more complex than under Windows 98. Both these newer versions of the `Windows operating system are designed for multiuser corporate environments; therefore, they were designed with somewhat tighter security controls. Many security controls are based on the level of access permissions granted to each individual user as well as to groups of users. An important part of creating new users under Windows 2000 and Windows XP involves assigning users to groups and designating the level of access those users will have.

In Windows 2000, for example, the Control Panel for creating users and managing passwords has been merged into one (unlike in Windows 98, which has separate panels for Users and for Passwords). Under the combined Users and Passwords Control Panel, you can add a new user by simply clicking a button labeled Add. After designating a username and password, however, you get to the more complex task of managing access permissions and groups.

In Windows 2000, you can create users (Mom, Dad, Junior, and Sis, for example), assign them all to an access group named Family, and then give access to certain documents (such as Junior's soccer practice schedule). Mom and Dad can also be assigned to a group named Parents, which would have exclusive access to ChristmasShoppingList.doc. In this way, Windows 2000 provides flexible access controls, both file-by-file and directory-by-directory.

You should read up a little on how to manage groups before arbitrarily assigning users to them. Check out the Microsoft online documentation for Windows 2000 at

```
www.microsoft.com/windows2000/
en/professional/help/
usercpl_overview.htm
```

Windows XP takes a slightly different tack. User account controls are under one Control Panel item named User Accounts, where you click the option labeled Create a new account. You can create any number of accounts, but control over the type of account you create is limited to two choices: Administrator and Limited. Marking an account as Administrator lets you do pretty much anything with the account: install software; make systemwide changes; access non-private files; and create, modify, and delete other user accounts. A Limited account can change only its own password and other personal settings. If you trust all other users not to mess up your computer deliberately or accidentally, you can give them Administrator accounts; if not, give them limited accounts.

When you create an account, it has no password. On the User Accounts page, you click on the newly created icon for your new account and then on Create a password. There you find both the screen that lets you enter the password and a hint in case you forget the password. After the password is set, the account is ready to use.

Customizing your Windows 98 settings

After you provide a username and password, Windows 98 gives you the option to decide which settings you want to let users customize for themselves and whether you want to prepopulate some of those with existing settings.

Here are your basic choices:

✔ Putting check marks next to each item allows the user to personalize that feature, and Selecting the Create copies of the current items and their content option makes a duplicate copy of all the primary user's settings, documents, and Internet Explorer Favorites, for example. All changes a user makes after this point will be unique to that user. For example, a copy of the entire contents of the main system's My Documents folder is made especially for the user. After that point, anything the user changes in that folder is visible to only that user.

✔ Putting check marks next to each of the items but selecting the Create new items to save disk space option creates a clean slate for the user. The Start menu contents are reset to their defaults, the My Documents folder is empty, and Favorites are restored to their defaults, for example. All changes made by the user are unique to that user.

✔ If you don't put check marks next to certain items, any changes made to those items aren't unique to the user. For example, if you don't allow users to have their own My Documents folder, they continue to have access to the systemwide version of My Documents and every time that user makes a change to a document, that changed document can be accessed by everyone. Removing the check marks from all items (regardless of whether you select Create copies or Create new items) means that any changes made by that user are also registered systemwide. For example, any change to the systemwide Favorites list can be seen by any other user who doesn't have a check mark next to Favorites.

If those options sound a little confusing, you're not alone. In the next couple of sections, we look at what those choices mean and how they affect user privacy. (If you don't care what's happening behind the scenes when you create new users, skip the following section.)

What's really going on

For each user you create, Windows is generating a folder in C:\Windows\ Profiles for that user. In each of those folders, depending on the level of personalization you choose for that user, are copies of their personalized settings, documents, Favorites, and other settings.

For example, you may create a user named Joe and choose to allow Joe to have his own version of the My Documents folder. Normally, the My Documents folder is located directly under your drive C: (C:\My Documents, for example).

If you choose Create copies, however, the system makes a copy of the entire contents of C:\My Documents and puts that copy in C:\Windows\Profiles\ Joe. Or, if you choose Create new items, the system creates a brand-new (empty) folder named My Documents and puts it under C:\Windows\Profiles\Joe.

From now on, every time Joe logs in, he still sees on his desktop a folder named My Documents; when he clicks on it, however, the system seamlessly routes him to C:\Windows\Profiles\Joe\My Documents.

If you have chosen *not* to allow Joe to have his own version of My Documents, the system continues to route the desktop icon for My Documents to C:\My Documents.

Nifty, huh?

If your account has been set to permit you to maintain your own, personalized settings, personalizing your desktop settings is as simple as logging in, right-clicking on the desktop, and choosing Properties.

Because of this capability, you can have many copies of a folder named My Documents and have many versions of the documents stored therein. This situation can prove to be confusing if multiple users are working on the same set of documents or on documents with similar names. That's why Windows gives you the option of allowing a user to have her own version of My Documents or to continue having her account access the main My Documents folder in C:\.

You can have per-user versions of all the other choices that are available when you create a new user. Depending on your choices, Windows either makes copies of items such as your Favorites file, generates fresh ones, or keeps them pointing to the systemwide versions.

Our recommendations

Because these choices can be confusing, here are our recommendations:

- ✔ If you're setting up a new system and want every user to be able to build her own documents, Favorites, and other items from scratch, put check marks next to all the items and choose Create new items.

- ✔ If you have an existing system with lots of preferences already set, you may want your "new" users to be able to customize their own settings in the future, but let them start out with all the current system settings they're used to. So put check marks next to those items you want them to be able to customize and select Create copies.

Three tips for logging on to and off the computer

After you've set up multiple users, every time you boot up the computer it asks you to log in. Just type your username and password. On Windows XP, it displays icons for each user (see those cute little pictures in the figure in this sidebar), so you click on your icon and then type your password.

When you don't want to shut down the computer, but need to let someone else log on, click the Start button. The option just above Shut Down is Log Off followed by the username of the person now logged in. Choosing Log Off takes you to a dialog box that asks for your username and password.

Here's a third way to log off under both Windows XP and Windows 2000. Pressing Ctrl+Alt+Del brings up a dialog box named Windows Security in Windows 2002 or Windows Task Manager in Windows XP. Among the items is a button labeled Log Off.

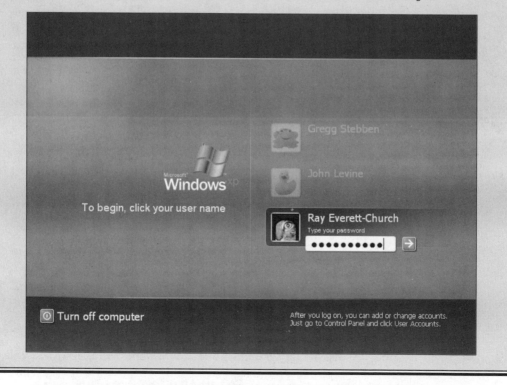

Protecting and sharing files on a shared PC

As we explain earlier in this chapter, Windows keeps track of different users on a system by designating a separate folder for each user and keeping the unique settings and documents in those separate folders. However, because those are all located under C:\Windows\Profiles\(username), hardly any security is inherent in this arrangement because anyone with access to the computer also has access to your C:\Windows\Profiles\ file. Therefore, if you want to protect your files, you need to get a little more sneaky.

Password-protecting your files

Many applications, including Word, Excel, Quicken, WordPerfect, and other popular programs, allow you to set passwords on files created in those programs. Consult the documentation for your favorite programs to see whether they allow password protection and, if so, how to turn it on.

Many Microsoft products, like Word, let you designate passwords for files at the time you first save the document. In Word, after you create a document, clicking Save As calls up a dialog box that asks for a filename and location in which you want to save it. At the top of that box is a pull-down menu named Tools; from that menu, choose General Options (which we discuss in Chapter 3).

A new box appears in which you can set various options related to saving the document. Included at the bottom of this box is an option labeled File sharing options. You have several options:

- **Password to open:** Type the password needed to open the file. After the file is open, the person reading it can change the contents of the document, unless you assign the option in the following bullet.

- **Password to modify:** You can require a password before any changes can be made to the document.

- **Read-only recommended:** You can alert the user that he shouldn't be fiddling with the contents of the file.

If you don't care who reads the file, but don't want anyone to change the contents, you can check the Password to modify option but and leave the Password to open option blank.

Alternative file-protection methods

The simplest way to protect files from unauthorized access is not to have the files on your computer in the first place. If you have only a few files that you need to protect, floppy disks and zip disks work well.

If you're worried mostly about unauthorized access by people sharing your computer, you can also consider storing sensitive files at an online storage site, like X-Drive. These sites offer reasonable promises of security, but in the end offer less control than keeping files in a secure place, like on a disk in your shirt pocket. If you have more files than will fit on a floppy or Zip disk, these services may be worth a look.

A number of third-party utilities are also available that allow you to block access to certain files, or even to entire directories. In Chapter 3, we provide some suggestions on how to locate shareware and freeware locking programs. These software packages offer differing levels of security, and you have no guarantee that whatever they do to prevent access won't go haywire and keep you locked out too. But even modest protection is better than none.

Sharing files on a shared PC

In this section, when we say *file sharing*, we mean sharing files between users of a single PC. This situation is different from File Sharing between computers on a Windows-based network, which we talk about later in this chapter.

As we mention earlier in this chapter, because of the way Windows keeps track of the users' personalization settings, users may have access to potentially many different desktop configurations and many different My Documents folders. Therefore, if you're regularly collaborating on files with other users of the same computer, it may make more sense for you to store those shared files in places other than on the desktop or in My Documents.

For example, you may want to create a new folder on drive C: that can be your designated file sharing location. To create a folder that won't be mistaken for something else, double-click on My Computer and then on C:. Choose New⇨Folder from the File menu and give the folder a name like Family Shared Files.

Sharing Internet access

After a computer is configured for Internet access, that capability is available to all users on that PC. However, depending on how you connect to the Internet, you can limit access. The simplest way to prevent the unauthorized use of a computer's Internet connection is not to store the login password for your ISP in your settings.

If you use the Internet dialer that is built into Windows, you should see whether your password has been saved in your settings. To access it, click the Start button and choose Settings⇨Control Panel⇨Internet Options. Click on the Connections tab, and under Dial-up settings (and Virtual Private Network, if you have that feature installed), find your default connection, click Settings, and look under Dial-up setting to see whether your username and password are stored there.

Deleting your password makes Windows ask you for your password each time you attempt to log on. If you want to prevent unauthorized Internet access, don't give anyone that password!

If your ISP uses a proprietary dialing program to access its service, you need to check to see whether its software permits you to remove your stored password. Most ISP dial-up software offers to store your password for you, but can be set to require it each time you log on.

One computer/multiple e-mail accounts

Many popular e-mail programs allow you to configure them for use with multiple e-mail accounts. America Online lets you maintain multiple e-mail accounts under each master account, allowing you to give everybody in the family their own e-mail address. This arrangement is also convenient because it allows parents to use the AOL Parental Control settings to manage how their kids use their e-mail accounts. AOL also lets you password-protect mail stored in your offline Filing Cabinet. Follow these steps:

1. Sign on using the screen name you want to protect.

2. Choose Settings⇨ Preferences from the menu on the AOL toolbar.

3. In the Preferences window, under Account Controls, click Passwords.

4. Put a check mark next to Filing Cabinet.

Other software packages also offer the capability to set up multiple users. For example, Outlook Express lets you create multiple identities, allowing each identity to have its own mailbox and settings, as shown in Figure 4-3. In Outlook Express, choose Identities⇨Add New Identity from the File menu.

When you specify an identity, you also get to choose whether to require a password in order to access that identity. Choosing Manage Identities also allows you to designate which identity Outlook Express uses when you first start it. After you've given the identity a name, you then provide the e-mail settings for that account, as provided by your ISP.

Using Web-based e-mail

Perhaps the best, easiest, and most secure way of keeping your e-mail out of the unwanted view of others who share your computer is to not keep your e-mail on your computer. Web-based e-mail, such as Hotmail, Yahoo! Mail, and others, offer a simple solution. It also has the benefit of not being tied to just one computer, so if you want to access your e-mail from elsewhere, all you need is a Web browser.

In Chapter 10, we talk more about the privacy pros and cons of using Web-based e-mail.

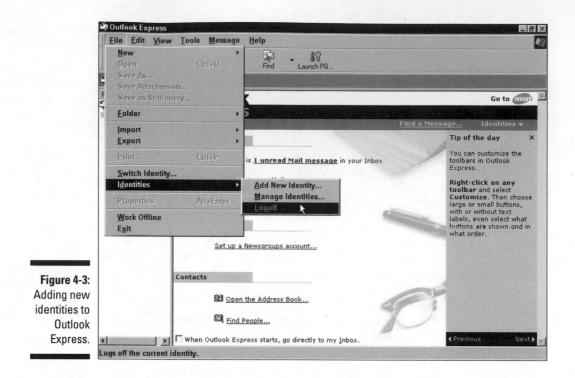

Figure 4-3:
Adding new
identities to
Outlook
Express.

One Network/Multiple Users

Now that computers have become so cheap, it's increasingly common for everyone to have their own computer, all connected by a network.

"Am I on a network?"

The answer to that question is an unequivocal "maybe." The answer for most of us is "if you're connected to the Internet, you're on a network." But, depending on how you're connected to the network can make a great deal of difference in terms of how your privacy is affected.

First, you need to spend a few moments delving into the geek realm to understand some things about networks. Most modern home and office networks use a *star* layout, as shown in Figure 4-4.

The star configuration has the benefit of being much efficient, expandable, and easy to set up. This kind of network has a simple premise: a computer, connected to many other computers, connected via some kind of traffic-control device (usually a network *hub* or *switch*.)

The term *Internet* refers to a network of interconnected networks. In fact, so many networks connect to make up the Internet that many illustrations of the Internet feature the "cloud" image shown in Figure 4-5. The cloud is in many ways similar to the puff of smoke used by a magician to disguise his skillful manipulations. Whatever goes on inside the cloud is something too complex and mysterious for mere mortals to understand!

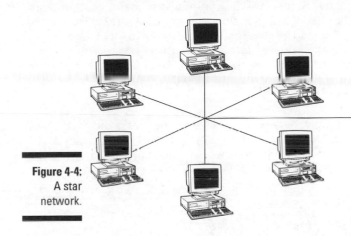

Figure 4-4:
A star network.

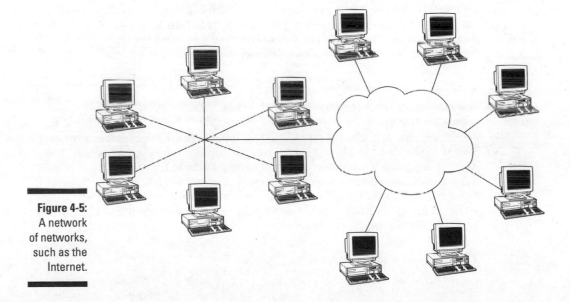

Figure 4-5:
A network of networks, such as the Internet.

Your own chunk of the cloud

When you connect to the Internet, whether it's via a modem or through a high-speed connection like a cable or DSL modem, you're little PC is becoming one of dozens of computers connected to your ISP's network. That network is in turn one of hundreds of networks connected to the network of so-called "network backbone" providers.

Some networks belong to places like Amazon or Yahoo! or Microsoft and are full of content. Other networks contain the computers of major corporations, like Boeing or General Electric, where the business of the world is conducted. And some networks belong to the government and to universities and research institutions. Finally, some networks are networks of networked computers, such as AOL and Earthlink, which contain connections to the computers of your friends and loved ones, where they send and receive e-mails and do their own Web surfing.

Unfortunately, that amazing variety of networks upon networks means that, as a great thinker once said, "No man is an island." In terms of your privacy and security, connecting your computer to a network is much like lowering the drawbridge on a fortress: It lets in both the kindly villagers and the barbarians.

Networks and file sharing

One key benefit of being connected to a network is the speed and ease of sharing data. Whether you have Web pages, memos for work, or the latest MP3 file from The Backstreet Boys, being connected to a network means never having to put a file on a disk and walk or drive or mail it to someone else!

First, a word of caution

If you stop and consider the ease with which you can grab files from other computers, you will immediately understand just how easy it could be for someone else to grab files off your computer. Unless you're absolutely certain that you need to share files between computers on your network, you should not open the Pandora's box of network-based file sharing. As we privacy geeks say: The most secure computer is one that isn't connected to a network, but then that also makes it a much less useful computer. The utility of file sharing can outweigh the danger, but you have to decide for yourself whether it's worth the risk.

Private and public directories

As we mention in a sidebar in the first part of this chapter, some operating systems, like Windows 2000, allow you to set restrictions and assign permissions based on individual users and groups. Just as you can limit access, you can also throw open access to the entire world. Obviously, it's not a good idea to do that if you're hoping to keep any of your private files private. But sometimes you may want to. When? For example, when you're building a site for the World Wide Web, which is by definition a place where you publish pages and documents you want the rest of the world to see.

Often the most efficient way to handle access restrictions is to designate some directories as Public and others as Private. By doing so, everything you toss into the public directory can be seen by the world while things you file privately remain hidden.

Luckily, complex operating systems, like Windows 2000 and all Unix-based systems (including Linux), have intricate ways of controlling file access permissions. In fact, on those operating systems, every file and directory has nine possible settings:

	Read	*Write*	*Execute*
Owner	r	w	x
Group	r	w	x
World	r	w	x

The possibilities for who can access a file are

- **Owner:** The person who created the file or was otherwise assigned ownership of it
- **Group:** A set of users (defined by the system administrator) who are permitted access to the file, such as "students in Chemistry 101"
- **World:** Just like it sounds — everybody

The possibilities for what kinds of access are permitted are

- **Read:** You can see the contents of a file.
- **Write:** You can change or delete the contents of a file.
- **Execute:** You can run the file, if it happens to be a program.

"Why," you may ask, "is it important for me to know this information?" Because this is how Windows controls access to files and directories, and it's how you decide who gets access to which files on your system.

If your ISP allows you to post Web pages on its server, you may have been instructed to place your Web pages in a directory named public_html. Although the rest of your file space is private — such as where your mail gets stored until you retrieve it — your files on public_html will have permissions set so that the world can read the files in there. The permissions also are set so that only you and the system administrator have the right to modify or delete files in that directory. Or, in terms of the preceding little table, it will be Owner Read/Write/Execute, but only World Read.

A beautiful day in the Network Neighborhood

When you connect two or more computers via a network, you have the capability to share files between them. But the computers have to know how to talk to one another first. Computers use many different *protocols* (languages, of a sort), to speak to each other in order to communicate with one another. Some of these protocols, you have heard of, such as Hypertext Transport Protocol (HTTP) and File Transfer Protocol (FTP).

Windows-based computers have their own flavor of networking protocol, named SMB, and every Windows machine has something named the Client for Microsoft Networks, which allows it to communicate with other Windows machines to share files, printers, and other network resources. Some versions of Macintosh computers also have something similar, named AppleShare, which serves exactly the same purpose.

When you connect your Windows computer to a network, the configuration process asks you for a number of things, including network addresses and the domain (the last part of the computer's name) of the computer. If you're connecting to the Internet, your ISP will have given you all these settings.

But when you're setting up a network between two or more Windows computers, you can specify your own local domain, which lets you set your computers apart from the larger domain, like Earthlink.com. The Windows domain is like a special nametag that your computer wears so that other Windows computers on your network can know that you're part of the same club.

When two or more Windows computers are connected to a network, they broadcast their existence to the network, including what domain they belong to. If your computer is designated as belonging to the same domain, clicking the Network Neighborhood icon on your desktop shows you the other computers claiming to be part of your domain.

After you have your computers connected to the network and they have broadcast their existence to everybody else on the network, it's time to share some files and other resources! You can easily accomplish this task by using Windows File Sharing and Print Sharing.

If you're connected to the Internet and click Network Neighborhood, why don't you see every single Windows computer that's connected from all over the world? Two reasons: First, not every computer is advertising itself as being in the same domain as your computer. Second, most ISPs operate firewalls that block the Client for Microsoft Networks from broadcasting its existence outside of a narrow part of its network.

When they call it a Network Neighborhood, they ain't kidding! Many cable modem and DSL providers recommend that Windows users put the same domain into their network settings. Because many of these ISPs put their firewalls at their main network connection point, you can often see that other users are connected to the same provider — for example, other people on your street or in your apartment complex! Imagine that: You could *accidentally* print that love letter or tax return on your next-door neighbor's printer! Why wait until you have made this mistake? Make sure that you turn on sharing only when you need it, and always set passwords.

Installing File Sharing and Print Sharing

Because file sharing is a potentially dangerous occurrence, many companies don't ship their computers with sharing installed. The quickest way to determine whether File Sharing and Print Sharing are installed is to click the Start button and choose Settings⇨Control Panels⇨Network. Near the middle of the dialog box is a button labeled File and Print Sharing, as shown in Figure 4-6. Click this button and turn the check boxes on.

Depending on your original installation, you may need your Windows installation CD or disks handy, in case the system needs to load new system files. If your computer doesn't ask for additional files, you can simply click OK and you're ready to set up sharing.

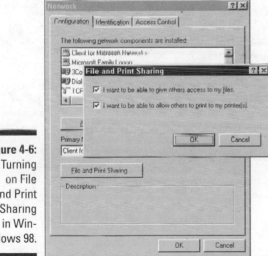

Figure 4-6: Turning on File and Print Sharing in Windows 98.

Turning on File Sharing

After you have installed File Sharing, it's time to share! But before you do, you need to keep a few things in mind:

✔ Windows allows you to designate entire disk drives as well as specific folders as "shared."

✔ If you choose to share an entire disk drive, take a moment to reflect on what kinds of personal information are stored on your computer because it's all about to become public information that anyone can see.

✔ Likewise, if you choose to share a particular folder, make sure that the subfolders don't have in them anything that you don't want the world to see. For example, sharing your C:\Windows folder could make all the Web page viewing history and page cache for your browser visible to the world because they're both stored under C:\Windows.

Not sure about the privacy and security impact of sharing certain folders? Then consider creating a special folder that is just for files you want to be shared, such as C:\Shared. Then, when you have files you want to share, you can simply move copies of them to that folder without fear that other files may also be seen.

Some versions of the Windows operating system (most notably, Windows 2000), suffer from a security bug that makes your entire hard drive visible to others on your network, regardless of which folders you choose to share. To see whether computers on your network are susceptible, open Internet Explorer and type *<computer-name>*\c$ (replace *<computer-name>* with the name of the computer you're trying to view).

After you have decided exactly which folder or folders you want to share with others on your network, select that folder in Windows Explorer and right-click on it. A menu appears, with an option labeled Sharing.

In Windows 2000 and Windows XP, the process of sharing folders or files is almost identical. In Windows 2000, right-clicking on a folder displays a Sharing menu. In Windows XP, however, it's named Sharing and Security.

In the Shared Properties window, you're given many choices:

✔ Turn sharing on and off for that folder.

✔ Choose the name and a comment that users see when they try to access the folder.

✔ Choose whether users can just read the files in the directory or whether they can have full access.

✔ Set a password for Read-Only access as well as Full access.

After you've made those choices and click Apply, a hand appears underneath the icon of the folder, as shown in Figure 4-7, indicating that it is now available for sharing.

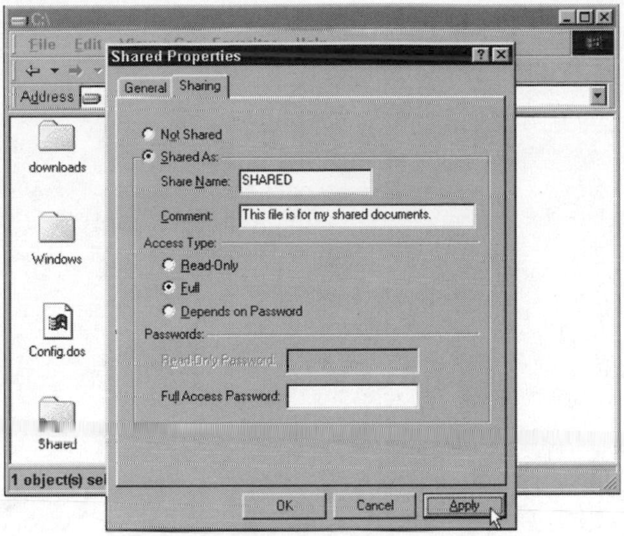

Figure 4-7:
After you've
set the
File Sharing
features
you want
and clicked
Apply,
a hand
appears
underneath
the file icon
to show that
the file
is being
shared.

Turning on Print Sharing

After making sure that Print Sharing has been installed (as we discuss earlier in this chapter), designating a printer to be shared is simple: Click the Start button and choose Settings➪Printers. You see any printers that have been installed and are active on your system. Right-click your mouse on the printer you want to share and choose Sharing from the menu. You're given the option to turn sharing on or off as well as to designate a name for the printer. Click Apply, and you're set!

The trade-off

A trade-off always exists between privacy and convenience, and rarely so clearly as when you're deciding how to set up your computer on a network. On one hand, the more networked resources you have, the easier it is for you and your friends to use your computer. On the other hand, your enemies and other miscreants will also find it potentially easier for them to use.

Balancing privacy and convenience is something you have to do continually, so don't just turn on file sharing and forget it. Turning it on when somebody needs it and off again when they're done is safer than leaving it wide open at all times. Share only what you need to, and double-check every week or so to see whether you're still sharing just what you need and no more.

Chapter 5

Privacy for Laptops and Handheld Devices

*W*hy is it that no matter what you're looking at on your laptop screen, what's on the screen of the guy across the airplane aisle always looks more interesting? And wouldn't it be nice if computer etiquette allowed for you to casually lean over and say "Hey, that looks really fascinating. Mind if I take a read?"

Of course, computer etiquette *doesn't* allow for such invasions of privacy — so if you're one of those people who insists on carrying *some* sort of electronic device around with you all the time so that you can read your e-mail or type a memo to staff members or sneak in a day's work while you wait for your latté to be served, you should be aware of some special privacy concerns,

First, a few words about mobile devices and passwords.

Although it certainly makes sense to use a password whenever the option exists — particularly on mobile devices like laptops, handhelds, and cellular phones — don't let the fact that you've set a password lull you into a false sense of security. Consider, for example, that although 10,000 combinations are possible for a 4-digit password — a hacker with a password-cracking program can cycle through all 10,000 of those combinations in less than a minute! You can read more about passwords later in this chapter.

Protecting Laptops

Take a moment to reflect on the number of hours you spend with your laptop and the number of intimate details about your life that you have shared with it, and you realize that it's really one of the most precious possessions of your life. Here's how to give your laptop the respect and protection it deserves.

Laptop theft

Those in the know estimate that more than 400,000 laptops a year are stolen. It's such a common occurrence that many companies don't even bother to report the loss, or they wait and report a whole bunch of them missing all at the same time.

The best places to get your laptop lifted

Business travelers, take note. These are the best places to get your laptop swiped:

- ✔ **At the airport, after your laptop has gone through the scanner, but while you're stuck behind a guy who keeps setting off the x-ray machine with all the electronic gizmos he has stashed in his pockets.** In fact, it may be his accomplice who has just made off with your laptop while you patiently wait your turn in line.

- ✔ **From your hotel room, while you're at dinner.** So maybe the next time your worry-wart significant other suggests that you not just leave your laptop lying on the bed, you should listen rather than get indignant.

- ✔ **From your car, especially a car that is fresh off a rental lot.**

- ✔ **From any public place where you've "just set it down for a second."**

How will you suffer if someone steals your laptop?

If someone steals your laptop, you will suffer. Let us count the ways:

- ✔ **If it's your own personal laptop:** Of course, you lose your machine, which is expensive to replace. But the data on the laptop is probably worth much more. If you're like many people, you keep on the machine all your financial information (bank account numbers, bank statements, credit and debit card numbers, stock and mutual fund information, tax information, your passwords for accessing your financial accounts online, your long-distance calling card number — maybe even your Social Security number). If you're like many others, you also keep information about your health and health insurance and other sensitive personal information on the machine. After all, that's what it was made for, right? What a shame it would be to lose it all — but even more of a shame if all that valuable information were to fall into the hands of the wrong people.

✔ **If it's the company's laptop:** You probably keep on your laptop all the personal information mentioned in the preceding bullet plus loads of valuable insider information about your company, including trade secrets, corporate intranet passwords, business plans, financial information, proposals, and e-mail. Do you really want to be responsible for letting all that information slip into a competitor's hands? In one case in Silicon Valley, the contents of a stolen corporate laptop theft were valued at more than a billion dollars.

✔ **Restoration comedy — or nightmare?** Ask anyone who has ever had a laptop stolen and that person will tell you that the worst part is rebuilding your digital life without it — especially if you weren't in the habit of backing up your data regularly. Reconfiguring a new machine with the right hardware and software and settings and passwords eats up hours and hours of your life. Meanwhile, a stolen laptop has a way of haunting you for years to come — because the time will come when you think, "Where did I put that file?" You'll get a sinking feeling down deep in your stomach when you realize that no matter how desperately you need that file *right now,* it's gone, gone, gone.

✔ **"First I lost my laptop, and then I lost my job":** We have unconfirmed rumors about some companies that make you walk the plank if your laptop takes a walk and it has company documents on it that, according to company privacy and security policies, shouldn't have been there in the first place.

How to foil the spoilers

Here's the laptop golden rule: When you're in a public place, don't *ever* let your laptop out of your sight — not even when you think you're in the safest public place in the world. We would bet that the CEO of Qualcomm, Irwin Jacobs, wishes he had followed the golden rule. After giving a speech to a room full of business writers at a conference, he walked into the crowd to shake hands and mingle. Just moments later, the laptop he had used to present his slides during the speech vanished from the room. You'll never guess what was on his hard drive: Qualcomm financial statements, e-mail, and other sensitive corporate information dating back several years.

Here's the laptop golden rule at the airport: You should always hand your laptop to security personnel for a "hand check" rather than let it ride on the luggage conveyor belt. If the security folks balk, make sure that your laptop is the *last* bag you put on the conveyor to reduce the time it spends on the other side unattended. And don't *ever* check your laptop as luggage — because if the thieves don't get it, the luggage-handling equipment will.

Here are some laptop essentials:

✔ **Use a bag that's not so obvious.** When your company assigned your laptop to you, it probably came in one of those black nylon bags that everyone else in corporate America carries a laptop in. That's a real mistake because using that bag telegraphs to the whole wide world that you have a laptop just waiting to be heisted. Instead, learn from one of your authors who violated the laptop golden rule but still came out on top: While on a commuter train from New York to Washington, D.C., he stowed two bags overhead. In one bag he had an inexpensive printer in a videocamera bag and in a worn-out, green college backpack he had a laptop computer. Which one do you think the thief walked off with? (John keeps his laptop in an old, beat-up briefcase that looks like only a geezer who still writes his documents with a fountain pen would own.)

✔ **Use a bag that's so, so obvious:** Regardless of what kind of bag you carry your laptop in, do something so that you can quickly pick it out in a crowd. Put a company sticker on the side of the bag or tie a bright piece of yarn around the handle. Why? If someone walks off with the case, you can quickly identify it and know for certain that it's yours, and you can take off after the person (while also yelling for the cops).

✔ **Use a bag with a strap.** You can throw the strap over your shoulder when standing and walking or drape it over your knee or wrap it around your foot while sitting.

✔ **Write down the serial number at home or at the office or both.** You can usually find the number on the bottom of your machine. Police officers, insurance employees, and who knows who else will want this number. This advice may seem obvious, folks, but if the *only* place you record the serial number is on your laptop, it doesn't really do you much good if the laptop's stolen, does it?

Here are a couple of smart, but optional, options:

✔ **Deface the machine:** One security expert suggests that having the machine's serial number engraved not just on the underside of the laptop but in big, humongous type on the outside of your machine is sort of like securing your car by putting The Club on your steering wheel: Its large and hideous presence may just scare off a potential thief because it's permanent and makes the machine much easier to identify.

✔ **Use a lock and an alarm to discourage theft.**

First, look on the back and sides of your laptop for a small padlock icon alongside a small slit in the plastic. If you find this security slot (a standard feature on most laptops today), you can quickly and easily attach a security lock and then wrap the cable around a fixed object. Laptop locks can be found online and at most computer and office supply stores.

Alarms come in many flavors. Some attach directly to your laptop or bag, others use cables, and most have motion-sensitive alarms. You can shop around, or you can make life easy and buy the Targus Defcon1, which can be attached directly to your bag or machine. It also comes with a built-in retractable cable. In addition to its motion-sensitive alarm, the DefCon1 also goes off if someone tampers with the cable. Finally, you want to get an alarm with lots of flashing lights so that it scares thieves away early, before they have even had a chance to think twice about trying to steal your machine.

If you really have something to lose

It's probably true that if someone *really* wants to steal *your* laptop, chances are good that he will eventually be successful. But that doesn't mean that you have to make it easy for that person to read what's on the hard drive, does it? Try these tips:

- **Use locking software:** Locking software locks up your operating system and hard drive so that no one can access it without the right password. We used the keywords *locking software* to search at www.cnet.com and found more than 60 different programs to choose from. As always with freeware and shareware, caveat emptor and other privacy rules apply: Choose software that is highly rated by others, and use the Web to do a little investigation into its programmer and the company that offers it. After all, bug-ridden software can cause you to be locked out of your own computer! (This advice applies to the software you find with the searches we suggest in the rest of this section, too.)

- **Hide those important files!** If a thief can't see your files, how will he know to read them? A variety of programs encrypt and then hide sensitive files and directories in secret places on your hard drive, out of sight and out of reach of anyone without the password. We used the keywords *hide files* to search at www.cnet.com and found more than 30 different programs to choose from.

- **Use a tracking program to relocate your stolen laptop:** A variety of freeware and shareware products are available that use the Internet as a tracking mechanism for stolen laptops. Although these products work in a variety of different ways, the principle is always the same: Install one of these programs on your machine, and every time it's connected to the Internet, it reports its location to a specified e-mail address or Web site. If the laptop has been stolen, this information may enable police to recover the stolen unit. We found a handful of these utilities by searching for the keywords *laptop theft* at www.cnet.com.

- **Go biometric:** The SecuGen EyeD Mouse II lets you record your own fingerprint on your hard drive — and we would bet that you can figure out what happens — or doesn't happen — after that. Meanwhile, before you get too excited about this foolproof locking system, keep this information in mind: If you use the SecuGen EyeD system and someone walks off with your computer and then is able to hack into the security software — you have just lost control of the most unique personal identifier you have, which should send shivers down the spine of anyone who is worried about identity theft.

"Is it safe to store Quicken or Microsoft Money files on a laptop?"

The real question is "Is it safe to store *anything* on a laptop?"

If you've read the section "How will you suffer if someone steals your laptop?" earlier in this chapter, you know that if someone gets hold of your machine, he will probably get access to everything there, including any Quicken or QuickBooks or Microsoft Money files you keep on your hard drive. It's up to you decide whether you want to take the risk.

Our recommendation: If you use financial software, like Quicken or Microsoft Money, you should use the software on a desktop machine, not on a laptop. But if you use one of these software programs on a laptop, at least set a password within the program to deter anyone who may get hold of your computer.

To do this in Quicken, choose File⇨Passwords⇨ File and type your password twice.

Whoa! Stop those straying eyeballs!!

From a Starbucks in downtown San Francisco to Seattle-Tacoma International Airport, you may spend a great deal of time working on a laptop out in public and be concerned about "eyeball eavesdropping." Because growling and grumbling no longer seems to ward snoops away, we suggest that you consider installing the 3M privacy screen filter on your machine:

www.3m.com/us/about3M/innovation/computerfilter/index.html

As hard as peeping Toms may try to get into the right position to read what's on your screen, it always looks blank to them — even as you continue to type away. Designed for use at airports and on airplanes and other public places, these privacy filters also make for a great practical joke for those who have snoopy co-workers or bosses.

For more information on protecting the data on your laptop, see Chapter 3.

What about Pocket Computers?

Tiny computers that fit in your pocket contain data just as important as their larger cousins, so here are some suggestions to keep your pocket computer secure.

Protecting Palm and Microsoft Handheld devices: If you can dream of a privacy or security application for your Palm or Windows CE device, the odds are in favor that someone has already written it. And, as the need for other applications arises, it's a good bet that someone will quickly fill them.

Software solutions for your Palm: By visiting the Software & Add-ons area of www.palm.com, you can find software products that let you protect the data on your Palm, generate random passwords, encrypt and memorize passwords, write encrypted memos, search and eliminate viruses, and automatically lock your Palm. Much of this software is freeware or shareware. Other resources for finding software for your Palm include the download areas of www.zdnet.com, www.cnet.com, and www.tucows.com. As always, your responsibility as a freeware or shareware user is to make sure that the software you're using is safe and stable and is provided by a legitimate source. We noted with interest that some of the software available from the Palm Web site has been downloaded as many as 40,000 times — which is probably a good indication of the software's reliability.

Software solutions for your Microsoft CE device: The Microsoft Web site also offers privacy and security applications that you can download, but not nearly as many. You can also find applications for your CE device if you search for *Windows CE software* at www.zdnet.com, www.cnet.com, and www.tucows.com.

Lock it up: You've entered your life into your handheld computer — now the worst thing that could happen is for you to have the unit and all your personal data stolen. With that in mind, Kensington (www.kensington.com) has designed a lock similar to the locks for laptops we described a little earlier; It allows you to use a cable to lock down your handheld computer to your desk without obstructing your access to the screen, buttons, and stylus.

Back it up: One of the great things about a handheld computer is that by simply syncing it with your desktop computer on a regular basis, you're effortlessly creating a backup file. Keep in mind that passwords must be used on both machines to ensure that your data is safe from privacy intruders.

Securing Your Cell Phone

Have you ever thought about how damaging it would be if your cell phone were to fall into the wrong hands? If someone gets your phone, she can quickly run up charges totaling hundreds or even thousands of dollars. Because it's your phone, you're probably liable for the charges. The phone numbers (and privacy) of your friends and family will be easily accessible from your cell phone's phone book. To protect yourself, your phone, and your data, take our advice:

You change phone settings differently on every phone, so if you don't know how to make the changes we suggest in the next few paragraphs, see your owner's manual, dial 6-1-1 (usually) on your cellular phone to reach customer service, or ask for help from the store where you bought your phone:

- **Activate your phone's password:** A password prevents unauthorized people from turning on the phone and making calls (although most phones now still complete a call to the 911 emergency service). Keep in mind that the password protects you only when the phone is turned off. Setting your phone's security codes (see the following bullet) protects you if your phone is lost or stolen when it is already turned on.

- **Use security codes:** Your phone's security codes prevent others from changing your password and altering other phone settings. If your phone is set to restrict incoming and outgoing calls (see the next bullet), your security code is what prevents someone from making unauthorized calls.

- **Restrict calls:** If your phone is stolen or you lose it while it is turned on, the password and security codes don't help prevent unauthorized calls. However, you can set your phone to restrict incoming and outgoing calls, thus rendering the phone useless.

- **Restrict international calls:** Often, cell phones are stolen so that they can be used to make expensive international calls. Therefore, unless you make a large number of international calls from your cell phone, you should call your cellular provider and ask someone there to restrict your account to domestic calling only.

- **Hiding phone numbers:** Some phones let you hide numbers that are stored in the phone book. This feature is particularly useful when you're storing numbers that include passwords; for example, access to a voice-mail account.

Part III
Privacy on the Internet

The 5th Wave   By Rich Tennant

@RICHTENNANT

"Hey Philip! I think we're in. I'm gonna try linking directly to the screen, but gimme a disguise in case it works. I don't want all of New York to know Jerry DeMarco of 14 Queensberry, Bronx NY, hacked into the Times Square video screen."

In this part . . .

When most people think "privacy," they think
"Internet" — and for good reason: When you plug
into the World Wide Web, you're becoming part of a world-
wide *network* of computers to which you are granted limited access. And, because your computer is then hooked
into all the other computers on this huge global network,
you're granting others limited access to your computer
as well. In this part, we look at how others (people, businesses, governments) can get access to your computer
and data on your computer and how you can limit this
access to your data so that your personal information
remains private and safe.

Chapter 6

You and Your Internet Service Provider (ISP)

In This Chapter

▶ What your ISP knows about you

▶ Special issues with cable and DSL

▶ How free are free ISPs?

A sk any farmer and he or she will tell you: Only a fool lets a fox guard the henhouse door.

As an Internet user, you have to remember that every time you go online, you do so while sitting on a pile of information that's *very* valuable. And It's your Internet Service Provider that's guarding the door — so read this first section carefully and choose wisely.

What Your Mother and Your ISP Have in Common

No one knows you quite like Mom does: She knows who your friends are. She knows where you like to go to hang out. She knows what you're afraid of. She knows what you like to wear.

Now, forget Mom for a minute and focus on your Internet Service Provider: If you think of the Internet as a tree with many branches (with each of your e-mail accounts as separate branches and your Web browsing and your instant messenger and favorite chat rooms and everything else you do on the Internet as other branches), your ISP is the trunk of the tree. From that trunk, all your other uses of the Internet grow.

What else does this mean? Unlike your Web browser software and your instant messenger software and other software applications that may have filed away some limited information about you and what you do on the Internet, your ISP knows about *everything* you do online. Like Mom, it knows who your friends are, where you like to hang out, what you're afraid of, what you like to wear. Yet, unlike Mom, it also knows when you're going on vacation, where you bank, what stocks you own, and whom you're mad at.

Seven things your ISP doesn't want you to know it knows

In addition to the obvious stuff, like your name, address, and credit card number:

- Every Web site you've ever visited (including the ones you went to by mistake — and then were very embarrassed when you saw what was there)
- Every e-mail and instant message you've ever sent and received and perhaps even written but then thought better of sending
- Everything you've ever said in every chat session you've ever had
- Everything you've ever bought over the Internet
- Everything you've ever considered buying over the Internet
- Possibly, who and how much you have paid if you pay your bills online
- Possibly, if you bank online, your account numbers, account balances, and the amount of your paycheck if you use direct deposit

Two ways to stop your ISP from finding out more

A little common sense begs you to remember that although your ISP may be able to capture your credit card number as you buy a sweater online, in most cases it already has the number and therefore could have long ago bought itself a sweater on your dime. In reality, the odds of your ISP doing something truly sinister with all your data are much smaller than the odds that your waiter is running next door to buy a sweater with your credit card right now while you drink your coffee and wait for the receipt. Still, common sense also tells you that you would be prudent to take the following steps to do everything possible to deprive your ISP of finding out more about you than it reasonably needs to know:

- **The facts, ma'am — just the facts:** To open an account, your ISP legitimately needs to know your name, address, and credit card number. If an ISP asks you for any more information, simply refuse to provide it. If it refuses to open an account without more information, your best bet is to start shopping for another ISP. (You can find a list of regional and national ISPs at `thelist.internet.com/`.)

✔ **Choose an ISP with a strong privacy policy:** In most cases, you can find a link to an ISP's privacy policy (if it has one) at the bottom of its home page. Be wary of "stickers" on the page that tout the ISP's membership in organizations like BBBOnline and TRUSTe — these organizations require its members to post and follow a privacy policy but don't ensure that the policy has any teeth. Don't ever fill out member profiles: When you do, you're literally hand-feeding the fox the personal information it most wants to know.

What happens when your ISP is slapped with a subpoena with your name on it?

Take the case of four John Does who were anonymously chatting in a Yahoo! financial chat room. They thought that their identities were hidden when they made defamatory remarks about Eric Hvide, the CEO of the Fort Lauderdale, Florida, company Hvide Marine. Claiming that the anonymous posts harmed both himself and his company, Hvide went to court to force the chatters' ISPs to reveal their identities so that he could sue them for defamation.

"They ruined this guy's life and career," Hvide's attorney said, defending the lawsuit. "You've got the right to know who's attacking you." A Florida appeals court agreed and ruled that Internet Service Providers must identify the source of defamatory messages.

The moral of the story: If we were to choose a privacy theme song for the Internet, we would probably pick the opening number for the TV show "Cheers" — because try as you might, it's awfully hard to go anywhere in cyberspace without everyone knowing your name.

"So where can I hide?"

If you want to use the Internet to send a truly anonymous message, don't use your own computer and don't use your own ISP. Your best bet is to use a computer at your local library or Internet café or some other location where you can get online without revealing your identity. Keep in mind that anonymity may be harder to achieve than you think. For example, if you use a credit card to pay for Internet access at an Internet café, you may have just created a paper trail that could enable your "anonymous" message to be traced back to you. (See our discussion of anonymous remailers in Chapter 10.)

Assessing Dial-Up versus DSL versus Cable Modem Connections

For many people, driving on the information superhighway is an extension of their personalities when they're driving on the interstate: They want to go where they want to go, and they want to get there fast!

When you've just got to have speed, you've just got to have DSL (Digital Subscriber Line) or cable. Before you sign up for the broadband revolution, though, keep in mind that cable and DSL access bring to the privacy equation the following problems to which pokey little dial-up connections are immune.

DSL and cable: Suffering from 7-11 syndrome

What do your broadband connection and your local convenience store have in common? Both are always open — which means that both are always vulnerable to attack.

You're like a beacon in the night, and day, and night, and day. The good news is that your DSL or cable access is always on. So you get to spend more time surfing the Web and less time drumming your fingers on the desktop, rolling your eyes and sighing heavily while waiting for your modem to dial up and make a connection every time you want to get online. The bad news is that your DSL or cable access is always on. So bad people who want to hack their way into your system can go at it any time they please, chipping away at your system whenever their schedules permit. If a hacker is successful, he gains a steadily reachable, high-speed-connected, probably unattended, probably unsecured computer to poke and prod into becoming what the security specialists call a *zombie* — a powerful, mindless drone who faithfully executes any command he chooses to gives it.

The trouble with cable

Did the cable guy forget to mention just how easy it would be for you to look at all the files on all your neighbors' hard drives — and for them to spend a leisurely evening letting their mice do the walking through your hard drive and files?

To keep strangers out of your computer — 24/7 — you need to install a personal firewall, which prevents outsiders from gaining entry into your computer by making your computer's ports invisible to anyone trawling the Web looking for open doors. We recommend ZoneAlarm, at www.zonelabs.com, which is free.

IP addresses don't change to protect the innocent. Your *IP address* is a unique string of numbers that identifies your computer on the Internet. With most dial-up accounts, you get assigned a new Internet protocol address (when you're showing off for friends, you want to call it an IP address) every time you log on. But if you access the Internet through cable or DSL service, you may have a permanent IP address. From a privacy perspective, this address is a dangerous thing because it means that someone determined to invade your privacy always knows where to find you.

Here's the cure:

- ✔ Ask your ISP whether it can provide you with a dynamic IP address. Even if the answer is yes, you still need to install a personal firewall.

- ✔ Just because your access is 24/7 doesn't mean that you have to stay connected to it. Consider turning off your modem or just disconnecting it when you don't need to be online — but check with your ISP first because this solution can cause problems for some systems.

- ✔ Still nervous? As an added security measure, shut down your computer when you aren't using it for long periods.

- ✔ Operate in stealth mode. Many excellent routers not only let you connect more than one computer to your cable or DSL line but also act as a firewall to screen out potentially invasive activities by hackers. Use an inexpensive DSL/cable router, like those made by Linksys or Netgear. The router takes the IP address from your ISP, and each of the computers behind the router gets its own, private IP address, which remains shielded from the outside world by the router itself.

File sharing with the Joneses

Whenever you and your neighbors use cable to look at the Internet, you're all sharing the same Local Area Network (LAN). As with any other LAN, your computer (yes, this means all the files on your hard drive, including your e-mail and your pictures of Aunt Betty's vacation to Coral Gables and your favorite MP3s and your banking records) can be accessed simply by clicking on Network Neighborhood in Windows 95 or later.

Even if you've installed a firewall, you want to make sure that your neighbors don't have access to your computer. Here's how:

If you're using only one computer with your cable modem: You can keep your neighbors from snooping around inside your computer by eliminating File and Print Sharing. Unless you have specific reasons to share files or printer resources with others on your network, you should turn off sharing. If you're behind a well-secured firewall and need to share files, you may turn file sharing on when needed. To do this in Windows 95 or later, turn off network access to your computer. How you do this task depends on which operating system you're using.

In Windows 98:

1. **From the Start menu, choose Settings⇨Control Panel⇨Network.**

2. **Click on the button for File and Print Sharing, as shown in Figure 6-1.**

3. **If the boxes on the File and Print Sharing panel are checked, uncheck them and click OK.**

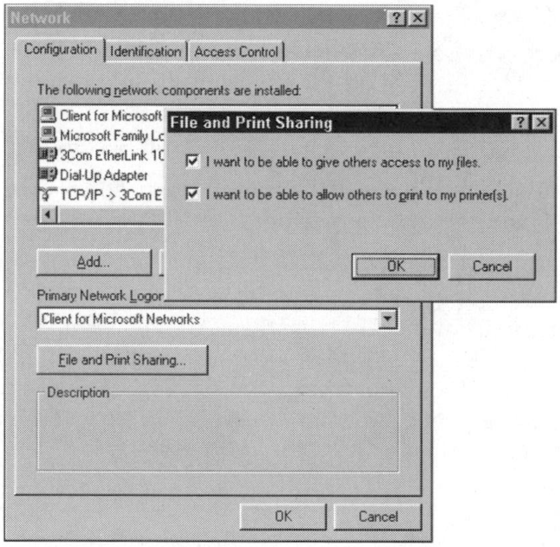

Figure 6-1:
Turning File and Print Sharing on and off in Windows 98.

In Windows 2000:

1. **Click on the Start button and choose Settings⇨Network and Dial-up Connections.**

2. **Right-click your cable connection and choose Properties.**

3. **On the General tab, uncheck the File and Printer Sharing for Microsoft Networks box.**

In Windows XP:

1. **From the Start menu, Choose Settings⇨Network Connections.**

2. **Click on the icon for your Local Area Connection to call up the Local Area Connection Status dialog box.**

3. **Click Properties to open the Local Area Connection Properties dialog box, where you can check or uncheck File and Printer Sharing for Microsoft Network, as shown in Figure 6-2. (You may have spotted this figure in Chapter 4.)**

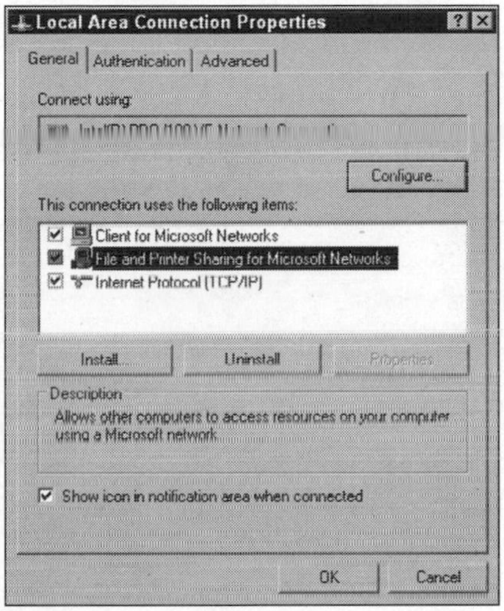

Figure 6-2: The Windows XP Local Area Connection Properties dialog box.

Running more than one computer off the same modem? You want to give your own computers access without giving your neighbors access, too. Be sure to put passwords (ones that aren't obvious) on any resource you share among your computers, and use a router with a firewall to connect your network to the cable.

Free ISPs: A Good Idea?

In our free-market system, whenever someone promises you something for free, you had better look long and hard because eventually you see that you're paying for it somehow. In the case of a "free" ISP, you get access to the Internet without dipping into your wallet, but you still pay for that free access by giving up some of your privacy and personal information.

Here's what you're often trading for "free" access:

- ✔ **Is free on the Internet really free?** As long as you're on the Internet using your free access, your free ISP gets to display an advertising bar (typically about an inch high) across the top or bottom of your screen. Right away, you can see that what you have just done is agree to let your free ISP erect a billboard on your desktop. If you own a piece of land next to the freeway and build a billboard there, companies pay you for the right to use your billboard to display their ads. Meanwhile, with a free ISP, the same exchange is being made — a billboard is on your screen, and your free ISP pays you to display ads on it by letting you access the Internet for free.

- ✔ **Ah, but the exchange of values may not stop there.** In many cases, a free ISP uses its billboard window on your screen to not only display ads but also build a record of where you go on the Internet (sort of like your ISP can do, remember?), which then enables it to not only send ads to your billboard window but also target those ads to you based on where you surf on the Web. Obviously, whenever a free ISP begins to collect information about you — versus sending information *to* you — a whole new set of privacy issues are raised.

- ✔ **"No, really — you'll *like* the ads!"** Some free ISPs not only require you to display ads on your screen but also require you to click on them whether you're interested or not. If you refuse? They turn off your Internet access, and you have to log on again.

- ✔ **Sometimes, it's free — unless you want to use it:** Some free ISPs charge for technical support.

Ultimately, the choice is yours: Are you willing to have a stream of ads scroll across your screen as you surf the Web, in exchange for free Internet service? And are you willing to have a company "follow" you around, recording every move you make on the Web, in exchange for that free Internet service? If the answer to one or both of these questions is Yes, free Internet access may be right for you. Yet, as always, you must carefully read a free ISP's privacy policy to ensure that you fully understand what you're giving up in exchange for that "free" Internet access.

The decision about whether to use a free ISP — in the United States, at least — is rapidly becoming moot as free providers go out of business or greatly limit how much time you can spend online per month before they start charging you. If you really need only an hour or two a month, you may find that using the computers at your local public library is easier.

Chapter 7

Fighting Back against Hackers

In This Chapter
▶ The hacking and cracking cast of characters
▶ The hacker's bag of tricks
▶ Keeping them out with a firewall

Feeling safe on the Internet is easy if you think of yourself as just one little surfer out in the middle of a giant ocean of networks, computers, and users. "I'll bet the odds of someone seeing me, let alone picking me out as a victim, are about as slim as the odds of getting bitten by a shark," you may think.

The problem with this analogy is that your average Internet bad guy is lots more technologically advanced than your average shark. Think about it: When you're a shark, you have only one mouth. You can chomp down on only one surfer at a time. The situation is completely different for someone who wants to wreak havoc on your computer.

Introducing Hackers, Crackers, White Hats, and Script Kiddies

A rose by any other name — on the Internet — can sometimes smell sweet and sometimes smell foul. What you may think of as a "hacker" is often known by another name within the hacking and computing communities. Here's how to know who is whom.

Technically speaking, a *hacker* is someone who is *really* good at pushing computers to their limits. These days, the definition has been expanded to mean someone who is *really* good at pushing computers to their limits as a way to get access to something he shouldn't have.

Because some hackers are good, the good ones have suggested that an alternative word, *cracker,* be applied to hackers who are bad. The problem is that the hackers didn't do a good job of telling the rest of the world that there's a difference between a hacker and a cracker, so the two words are used pretty much interchangeably. When the news media makes any distinction between the two words, they usually call a hacker someone who has some larger scheme in mind when breaking into a computer or network and refer to a cracker as someone who generally breaks into computers for the thrill of it.

Just as in John Wayne's world, the world of computer hacking has white hats and black hats. The *black hats* are the bad-guy hackers and crackers, of course — but the role of the white hats isn't as clear as it was in John Wayne's day.

White hats are good guys, mostly. The problem is that the way many white hats do their good deeds is by doing many of the same things that crackers do, but often while working as consultants for the networks they're trying to crack (known as ethical hacking). Meanwhile, some white hats don't wait to be hired, instead preferring to go ahead and ply their craft (pulling off the hack) and then telling the owners of the site after the fact that they've conquered the site.

What differentiates these self-proclaimed white hats from the bad-guy black hats is that they don't abuse the companies whose soft underbellies they've just exposed. But problems still exist. For example, sometimes after a white hat successfully pulls off a hack and then notifies the company of the security hole, the company doesn't take the hint and fix the problem. This neglect enrages some white hats, who then feel justified in publicizing the vulnerability — and this, of course, then *forces* the company to fix the problem in a big-time hurry or risk being overrun by a horde of bad guys, all intent on taking advantage of the security leak.

For a great interactive simulation of a battle between a white hat and a black hat, go to www.msnbc.com/news/437641.asp

---

"Ethical" hacking?

"Ethical hacking" is at the center of a raging debate about whether using dastardly techniques, but not actually doing dastardly deeds, is much of a distinction. If you're a good person, the argument goes, you would not use evil tactics, even in pursuit of a greater good. But, the counter-argument runs, wouldn't you prefer that your vulnerabilities be discovered by someone who warns you about the problem and doesn't exploit it for mischief in the meantime?

For your average Internet user, script kiddies pose the greatest threat. Unlike hackers and crackers — who know what they're doing — *script kiddies* have merely lucked into the possession of harmful software programs called *scripts*. But these script kiddies don't really understand what the scripts do or how they work — all they know is how to unleash these dangerous little applications on the world at large.

As you may expect, script kiddies are most often teenagers — teenage boys, to be exact. At any time, hundreds of chat rooms and message boards on the Internet are swarming with these script kiddies, who are swapping the latest scripts. Unfortunately, the Internet makes it so easy for them to trade and distribute these scripts (later in this chapter, we describe in full detail what the scripts do) that it puts all our computers at greater risk of falling victim to one of their random attacks.

The "coolest" kiddies are 31337 II4X0rZ (which, believe it or not, stands for ELEET HAXORZ or elite hackers). Does that leave you feeling clueless? If you turn the 3s around into capital *E*s, the number 1 into a lowercase *l*, and look at the 7 as sort of a cursive capital T, you see ELEET. You can figure out the rest. What does it mean? Simply that they think they're better than the next kiddies at doing things like downloading hacking software, even though most of them still don't know how it works.

Hacking 101

What makes a hacker tick? We've seen several, often overlapping, goals.

Trouble is my business

Today's cybertroublemakers are always on the lookout for computers (like yours!) that they can attack and remotely take control of, or "own."

How's this for creepy? After they take control of a computer, they call it a *zombie* because they can remotely make it do all sorts of nefarious things, ranging from the cyberequivalent of teenage mischief all the way up to cybertheft, cyberterrorism, and corporate and governmental espionage.

After a hacker takes control over your computer, he can do just about anything he wants with it, including reading your mail and stealing your financial data and other private information. When he's done with all that, he can even set your computer to reformat its own hard drive if he wants.

Why your computer may be in denial

Recently, hackers have been hijacking home computers with another particular purpose in mind: committing a federal crime called a distributed denial of service attack.

To launch one of these attacks, a hacker (or group of hackers working in concert) commandeers computers all over the world, turns them into zombies (see the preceding section), and then orders them to flood a targeted Web site with millions of simultaneous data requests that choke the Web sites' servers and make them unable to serve up pages.

This kind of attack is called *distributed denial of service* because the zombies' data requests get sent or distributed to the victim's servers around the world, forcing the servers to stay so busy that they deny regular service to legitimate customers and surfers like you and us. And this happens more often than you may think; in fact, Microsoft, Yahoo!, eBay, ZDNet, CNN, and many other large companies have all been victims of denial-of-service attacks.

A few years ago, hackers didn't pose much of a threat for most people. But now, thanks to the Internet, we're all their potential victims.

In today's wired world, hackers use automated tools to scan the connections of thousands of online computers every hour and then focus their attention on the ones that appear to be the most vulnerable. Because some of these hacking tools are easy enough for even a child to use — surprise, surprise! — some of the biggest problems are caused by kids (yup, script kiddies) who get their hands on programs they can run, but cannot understand.

Catch them red-handed

One of the great things about the technology of our times is that in spite of the fact that it enables bad guys to do bad things like hacking, the same technology also enables good people like us to have a good time tracking down those bad guys.

Detecting an IP address stalker

As we discuss in Chapter 6, every computer on the Internet has a unique IP address. You may recall that if you have dial-up access, you probably get a new IP address every time you dial up (it called a *dynamically assigned* IP address). If you have cable or DSL, you may get a permanent, or *static,* IP address, which makes sense because you're online all the time.

A network (like your ISP) is commonly allocated a range of IP addresses, from which it assigns a unique IP number to each computer on the network. Because those IP addresses are sequentially numbered, a mischievous hacker can simply identify a range of IP addresses belonging to a DSL or cable modem service provider (versus a company that primarily offers dial-up service) and keep probing every computer at every IP address one by one, until it finds a computer that is vulnerable. ("Vulnerable? Me?" you may be thinking. Don't worry: You find out how to know whether you're vulnerable — and what to do about it — in the next section.)

To understand how a hacker does this, think of a row of houses along a street, with a burglar walking from door to door and rattling each doorknob until he finds one that opens. This is what devilish hackers spend their lives doing, running programs that electronically scan networks, looking for computers that open the door and let them in.

If you have cable or DSL (Digital Subscriber Line) access, how do you protect yourself? With a personal firewall, which you can read about later in this chapter.

Hacking in the danger (and the boredom) zone

As you soon see, network address scanning has its ups and downs for hackers.

Scanning a network that has firewalls installed can be dangerous because the firewall may set off an alarm when it detects someone trying to scan one computer after another after another after another. In fact, after a security expert is alerted, he can watch where the scans are coming from and gather enough evidence to send federal agents knocking on the hacker's door before the scanning is even complete.

Why your cable modem or DSL helps hackers

Hackers looking to cause trouble just love people who have cable modems or DSL connections because more and more users with these 24/7 connections leave their computers turned on day and night. Why?

Why not? What could be better than to be able to get up in the middle of the night to see whether you've gotten any e-mail or to see how your favorite soccer team in Australia is doing? This 24/7 connection offers an awful lot of convenience, but as you can see in Chapter 6, it often also offers a hacker a permanent IP address where you can be found, and an attractive target for attack.

Life can get pretty dull when you make the mistake of scanning ranges of IP addresses that are allocated to modem dial-up connections, and even if you find a computer that's vulnerable, you have no guarantee that the user will stay online long enough to enable you to cause much trouble.

The ultimate hacker payoff

With the dawn of entire neighborhoods connected via dedicated, superfast connections, and with poorly secured computers left on day and night, a clever hacker has fertile ground on which to go zombie farming. After he nails a few victims, he can send his new zombies out to do *all* his scanning and hacking for him. What a beautiful system for the hacker: His zombies report back to him with all their hits, and they take the fall if somebody gets wise to their shenanigans.

Think it can't happen to you?

Although your computer may not offer much of interest to attract most hackers and crackers, you can be sure that it gets probed regularly by script kiddies because they're sweeping thousands of computers at a time and probing every system they can get their little eyes on.

This probe even happens to the computers of smart techies, as you can see from one morning's log of probes from John's small home network. Using the built-in logging on the PC that connects his network to the outside world, John recorded the following probes between 9 a.m. and 10 a.m.:

```
02/04/10 09:03:49 !f 00 dream1.pracon.net ->    jclt.iecc.com
         D  TCP   3831 -> smtp  S
02/04/10 09:06:11 !f 00 ip61.eti.uva.nl ->    www.abuse.net  D
         TCP   1964 ->  smtp  S
02/04/10 09:06:29 !f 00 angora.blitzed.org ->    xuxa.iecc.com
         D  TCP   4680 -> telnet  S
02/04/10 09:06:31 !f 00  211.155.27.211 ->    www.abuse.net  D
         TCP   4162 ->  smtp  S
02/04/10 09:13:35 !f 00 grimlock.angmar.com ->
         xuxa.iecc.com     TCP  50307 ->  smtp  S
02/04/10 09:13:36 !f 00 grimlock.angmar.com ->
         xuxa.iecc.com     TCP  50312 ->  smtp  S
02/04/10 09:14:09 !f 00 rrcs-nys-24-97-64-10.biz.rr.com ->
         xuxa.iecc.com     UDP  33667 ->   137
02/04/10 09:15:58 !f 00  218.233.38.228 ->    ivan.iecc.com  D
         TCP   3648 ->  smtp  S
```

```
02/04/10 09:18:52 !f 00 ip61.eti.uva.nl ->   www.abuse.net  D
          TCP  2033 ->  smtp  S
02/04/10 09:19:30 !f 00 smtp.interaccess.com ->
          www.abuse.net  D TCP 56482 ->   smtp  S
02/04/10 09:20:56 !f 00   64.86.192.65 ->   xuxa.iecc.com
          UDP  4421 ->   137
02/04/10 09:21:43 !f 00      borrell.net ->   xuxa.iecc.com
          UDP  137 ->   137
02/04/10 09:21:51 !f 00 smtp.interaccess.com ->
          www.abuse.net  D TCP 56482 ->   smtp  S
02/04/10 09:26:10 !f 00    gnat.k12.com ->  mail2.iecc.com
          UDP  412 ->   137
02/04/10 09:26:33 !f 00    12.35.167.4 ->   www.abuse.net
          UDP  137 ->   137
02/04/10 09:31:34 !f 00 ip61.eti.uva.nl ->   www.abuse.net  D
          TCP  2140 ->  smtp  S
02/04/10 09:32:10 !f 00 mail.bankofcastile.com ->
          xuxa.iecc.com    UDP   137 ->   137
02/04/10 09:39:20 !f 00 ypw2k6.yukselproje.com.tr ->
          www.spidergraphics.com  D TCP 43910 ->  smtp  S
02/04/10 09:41:58 !f 00   208.31.41.123 ->  mail.iecc.com
          UDP  137 ->   137
02/04/10 09:42:00 !f 00   208.31.41.123 ->   tom.iecc.com
          UDP  137 ->   137
02/04/10 09:42:03 !f 00   208.31.41.123 ->   tom.iecc.com
          UDP  137 ->   137
02/04/10 09:43:17 !f 00 h213-109-165.RM.albacom.net ->
          www.abuse.net    UDP   137 ->   137
02/04/10 09:44:12 !f 00 smtp.interaccess.com ->
          www.abuse.net  D TCP 59605 ->  smtp  S
02/04/10 09:44:15 !f 00 ip61.eti.uva.nl  ->  www.abuse.net  D
          TCP  2213 ->  smtp  S
02/04/10 09:44:24 !f 00 ip61.eti.uva.nl ->   www.abuse.net  D
          TCP  2213 ->  smtp  S
02/04/10 09:46:45 !f 00      10.0.1.101  ->   wap.iecc.com  D
          TCP  2799 ->  http  S
02/04/10 09:48:13 !f 00 ip86-113.dialup.wplus.net ->
          www.iecc.com    UDP   137 ->   137
02/04/10 09:48:31 !f 00  139.177.224.71 ->
          pro.spidergraphics.com    UDP   393 >   137
02/04/10 09:51:20 !f 00   64.80.33.202  >
          www.swedishhill.com    UDP   137 ->   137
02/04/10 09:53:00 !f 00 host244124.arnet.net.ar ->
          www.telecom-digest.org   UDP   137 ->   137
02/04/10 09:54:56 !f 00 angora.blitzed.org ->  xuxa.iecc.com
          D TCP  4782 -> telnet  S
02/04/10 09:57:00 !f 00 ip61.eti.uva.nl ->   www.abuse.net  D
          TCP  2292 ->  smtp  S
02/04/10 09:59:43 !f 00 deloitte1.everestbbn.com  >
          www.abuse.net  D TCP  3671 ->  smtp  S
```

In the preceding example, the IP address of the computer doing the probing (the attacker) is listed first, and the IP address of the computer being probed is second. The numbers or names following TCP or UDP are the ports. More information about ports is coming up next.

Any port in a probe

So what are the probes probing for?

They're checking to see whether anything running on your computer will respond to their electronic "knock-knock." Operating systems such as Unix or Windows have lots of little applications (called *services*) that run continuously in the background, even though you never asked them to. In Windows 98, for example, an application regularly checks to see what other computers (if any) are attached to your Network Neighborhood — and it checks to see what other computers may be networked to yours even if you've never even heard of a networked computer or you live 500 miles from the nearest DSL line or cable modem. In Windows 2000, a networking application lets other users access certain directories or devices (like a printer) on your computer, depending on what level of permission you've granted them.

The bottom line: Most people have these little services (and security holes) running on their computers at all times, whether a modem or network card is in their computer or not — and it takes expertise in networking to make these services *stop*. You can find out in Chapter 4 more about these kinds of services and what security risks they pose.

Each of these services listens for a slightly different kind of connection, called a port, and each port is used for a special purpose. Think of *ports* as special little doors, some of which have locks that are susceptible to being jimmied, allowing a hacker to sneak in and tinker with your computer.

By *port scanning,* a wily hacker is essentially rattling all the doorknobs of all the ports on your computer and hoping that he can find one that welcomes him in. For example, port 80, which you occasionally see in Web addresses, is the port that Web servers use to talk to Web browsers, and port 137 is the one Windows systems use for the Network Neighborhood check. Dozens of other ports are designated for things like sending and receiving e-mail, transferring files, updating domain name information, using Internet chat systems, and playing network-based games, for example.

Here's some gallows port humor: In the dark and creepy "shoot-'em-up" video game Doom, players compete with friends via the Internet to zap the game's evil, devilish enemies. The port you use on your computer to play the game online? Port 666, of course, which is also the biblical "number of the beast."

You can find a list of other reserved port numbers at www.isi.edu/in-notes/iana/assignments/port-numbers.

Welcome, Mr. Hacker — why don't you come on in?

It doesn't matter how you do it, from the minute you connect your computer to the Internet, you've hung out a giant neon Welcome sign in front of your humble little cyber-abode. Here's why:

Kick Me, Version 2.0. It seems ironic to us, but the most popular operating systems — especially Microsoft products, like Windows 95, Windows 98, Windows Me, and Windows XP — all come out of the box just full of built-in holes in their security. Why? Because security features cause operating systems to become complicated, and in the battle between high security and user friendliness, guess which one usually wins? Unfortunately, many of the holes are extremely difficult — if not impossible — for most users to find and turn off. On top of that, lots of popular Internet programs — like chat software, MP3 trading programs, instant-messaging services, and even some games — can unlock even more of your ports in the course of their normal operation. Meanwhile, even if you upgrade your operating system to Windows 2000, which comes out of the box slightly more secure than the others, you still are lacking the protection you need, which is a personal firewall.

Beware of Greeks (and geeks) bearing gifts. Most computer users don't know how to avoid setting loose Trojan horse e-mail attachments (documents or programs that look innocent, but do something nefarious when you open them) inside their computers. In fact, most people who are hosting these hacker's tools of destruction and maliciousness on their computers don't even know that they are there.

The only way to keep Trojan horses out of your computer is not to let them in there in the first place. You learn how to protect yourself against Trojan horses and other viruses in Chapter 8.

"Help me! I need an exorcist!" Unbeknownst to many people, while they sit at their computers playing Solitaire or balancing their checkbooks, their computers have been zombified (refer to the section "Trouble is my business," earlier in this chapter) and are secretly and quietly attacking other innocent people's computers, like blood-lusty vampires in the night.

The best way to make sure that your computer hasn't been hijacked is to run antivirus scans regularly. If your computer is connected to the Internet 24/7, you should also run a personal firewall program, which we talk about later in this chapter. A *personal firewall program,* among other safety features, helps you detect the presence of an intruder program by alerting you every time one of your programs — or, more importantly, a program being controlled by a hacker or zombie — tries to connect to the Internet. For example, if you download what you think is an innocuous game and it suddenly starts trying to connect to the Internet for no apparent reason, you may have downloaded a hidden hacker tool masquerading as a game, a kind of Trojan horse, or, worse, a piece of software that's spying on you! If your firewall software tells you that some software you don't recognize is trying to go online, it's time to start investigating.

For broadband users only: Hackers love your broadband access for all the same reasons you do — speed, speed, speed — and boy, do they have big plans for your bandwidth:

✔ After turning your computer into a zombie, they use your computer to flood other victims with port probes.

✔ They use both your bandwidth and your hard drive as a little secret hideaway for stashing pirated software and scripts.

✔ They use your bandwidth and hard drive to trade pirated software and scripts with friends all over the world.

Again, the solution is a properly configured firewall.

Is there life after zombification?

The good news is that no one's going to drive a stake through your heart or the heart of your hard drive if you discover a zombie living inside your computer. By the time you finish cleaning up the mess of zombification, however, you may wish that somebody had.

Here are our five steps for post-zombie cleansing and renewal (get a recent edition of *Windows For Dummies*, written by Andy Rathbone):

1. **Make copies of all your important documents and files (you have been backing up your hard drive like we tell you to in Chapter 3, right?).**

   The reason is that you're going to have to reload all your files (after you scan them with your antivirus software, of course!) as well as your software to make sure that you have eliminated all traces of the zombie.

2. **Reformat your hard drive (ouch!).**

3. **Reinstall your operating system and software from the original disks (ouch!).**

4. **Scan *everything* with your new antivirus software.**

   Scan all your files, including all backup disks and downloaded software —
   because who knows for how long your machine was "owned" by the
   hacker? If you skip this step and don't scan all your files for viruses, you
   could be restoring files that include the hacker's tools without even
   knowing it.

5. **We say it again: Get yourself a firewall so that you don't have to go
   through this process again in a few weeks.**

The Firestorm over Firewalls

In response to mass scanning and the zombification of innocent machines
and networks (introduced earlier in this chapter, in the section "Trouble is
my business"), a growing number of companies are producing personal firewall software that users can install on their always-on home computers.

Without a firewall, most users don't know that a hacker has hijacked their
systems until it's too late — and even *then* they may never notice that anything is wrong, even as their own computer is being used as home base for a
host of no-good deeds.

The easy way to firewall

If you have a DSL or cable modem and several computers, you should get a
router that connects the modem to your home network, with a firewall built
right into the router. This arrangement avoids the entire issue of having to
firewall your PCs one by one.

Using a personal firewall
to swat the probes

Earlier in this chapter (in the section "Think it can't happen to you?"), we
show you a log full of probes that were captured using a program named
Snort, which is used to listen for probe attempts. Snort is for computers running flavors of the Unix operating system, and if you're one of those technically adventurous readers who is running a Unix variant like Linux or
FreeBSD, you can check out www.snort.org for more information.

Should you use a personal firewall software?

Ray: If you've got a dedicated, high-speed connection, it's a good thing to have. My personal favorite is ZoneAlarm, and I've installed it on my home computers, and I even installed it on my parents' computer because they have a cable modem. For theirs, I turned off the alerts and logging, so it just quietly protects them and they never hear a peep from it.

Gregg: If you have a dial-up connection like I do, you probably don't need a personal firewall because your IP number is always changing and your connection is just too slow to interest most hackers. On the other hand, if like me you go online for hours at a time, your vulnerability increases. That's why I use a personal firewall, Norton Internet Security, which includes both a firewall and auto-updating antivirus software.

John: If you have a permanent connection and no firewalled router and you use easily hackable software (which includes any version of Windows), a firewall like ZoneAlarm is useful. If you use a dial-up connection, I wouldn't bother.

Not a certified cybergeek? Don't despair! A personal firewall product is out there to help everyone deflect the probes of evildoers.

One of the best products for zapping probes is the freeware alternative, ZoneAlarm, by Zone Labs (`www.zonelabs.com`). ZoneAlarm can be set to sound a warning (or not) every time your computer is probed, and it not only deflects probes (making your computer essentially "invisible" to the people doing the probing) but also keeps a log of everything it hears so that you can investigate and complain about the probes if you choose. (Investigating hacker probes uses many of the same investigative techniques we describe in Chapter 11, about spam hunting.) A personal firewall like ZoneAlarm can also be set to warn you when any program on your computer tries to connect to the Internet so that you know no zombies are going online without your knowledge. The best thing about ZoneAlarm? If you're using it for personal or nonprofit use, it's absolutely free!

If freeware makes you nervous or you would just rather pay for peace of mind, both Symantec (`www.symantec.com`) and McAfee (`www.mcafee.com`) offer high-quality, low-priced personal firewall products, although we don't think that either is as good as ZoneAlarm.

In some cases, you may *not* want your firewall software to report every probe it receives. Why? Because some cable modem and DSL providers are beginning to probe their own networks in attempts to identify unsecured computers before hackers do.

We mention BlackIce Defender (www.networkice.com) here because some hardware vendors and ISPs encourage their users to use it. Like ZoneAlarm, it's user friendly and easy to install, and it detects and logs everything that tries to connect to your computer. The problem: When we say BlackIce Defender detects everything, we mean *everything,* sometimes even including the pages where you're trying to go. Because of some poorly worded alert messages, some versions of the software give you the impression that when you surf over to a site like CNN, it may alert you that www.cnn.com is trying to hack you when all it's really doing is sending you the Web page you requested. With all the false alarms, you have no way to pick out the few real problems it may report. So, BlackIce Defender overall is more trouble than it's worth, when superior alternatives like ZoneAlarm are available.

Chapter 8

Viruses, Worms, Macro Viruses, and Trojan Horses

●●●

In This Chapter

▶ What are viruses and where do they come from?

▶ Keeping viruses away

▶ Using antivirus software

▶ Viruses in your pocket

●●●

Since the dawn of time, humans have been passing off some really disgusting stuff to one another: Lumps, bumps, unsightly sores and rashes; purplish splotches; little critters that are always looking for a new host — not to mention things that could be downright life threatening.

Broadly, these things are called social diseases. And just because the Internet is high-tech and impersonal (in other words, an appliance that, if used correctly, shouldn't involve any bodily fluids), it doesn't mean that the potential for nasty critters to pass from person to person has been eliminated. It just means that these nasty critters have gone high-tech too.

Because we're well-adjusted, happy-go-lucky guys, we wish that we could tell you that all these critters occur only as accidents or as odd freaks of nature. But the truth is that these devilish devastators of data are always manmade and created deliberately.

Why Are They Called Viruses, Anyway?

They may not make your nose stuffy, but computer viruses behave much like the viruses you catch during flu season. The cold virus is transmitted from one host to another (the server sneezes on your fruit plate at lunch), it reproduces in your body (usually by hijacking your body's cells and turning them into little carbon copies of the virus), and then it causes symptoms like coughing and sneezing to encourage transmission to another host, which eventually leads to the infection of someone else.

Similarly, a computer virus gets into your computer by being passed on from another infected machine — maybe through an e-mail or an infected disk. After it's inside your computer, it replicates itself and then attaches itself to yet another e-mail or disk to make sure that it gets passed along to more and more victims (like the Melissa virus, which e-mails itself to everybody in your address book).

As interesting as it may be to point out all the ways in which a virus in the natural world and one in the computer world are similar, the two have one *big* difference: The computer virus is *always* manmade and is *always* created with the goal of doing harm to someone else.

How to become a virus hunter: Perhaps not surprisingly, some of the world's best computer virus hunters have advanced degrees in biology and epidemiology (the study of disease epidemics). For a scholarly look at the parallels between biological and computer viruses, see www.research.ibm.com/antivirus/SciPapers/Kephart/Spectrum/Spectrum.html.

How *not* to be a virus hunter. We know that your heart is in the right place, but when you send virus alert e-mails to all 999,999,999 people in your address book every time you hear about some deadly new Internet plague, you're more often than not scaring the bejeebers out of everyone with news about a virus — that is a hoax!

Believe it or not, the amount of harm done by sending false alarms to your thousand closest friends can be just as damaging as the alleged virus (if it even exists!); if you remember the story of the boy who cried wolf, you understand why.

Perhaps the oldest and most tired virus hoax claims that if you open an e-mail message with the phrase "Good Times" in the subject line, your hard drive will explode. Hundreds of variations of this e-mail hoax circulate, and each one has a different subject line. For example, an e-mail with the subject line "Real men love Jesus" is another perennial favorite. Regardless of the subject line, these hoax e-mails always claim that if you open the wrong e-mail, something really awful will happen to your computer as a result.

You can learn two lessons from these hoax e-mails:

If you think you've got the scoop on the latest new devastating virus, check it out at the Web sites at the end of this section before taking it on yourself to alert the world. If the virus really is as terrible as you think it is, odds are the virus fighters already know about it and — good news here! — your antivirus software provider probably knows about it too and already has an update for it.

No known viruses can be unleashed by simply opening a plain-text-based e-mail. (E-mails containing HTML, the Web page language, are another story, which we discuss later in this chapter and in Chapter 9. That's not to say that this type of virus won't *someday* exist, but at the moment the only way you can contract a virus via e-mail is if it's hiding in a file or document that is *attached* to the e-mail and you make the mistake of opening the infected attachment.

Check out virus hoaxes and urban legends at these sites.

✔ urbanlegends.about.com/science/urbanlegends/cs/
   virushoaxes/

✔ www.snopes2.com/computer/virus/virus.htm

When is a virus not a virus?

Most *viruses* you hear about on the news are nothing of the sort. They're really worms and macro viruses and Trojan horses. (We always refer to the group — including viruses — as critters.) Yet the lowly virus is, in relationship to these other critters, a bit like vanilla ice cream in relationship to all other flavors in the Ben & Jerry's universe.

Vanilla meets all the basic requirements for ice cream (it's cold, it comes in a carton, and it's made from cream), but it surely lacks all the color and flavor that most of us have come to expect from ice cream. Yet, just as vanilla blandly provides the basic evolutionary building blocks for making all other ice cream flavors, the virus has played a key role in the evolution of all other critters.

These four different breeds of critter are like an assortment of ice cream flavors in another way, too: Given a choice, most people choose something richer and more flavorful than plain old vanilla. Yet if vanilla is the only choice available, most people would much rather have vanilla than no ice cream. The same is true for most virus writers. They may like to write a richer and more flavorful critter (like a worm or macro virus or Trojan horse), but for whatever reason (often having to do with their level of programming skill), they're stuck with the plain ol' vanilla of critters, the lowly virus. Meanwhile, understanding what these four types of critters have in common and how they differ can help you in the fight to protect your computer against them.

Even though we're about to go to an awful lot of trouble to explain the differences between viruses, worms, macro viruses, and Trojan horses, after you finish reading this chapter, you have our permission to wrongly refer to them all as viruses again, just like everyone else does. After all, do the people who make "antivirus software" call it "antivirus, antiworm, antimacro virus, anti-Trojan horse software"?

Meet the critters

As you read about viruses and all the other critters, you should remember that they're really just a means to an end.

So what's the end?

That depends on the goal of the writer. Some critters are written to annoy, others are written to destroy. This distinction is particularly important to keep in mind because, even as you read this chapter, you can safely bet that someone, somewhere, is diligently working at finding a new way to annoy or destroy that defies all the definitions in this section.

Viruses

A *virus* is a type of tiny little program that gets loaded onto your computer without your knowing it and then starts running amok. This section describes a few of the defining characteristics of a virus.

A virus can replicate itself and pass itself along to infect other computers — but only by burying itself inside something larger, such as a Microsoft Word document or the programming code of a piece of software, which then takes a ride to another computer on a disk or as an e-mail attachment or by some other method of file transfer.

In replicating themselves, viruses sometimes do their damage by making so many copies of themselves that they fill up your computer's memory and cause it to crash.

In many cases, the replication and spread of a virus are secondary to its primary function, which is to perform some other task (sometimes harmless, sometimes fatal) inside your computer. For example, a more malicious virus may take over complete control of your computer and order it to do something horrible, like delete its own hard drive. Other viruses are intended as mere pranks: A good example is the Merry Christmas virus that simply flashes a harmless season's greeting on your screen in December — end of story. Or so you think, but now it's April Fool's Day and the Merry Christmas virus doesn't let you boot up your computer. Ha-ha-ha!

Worms

Forgive us for the analogy, but think *tape*worm — like the ones your mom always thought you had in your gut when you were a kid. Let us explain why the analogy is so fitting.

Worms are similar to viruses in that they can copy themselves and do bad things to the computers they invade. Worms are also notorious loners, though, so they generally don't attach themselves to the programming code of files or dig deeply in the out-of-the-way corners of disks or hard drives, as viruses do. Instead, worms send copies of themselves over the Internet directly, or, as in the case of the ILOVEYOU worm, they can hitch a ride in an e-mail message.

A good example of a worm is FriendlyMess, which is similar to ILOVEYOU in that it travels as a little bit of programming code (called a *script*) attached to an e-mail message. If the recipient of the e-mail clicks on the code, it delivers a nice message saying that the recipient is a special friend. That's the friendly part. The mess? As the recipient reads this friendly little message, the worm quietly rewrites the computer's autoexec.bat file, which Windows uses to provide instructions and settings each time it starts or restarts your computer. In this case, the new instructions are "Delete your entire operating system (in other words, the contents of C:\Windows and a few other directories) and possibly some personal documents, depending on which directory you've been storing them in."

Macro viruses

A *macro virus* is a category of virus that's quite unique: Rather than be its own little program or application, it makes its appearance in the form of a *macro* embedded in a document file.

Some experts claim that nearly three-quarters of all viruses are macro viruses, in part because they can embed themselves in your software and attach themselves to every document you create, which allows them to be spread easily to others.

To understand macro viruses, you first have to understand macros. Many software applications (like Word, Excel, and PowerPoint) allow you to create

macros, which are nothing more than a way of recording long series of commands and then repeating the series of commands over and over again with
just a keystroke or two. To see how Word 2000 handles macro security,
choose Tools⇨Macro⇨Security from the menu bar, displaying the menus
shown in Figure 8-1.

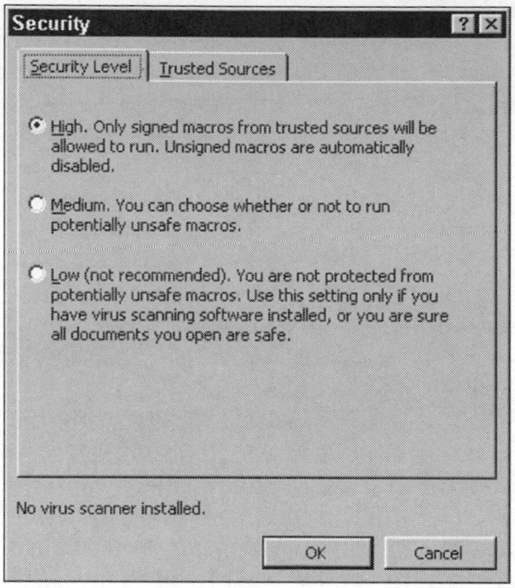

Figure 8-1:
Choosing
macro
security in
Word.

In some cases, macros add themselves to your default document template so
that they're executed automatically every time you open an existing document or create a new one. That's how most macro viruses get spread so
quickly: Every time you create a new document in Word, the document is
based on a default template named Normal.dot that can contain font choices,
margin settings, and, yes, even macros and macro viruses. If a macro virus is
in your default template, you spread the virus every time you open or create
a new document.

One of the first macro viruses created is named Concept, and it infects Word
documents. Although the Concept virus doesn't do any harm to your computer (in fact, the author of the virus makes clear inside the programming
code that he wrote Concept only to demonstrate that programming a macro
virus really can be done), the Concept programming code provided the
springboard for later macro viruses that were far more damaging. For example, the Akuma macro virus spreads like Concept, activates at a preprogrammed time, and then deletes all files you've recently edited with Word.

The original Trojan horse

If you remember your Greek history, you recall the many long battles between the Greeks and the people of Troy. After many months and years of fighting, the Greeks were unable to penetrate the walls of the city, so they decided to give up fighting and wheel up a peace offering to the gates of Troy: A *big* wooden model of a horse. The Trojans accepted the gift and promptly brought it inside, not realizing that inside the horse were hiding a bunch of Greek soldiers. After everyone had gone to sleep, out popped the soldiers, who threw open the city gates, letting in the Greeks to ransack the city. The legend of the Trojan horse was born, and the rest, as they say, is history.

Trojan horses

A *Trojan horse* program tricks you into loading and running it by pretending to be something that it's not. (Surely you remember this story from Greek mythology. If not, you can revisit the story in the nearby sidebar "The original Trojan horse.") The perfect example of a Trojan horse is a file that masquerades as an antivirus software patch but is really a virus.

Some Trojan horses are coupled with other types of viruses, such as macro viruses, which then generate new Trojan horses that get passed along to others.

The most famous example of a Trojan horse is the Melissa virus, which took the computer world by storm on March 26, 1999. Melissa arrived as an e-mail message with a Word document attached. Anyone foolish enough to open the attachment soon found out that the document was a Trojan horse for the macro virus embedded within the attached Word document.

The story of the first nasty critter

One of the earliest incidents of a virus — a worm, actually — was in 1988, when a young college kid named Robert Tappan Morris, the son of a computer security expert at the CIA, decided to have a little fun. Reading his story tells you a great deal about how virus authors think of themselves and their creations and what happens when the fun and games go sour.

According to federal court documents (can you tell where this story is going?), it was in the fall of 1988 that Morris, a Cornell University graduate student in computers, noticed that security on many of the networked computers at his school and elsewhere was pretty lax. So he went to work on a worm to demonstrate to the world just how poor the security really was. At that time, the Internet was mostly accessible only by university, government, and military people, mostly in the United States.

Morris thought that they all needed to be taught a lesson. He designed his worm to spread itself widely, but to do so without drawing attention to itself. He also wanted to make sure that the worm wouldn't copy itself to computers that had already been infected because he didn't want the hard drives to fill up. His solution? He programmed the worm to first ask computers whether they already had a copy. But then he realized that some system administrators might catch on and program their systems to say "Yes, I have a copy" even when they didn't. To overcome this possibility, he set the worm to copy itself every seventh time it heard a Yes response, guessing that one out of seven was a safe ratio to keep too many copies from being made. He also designed the worm to be killed whenever a computer was shut down, an event that he assumed would happen every couple of weeks and prevent the worm from filling up a system too many times.

How did Morris's worm get into computers? Four ways are possible:

- ✔ Through a hole in a mail server program that is widely used on Unix-based servers

- ✔ Through a bug in a program named Finger that allows you to ask a computer for basic information about users of another network

- ✔ Through a feature that permits administrators to designate a computer as "trusted," allowing it to connect to another without a password

- ✔ Through a process of randomly guessing passwords

On November 2, 1988, Morris broke into a computer at the rival Massachusetts Institute of Technology and released his worm. Within hours, it was clear to Morris — and to nearly everyone else connected to the Internet — that he had sadly miscalculated how quickly his worm would spread and how many times it would try to copy itself on each computer.

Very quickly, Morris tried to send out anonymous alerts to everyone he could on the Internet to warn them about the worm and tell them how to disable it. But his messages couldn't get through because computers all over the place were crashing, bringing large portions of the Internet to a grinding halt.

Morris was found guilty of violating several computer crime laws and sentenced to three years of probation and a fine of $10,000. In case you were wondering, he eventually did get a doctorate degree (from Harvard, though, not from Cornell) in 1999. His thesis? How to control network congestion on a large scale! (No kidding! Check it out at www.pdos.lcs.mit.edu/~rtm/papers/tp-abstract.html.)

From whence viruses come

After you know where viruses come from, you have a much better chance of not getting them in the first place:

Diskborne viruses

Some of the first computer viruses affecting PCs used floppy disks as their *vector* (a term used by both doctors and computer virus experts to describe ways infectious elements are transmitted). Why the floppy disk? Well, before the Internet, if you needed to get data from your computer to your office colleague, the only way to do it was to put the file on a disk and walk it over to the other guy's desk (traditionally known as sneakernet). Although some instances of diskborne viruses still exist, the Internet offers a virus writer an almost unlimited opportunity to spread his wares, so many fewer diskborne viruses exist than before.

The best way to prevent a virus-on-a-disk from infecting your data is to scan all disks before you open the files or software that's on them. Luckily, most major antivirus software programs now let you adjust the settings so that the software automatically scans every disk you put into your drive. Of course, it's up to you to make sure that this setting is turned on at all times.

Even though not as many diskborne viruses are being written any more, an awful lot of floppy disks are still floating around. (Can you guess how many of those disks got mailed to you from AOL?) You have to remember that although those dusty disks may be old, it doesn't mean that they don't carry viruses — so regardless of the vintage, make sure that you scan them or erase them before you use them.

ILOVEYOU, Melissa, and Bubbleboy: Who names these things?

Computer viruses often get their names from something in the programming code of the virus, like the LordZero virus, which is the nickname of the author. Viruses can also be named for something the critter does. For example, the e-mail-borne worm named Bubbleboy generates e-mails containing links to a Web site featuring excerpts from the "Seinfeld" episode of the same name. The ILOVEYOU virus was named after the subject line of the e-mail that spawned it, and the Melissa virus was named after a topless dancer the programmer once knew. And you thought that programmers wrote viruses because they otherwise were leading boring lives!

Boot-sector viruses

A *boot disk* is a specially formatted disk you can use to boot, or start, your computer. (Ever leave a disk in your drive and get the message that says "Non-system disk in drive?")

The reason you get that message is that the disk in the drive is not a boot disk. And yes, your hard drive is a boot disk, too.) Every disk has sections of it allocated for storing information about whether you can use it to boot a computer and how the boot files should be allocated.

Unfortunately, boot-disk viruses are particularly good at hiding in out-of-the-way corners of floppy disks, making them all but impossible to detect. Even using current antivirus software, these boot-sector viruses can be incredibly tricky. In fact, when antivirus software was in its infancy, you frequently had to use multiple scanning programs multiple times to sniff out all the boot-disk viruses that were hiding on top of each other.

Here's another reason to upgrade your antivirus software if you haven't done it in a few years: What was impossible then is easy as pie today. Just plop a floppy disk into your disk drive and if your antivirus definitions are current and a boot-sector virus is on the disk, your new antivirus program ferrets it out. (Later in this chapter, we cover two major antivirus programs and how to make sure that they do things like this automatically for you.)

Viruses in programs, software, and applications

Another popular hiding place for viruses is within other programs. Let us go back to our biology lesson and remind you of how viruses work. Viruses carry a little bit of genetic code inside them, which they paste into the genetic code in the cells of their host. Who's the host? *You* are!

Depression over compression?

To make sharing program files easier, people often use programs like WinZip or StuffIt to compress files and make them smaller, and therefore easier to fit on a floppy disk or faster to upload and download. But compressed program files look very different to an antivirus scanning program, adding new challenges to the antivirus programmers. Here's another reason to update your antivirus software: Most newer models are now adept at peering into the mysteriously compacted files and can detect whether something rotten is inside.

What happens when the virus replaces the code in your cells with its own? Ever see *Night of the Living Dead?* The cell becomes like a little zombie, doing the viruses' bidding, which usually includes making more copies of itself. With enough of that going on, you eventually begin to look and feel like you're part of the night of the living dead yourself.

Similarly, some computer viruses can hijack the code of a computer's operating system or software application, pasting its own sets of instructions into the code and making the program carry out the viruses' dastardly deeds.

Because the average person doesn't go poking around in the programming code of most software (and you probably wouldn't recognize virus programming from make-the-computer-go-beep! programming, anyway), the only way to discover viruses hidden inside programs is to have antivirus software that can detect changes in a program's code.

Always scan program files with your antivirus software to scan the file *before* you unzip or install them because whenever you unzip files automatically, the installer may also launch automatically, before you have a chance to do a virus scan.

Virus-infected documents

As you've probably already figured out, a document can get a virus in only one way, and that's if the virus is a macro virus.

Macro viruses are an evolutionary leap in computer viruses, a hybrid of previously known critters that combine aspects of a regular virus (hijacking the programming code of an existing program to do its bidding) and a Trojan horse (hiding inside an otherwise innocent-looking file).

What is it about the macro features in programs like Word, Excel, WordPerfect, and many other popular software packages that make them so easily hijacked by macro viruses?

Their advanced macro capabilities allow users to automate repetitive tasks. For example, Word has numerous template files that allow you to quickly create preformatted letters, faxes, and other documents. These template files use macros to ask you to enter certain data (like your name or the date) and then automatically enter that data into the right spots on the form. They can even launch other programs, like spreadsheets and databases. But, like many good things, these macro functions can also be used for evil — and, because macro viruses are fairly easily created and can even be programmed to modify themselves as they replicate — they have become the most common form of virus on the loose. It's also why they're the hardest to catch: because they come onto the scene quickly and change rapidly — much faster than the antivirus folks can keep up.

Virus problems aside, macros are now definitely one of the coolest and most useful features of many software programs. If you do lots of repetitive tasks, you owe it to yourself to investigate how macros work. Take it from us: Those aching "carpal tunnels" in your wrists will thank you for it.

Macro viruses: What's the cure?

Many software packages now offer you the ability to disable macros until you know who put the macro there and what it's supposed to do. If that information isn't available, don't run the macro!

Most popular antivirus software packages now scan inside documents to look for macro viruses. As we say elsewhere, though, one of the most frightening things about these viruses is that they can be programmed to modify themselves and therefore may elude detection. So make sure that you use your antivirus software, but don't depend on it. You also need to keep your macro security settings on high. When you receive files from others with macros in them, don't execute the macros until you can confirm their validity with the sender, and don't open attachments that arrive via e-mail from strangers.

Break yourself of the habit of opening documents that come attached to e-mail without questioning whom the e-mail is from or what the document may be because this technique is precisely how macro viruses spread so quickly.

Some early versions of Word 2000 and Excel 2000 and all versions of Word 97 and Excel 97 must be updated to allow you to turn off the feature that automatically runs macros. Check `www.microsoft.com/office` to get the latest updates. If your version of the software doesn't offer settings for controlling the auto-execution of macros or an update to provide those settings, you should consider changing software or upgrading immediately.

E-mail

When it comes to transmitting viruses, e-mail is the perfect medium. You can send an innocent-looking e-mail message and attach to it all sorts of evil programs, macro-virus-filled documents, or even little bits of programming code (*scripts*) that act just like miniature programs. (You can find out more about how hackers use scripts in Chapter 7.)

Melissa: Anatomy of a Successful E-Mail Virus

The best way to show you how e-mail can be used to spread viruses is to look at the case of the Melissa virus. Melissa, you may recall, was unleashed on the world on March 26, 1999, and within hours had spread around the world, clogging mail corporate mail servers and overloading networks with millions of pieces of infected e-mail. Let's take a look at how Melissa worked and see where smart antivirus prevention methods may have helped stop her in her tracks.

First, the Melissa virus was spread through an infected Word document, and by people using the Microsoft Outlook e-mail software

The Melissa virus message contained the Subject line "Subject: Important Message From <name>." The <name> part was the full name of the user sending the message, as shown in Figure 8-2.

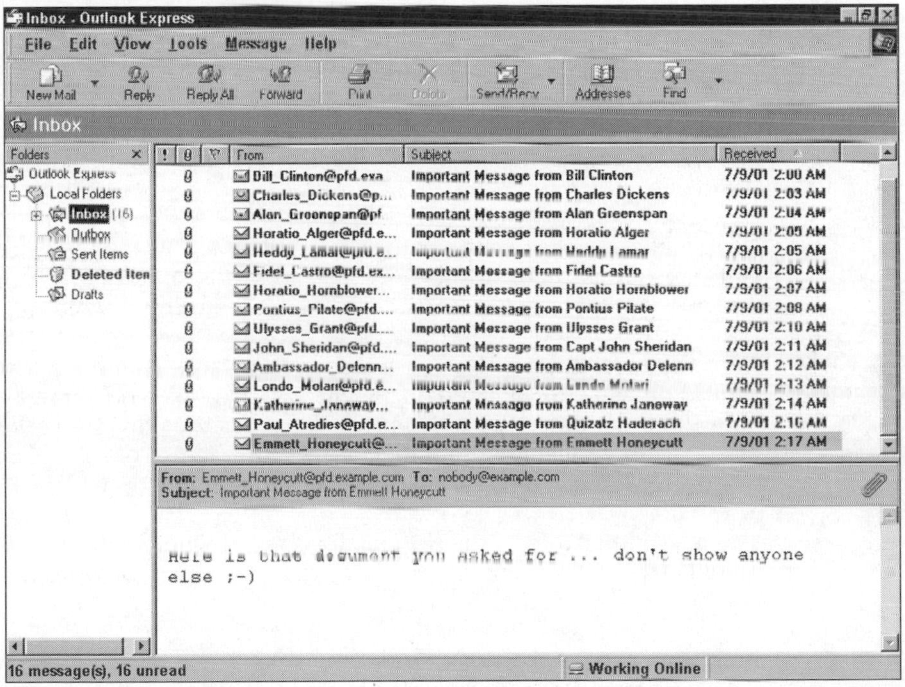

Figure 8-2: An e-mail inbox filled with Melissa mail. Melissa had the intriguing body text "Here is that document you asked for — don't show anyone else ;-)."

The message is intriguing; it's kind of like a pretty wooden horse rolled up outside the city gates, no?

For Melissa to spread, users had to open the infected document in Word 97 or Word 2000.

Just think: If everyone knew not to open strange attachments, Melissa never would have gotten past the first person who received it!

If the Word macro security settings were set to Low when the document was opened, the macro virus was immediately executed. If the macro security settings were set to Medium or High, the user was asked whether she wanted to run the macro. If the user clicked the Enable Macros button, the macro was executed anyway.

Oh, we told you so! Even if your macro security is set at the highest setting, you still have to use your head and say No to files with suspicious macros. All the security settings and antivirus protection in the world can't save you from a short-circuit between your ears!

After the virus is executed, it resets the Word macro security settings to their lowest settings (a brilliant defensive strategy) to permit all macros to run whenever a document is opened. This strategy keeps the user from being alerted every time a virus is executed in the future.

The virus then changes a few settings deep inside one of the Microsoft Windows configuration files and signs the changes with the virus author's nickname, Kwyjibo.

Next, Melissa looks to see whether the victim has any names stored in her Outlook address book. If she does, Melissa sends copies of the original e-mail and attachment to the first 50 addresses in the address book.

Here's the real genius of the virus writer. He hijacks your address book and sends copies of the infected document out to people you know, as though it's you who is sending it! This technique increases the odds that others will open the attachment without thinking about it. It also means, of course, that when people's machines are hijacked, you're the one they blame!

The macro then infects the Normal.dot template file. By default, all Word documents use the Normal.dot template; therefore, any new Word documents you create are also now infected.

Here's the bad news: Even after you think you're rid of Melissa, you can create a document and give it to somebody else (by e-mail or floppy disk or on a file server), and the moment they open it, the whole thing starts all over again.

Melissa, the sequel?

Old viruses like Melissa never really die; they just go dormant and fall out of circulation, sleeping on a floppy disk in the back of a desk drawer or lurking on a backup tape in some corporate computer room. In fact, anybody accessing these disks might wake her up and start passing her along again. But even if we don't see the likes of Melissa again, it doesn't mean that she's gone; she's just sleeping in a forgotten corner somewhere. Nor does this mean that we won't see a new generation of Melissa sometime soon. In fact, a very good chance exists that

Melissa's great-granddaughter will show up in a few years with lots of new features designed to outdo all the horrifying deeds of the original.

For more information about the Melissa virus, see

✍ **Info from the Computer Emergency Response Team (CERT) at Carnegie-Mellon:** `www.cert.org/advisories/CA-1999-04.html`

✍ **MelissaVirus.com.** `www.melissavirus.com/`

Finally, if the minute of the hour matches the day of the month at this point, the macro inserted into the current document displays the message "Twenty-two points plus triple-word-score plus fifty points for using all my letters. Game's over. I'm outta here."

Okay, smart-aleck, stop with the graffiti already.

Two More Thoughts about Attachments

As we mentioned earlier in this chapter, at the time this book was written, you *could not* get a virus by just opening an e-mail. For a virus to be transported or contracted using e-mail, it must be part of an attached file, which you then must make the mistake of opening or running, thus setting the virus free.

A file doesn't have to be a Word, Excel, PowerPoint, or WordPerfect document to contain a virus. In fact, dozens of file types, and scripting and programming languages, can be used to create viruses. When these files are attached to e-mail, they can infect your computer if you foolishly double-click on them.

If your e-mail software program displays a file-format icon for an attachment and you don't recognize the icon (in other words, it's not for Word or Excel or another program you commonly use), think twice before clicking.

If no icon is next to the filename, look at the file's *extension* (the part of the filename after the dot or period [.]). As Gregg worked on this chapter, the Word file was saved on his hard drive as

```
C:\Docs\Privacy4Dummies\VirusChapter\virus005.doc
```

You should be able to tell by looking at the filename that this document is being written in Word because the extension at the end is .doc. If the file were an Excel file, the extension would be .xls, and if the file were a PowerPoint file, the extension would be .ppt.

Other common extensions include .txt for a text file, .wpd for a Word Perfect document, and .gif or .jpg for pictures. If you get an e-mail with an attached file in an extension you don't recognize, don't open the file until you've scanned it for viruses.

Many recent viruses have been sent to victims as .vbs files, or files written in Visual Basic Script. Unless you're on a corporate network that distributes system updates by e-mail (not a good idea, but some do), never open a file that ends with .vbs as its extension.

Figure 8-3 shows what a .vbs file attachment looks like in Outlook Express. Some versions of Outlook Express automatically run file attachments, so make sure that you have applied the latest security patches for your version. You can find more information about patches and upgrades in Chapter 3.

If you see a filename or an extension that you don't recognize, try searching for it in the F-Secure database of virus information, at www.f-secure.com/v-descs/.

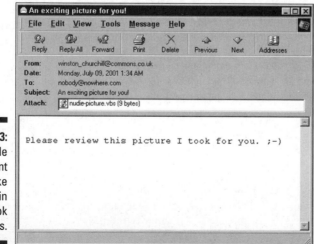

Figure 8-3:
A .vbs file attachment looks like this in Outlook Express.

Starve a Cold, Feed a Fever, Avoid a Virus: Seven Rules to Stop Critters in Their Tracks

You may not like hearing this statement, but it turns out that Mom was right: When it comes to fighting viruses, it's *much* better to take the proper precautions to avoid the virus in the first place than it is to be careless and have to fight the cold or virus later on. (Can't you just hear her shouting "Take a sweater!" from the porch right now?)

So with a tip o' the hat to dear old Mom, we offer you the seven tips in this section.

Someday, you're going to start taking all the proper precautions. Will that day be today, or the day *after* you lose all your data to a critter?

Got good antivirus software. This tip is hardly earth-shattering, but you would be surprised at how few people have functioning antivirus software on their computers. Frankly, the reason that many thousands of viruses are still roaming cyberspace even years after their introduction is that people don't take this most basic precaution.

If you don't have an antivirus software installed on your computer, get some!

See the section about practicing safe hex, later in this chapter, for information about two popular brands. Even if a fierce, new critter is taking cyberspace by storm and you don't have the money for antivirus software, If you go to the sites of most antivirus software makers, you can often download a trial version for free that protects you for at least a week or two until the existing crisis is over.

For a trial version of Symantec Antivirus, visit www.symantecstore.com/. For a trial version of McAfee Antivirus, visit download.mcafee.com/eval/evaluate2.asp.

Keep your antivirus software updated. If you bought your computer in the past three years, chances are that it shipped with some antivirus software preinstalled on it. That would be a good thing, except that antivirus software stops being current the day it's slapped on your machine. If you don't update the virus definitions regularly (we recommend at least once a month), you're really not protected. After all, with antivirus experts estimating dozens of new strains and variations of viruses appearing each month, relying on outdated antivirus software is a bit like placing your faith in a really good suit of Renaissance-era armor when everybody else is sporting a brand new "Star Trek" phaser.

When was the last time you downloaded the latest definitions for your antivirus software? To find out, click on the icon in your Windows system tray (on the opposite end from your Start button, near the clock) or click on the Start button, choose Programs, and look for the name of your antivirus software. If your software doesn't display the date of its most recent update on the main menu (see examples from McAfee and Norton later in this chapter), try choosing About from the Help menu. That should tell you what software version you have and may even say when it was last updated. The same set of Help menus should also give you instructions on how to update those antivirus definitions.

Virus-scan every floppy disk that goes into your computer. Back in college, Ray used to do lots of desktop publishing for neighborhood newsletters, local political groups, church bulletins, and his college newspaper. Every time he would get a batch of disks from contributors, at least one in five would have some kind of critter on it. It takes only a second to scan your floppy disks, and some antivirus software does it automatically whenever you insert a disk, so it's a no-brainer.

Treat attachments with care. Just as you wouldn't French kiss every stranger walking down the street for fear of what diseases you may catch, accepting unknown files from strangers is an equally bad idea. We talk more about file attachments later, but for now, just remember this advice: Don't open unexpected files or attachments from people you do know until you've confirmed why they sent them, and don't *ever* accept files or attachments from people you don't know.

Don't accept downloads from strange Web sites. Unless the Web site has a good reason for sending you something to download, you're wise to reject those automatic download boxes that sometimes pop up. If there's a legitimate reason for making you download some kind of program, Web sites usually tell you well in advance and give you the opportunity to download it yourself rather than force it on you. Even then, you may want to steer clear, for reasons we discuss in Chapter 9.

One automatic download that's usually acceptable: Shockwave Flash plug-ins. Many Web sites use Flash to enable rich menus. But if you're feeling skittish about accepting downloads from unfamiliar sites, you can always go to Shockwave.com on your own and get Flash directly from the source.

When Web browser plug-ins, like Shockwave, are downloaded, Internet Explorer alerts you to the impending installation and displays an authentication statement, as shown in Figure 8-4.

After the plug-in is installed, an animated graphic appears and you can continue browsing.

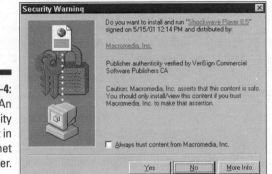

Figure 8-4:
An
authenticity
statement in
Internet
Explorer.

After you download files, scan them. Make sure that you scan all files or programs you download *before* you install or run them. Even if your favorite shareware Web site claims that they virus-scan everything (as Tucows.com and C|Net do), take the few extra seconds to run your own virus scan before installing new software. Likewise, you should also take the time to scan all files sent from coworkers and friends before opening them.

Many antivirus software packages let you right-click on a file to scan it instantly — and now that you know, you also know that you have no excuse not to.

Check your macros at the door. Make sure that any programs on your computer that use macros (most commonly Word, Excel, and WordPerfect) have their macro-related security settings set to their highest setting. This setting alerts you to the presence of a macro before it's executed, giving you a chance to run a virus scan on the file before executing the macro — and to possibly avert disaster. If your software program doesn't offer a security setting for macros, check with your software vendor for an upgrade security patch.

To turn macros off in Word 2000 and Excel 2000, choose Tools⇨Macro from the menu bar. You should see a Security submenu that lets you turn macro functions on and off (refer to Figures 8-2 and 8-3, earlier in this chapter). In WordPerfect versions 9 and 10 (part of Office 2000 and Office 2002), choose Tools⇨Visual Basic from the menu bar and then click on the Security tab to select it.

The Dangers of Chat, Instant Messenger-ing, and Music Trading

Even when you're trading files with others in a chat room, on Napster, or through your instant messenger software, you have to be just as vigilant about opening files you receive as you do about files you receive via e-mail. If you don't know the sender or don't recognize the file extension or you have *any* reason to be suspicious of the file, scan it with your antivirus software before opening or running it.

Although we haven't found any viruses targeting Napster yet, one is affecting the peer-to-peer sharing program Gnutella. Named GWV, this worm uses the Visual Basic Script (.vbs) language to make multiple copies of itself under different names. It can attack only if you double-click on it; but because the file extension on the worm files is .vbs rather than .mp3 or another recognizable music file type, you can easily avoid it as long as you stay alert and vigilant. Versions of this trick have also tried to infest other music-sharing programs, with limited success.

Practicing Safe Hex: Choosing and Using Antivirus Software

In the good old days, you could choose from a wide range of different antivirus software packages. Thanks to a great deal of consolidation and mergers, though, just two popular programs are left for personal use: McAfee and Norton. Of course, other packages are available, some of which we mention throughout this chapter, and some are even free or come as shareware. But looking for bargains in antivirus software is a little like looking for bargains in brain surgery. It's not exactly the kind of thing you should try to skimp on. Both McAfee and Norton work well, but we prefer Norton.

Safe *hex?* Peter Johnston, a co-author of the 1989 book *Computer Virus Crisis*, first used the term *safe hex* as a play on words on the term *safe sex,* which prevents the spread of other kinds of viruses. *Hex* refers to the hexadecimal data encoding found in the inner workings of most computer programs.

You can buy either the McAfee or Norton antivirus program online and download it, through `www.mcafee.com` and `www.symantec.com`, respectively. Or you can buy it from your local computer store. We recommend that you buy the program from your local store, because

- ✔ The full installations of McAfee and Norton are very large and could take hours to download over a modem (not to mention hours more if you get accidentally disconnected).

- ✔ If your computer is already infected, there's no telling what will happen if you try to install antivirus software on top of the virus. Both McAfee and Norton come with bootable disks, allowing you to restart your computer safely, knowing that it's virusfree before you begin to install.

Both software packages have easy-to-follow installation instructions. After you've installed one of them, you have lots of choices about how to use them. We describe some of those in a moment.

During installation, both programs give you the chance to select from various antivirus settings and options, which we discuss in more detail shortly. You're also asked whether you want to install some additional software and a few other add-ons. Whether you choose them is up to you, but in most cases they're not necessary; we stick with just the antivirus features in this chapter.

With both programs, you're also given several choices that we do recommend you take advantage of, including

- ✔ Make backup disks from which you can recover your system if a virus happens to slip past your defenses. The backup may require five or more floppy disks, so make sure that you have some handy.

- ✔ Immediately download updated virus definitions from the software maker's Web site.

- ✔ Immediately scan your entire system for infected software.

Sometimes, installing new software requires you to disable your antivirus software for the installation to work correctly. You should disable your antivirus software only if you have a great deal of confidence in the source of that software.

After you do that, you still have additional choices depending on which software package you've chosen.

McAfee VirusScan

McAfee was one of the earliest antivirus software packages. Several years ago, it was bought by a company named Network Associates, which now markets a bunch of security and privacy software under the McAfee brand. Its basic antivirus software package is McAfee VirusScan.

Configuration options

During installation, you have the option to turn on several types of protection and configure the actions it performs when it finds a virus (how it alerts you and whether it cleans the infected item automatically or waits for your intervention, for example). Together, McAfee calls these functions the VShield, with each choice corresponding to different ways that viruses can get into your computer.

The VirusScan Central console

After the installation and initial configuration, an icon for McAfee VirusScan Central is automatically installed on your desktop. Double-clicking this icon launches a control panel that lets you

- Review the date of your last systemwide virus scan
- Review the current VShield settings
- Review which version you're running and when the last virus update was installed
- Run a disk scan manually
- Set up a regular scanning schedule
- Scan files that you have put in a Quarantine folder to await scanning
- Download and install updates to the software and virus definition (DAT) files

You can also access the VirusScan control panels by right-clicking on the icons in the system tray in the lower-right corner of your taskbar (the little icons near the clock).

Installing updated DAT files manually

McAfee stores updated information about the latest viruses in a DAT file. Because new viruses are released frequently, you *must* keep the latest DAT file installed. You can use the automatic-update button on the McAfee VirusScan Central console or update the program manually. The automatic-update button is quick and easy to use.

Sometimes, you may want to do the update manually, for these reasons:

- **If for any reason your VirusScan Central software has problems connecting to the update server.** (This problem is more common with McAfee than it probably ought to be.)

- **If you have several networked computers running VirusScan.** You can download the update file once and put it in a shared directory for quicker installation by all users. (See Chapter 4 for information about sharing files on networks.)

To download the latest DAT file, browse to `http://download.mcafee.com/updates/updates.asp`. You see links for downloading the latest update.

The DAT file comes in the form of a self-installing program. Double-clicking on the program file launches the installation process. At the end of the installation, you may have to reboot your computer.

Scheduling system scans

A good way to avoid forgetting to run virus scans is not to have to remember to do them in the first place. Using the VirusScan Central console to schedule regular system scans lets you avoid the hassle of remembering.

When you install VirusScan, it adds a schedule scan named Scan Drive C, but doesn't turn it on. To turn on the scan, open the VirusScan Central console and choose Schedule. You see two scheduled items: VShield is set to run a scan at system startup (the default), and the Scan Drive C option is set to Not Scheduled. Select the Drive C scan and choose Edit to display the properties of this task. Selecting the Schedule tab gives you an array of choices.

Make sure that you choose a time that you know your computer is likely to be turned on but when you won't be working (during your lunch hour, for example). Scanning the computer can take some time and may disrupt you when it starts up while you're working on something else.

Norton AntiVirus

Another popular antivirus package is Norton AntiVirus, made by Symantec. Like Network Associates, Symantec offers a wide assortment of popular computer utilities and security products for consumers, marketed under the Norton brand name.

During installation, Norton AntiVirus adds an icon for Norton AntiVirus to your desktop. Clicking that icon calls up the Norton AntiVirus control panel.

Antivirus for corporate bugs

Sophos Anti-Virus (www.sophos.com) is a very good antivirus package, designed primarily for corporate applications, with excellent round-the-clock service and support.

Trend Micro (www.antivirus.com) is another excellent antivirus package for corporate settings, with an emphasis on server-based functions, such as scanning all e-mail coming into a company.

Should you use antivirus software?

John: I'm probably the last person on the planet who doesn't use antivirus software on his Windows laptop. But that's because I only use about four programs on it, and most importantly I don't read my mail on Windows. If I did, I would certainly use an antivirus program.

Ray: Let me put it this way — the only way I would recommend not using antivirus software is if the computer's only use is as a door stop or plant stand. Given a choice between McAfee and Norton, I would give the nod to Norton.

Gregg: Unequivocally, yes.

You can also access the control panel by double-clicking on the antivirus icon in the system tray.

E-mail protection

Most antivirus software programs know how to communicate with most popular e-mail software packages, and they scan the contents of e-mail messages after you've downloaded the mail to your system. But Norton does something a little different. If you choose to enable the E-mail Protection option during the installation process, Norton works as a *proxy* (a kind of go-between) between your ISP's e-mail server and your e-mail program. By placing itself as a pass-through for all your e-mail, it can catch infected, virus-laden attachments before they even get saved to your computer.

Before you turn e-mail protection on, make sure that you have written down your e-mail server settings. Norton AntiVirus adjusts those settings, so you want a copy of them as they used to be, in case anything goes wrong.

The Norton AntiVirus Control Panel

The Norton AntiVirus control panel is a gateway to all the important features of the Norton package:

- **System Status:** Indicates whether the antivirus program is running, when you last updated the virus definitions, and whether the automatic-updating feature is turned on; also displays several performance statistics.

- **E-mail Status:** If you have enabled e-mail protection, shows whether it is turned on, for which e-mail accounts, and for which e-mail software.

- **Scan for Viruses:** Allows you to specify drives, folders, and even specific files to be scanned.

TIP

✔ Choosing Add Scan lets you specify a group of folders or files to be scanned and then save that selection so that you don't have to configure those choices again. This option can be helpful if you have a folder in which you frequently put new files and want to scan just those, without having to run a full system scan.

✔ **Reports:** Allows you to view logs of earlier scans and to manage which folder is designated for holding "quarantined" files waiting to be scanned.

✔ **Scheduling:** Helps you schedule system scans and check for updates and other events.

✔ **Live Update:** Makes a connection over the Internet to the Symantec Web site and then downloads and installs the most recent updates to both the antivirus software and the virus definition files.

✔ **Rescue:** Creates new rescue disks, just like during the installation process.

✔ **Options:** Allows you to modify a wide variety of settings. We recommend that you keep all the default settings. We don't have room to describe all the settings, but a few are noteworthy:

- **Auto-Protect:** You can decide when to scan for viruses, such as when files are run, opened, created, or downloaded.

- **Manual Scans:** You can choose file types, programs, and various parts of your system (such as the computer's active memory) to include when running scans.

- **Live Update:** The program automatically checks for new virus definitions without your intervention.

What's That Crawling in Your Palm?

In late September 2000, the first-ever virus for the Palm operating system was discovered — and more have followed:

PDA viruses we have known

The first Palm virus is named Phage, and it's a true virus, capable of infecting applications and being transferred with them, including when they're "beamed" via the Palm infrared data port.

Luckily, Phage is fairly easy to notice because it lists itself right there in your directory with all your other applications. Second, after it infects other applications on your PDA, they're stopped in their tracks. (Gee, that should increase the odds that you notice Phage quickly.)

All good Trekkers know that the name Phage comes from the television show "Star Trek: Voyager." According to Trekkie lore, the Phage is a deadly plague that is destroying an entire race called the Vidiians. Those nasty Vidiians are the ones who stole Neelix's lung!

Technically not a virus, the Liberty virus Trojan horse pretends to be a program for "cracking" a GameBoy emulator program named Liberty. After victims of the Liberty virus download it onto their PDAs and click on it, it deletes all applications on the device.

If you don't know what a GameBoy is or why anyone would want to use a Palm to emulate or "crack" one, read on. An *emulator* lets you run Nintendo GameBoy-style games on your Palm, and a *crack* is a means of disabling copy-protection schemes (such as requiring you to enter a code or a password in order to install the software) so that you can make copies of the games and use them without paying for them.

If you're a victim of Liberty and lost all your files to this Trojan horse, we say "That's what you get for trying to cheat those nice folks at Gambit Studios (www.gambitstudios.com) out of the $17 they ask for in exchange for creating this cool utility." Luckily for you, you can delete the Liberty virus and reinstall all your applications using your PC connection.

Protecting your PDA

Phage and Liberty were the first, but certainly not the last, Palm viruses. As with all other viruses, avoiding them is a better bet than trying to get rid of them later. Here are some tips for keeping your PDA clean:

- ✔ **For wireless PDAs:** The same rules that apply to your PC apply here. Don't download files from people you don't know, and don't run files until you've scanned them.

- ✔ **For PDAs with infrared capability:** Ditto.

- ✔ **For all PDAs:** Since the emergence of Phage, the major antivirus software makers have started to get serious about antivirus software for PDAs. By the time this book falls into your hands, you should be able to go to http://www.palmgear.com and have a choice of several antivirus products to choose from.

Some antivirus programs for your PC are being updated to allow you to scan Palm applications before downloading them to your PDA. Check with your favorite antivirus software vendor to see whether its software offers this feature.

Another word on viruses

As we have tried to make clear in this chapter, unlike the common cold virus, computer viruses are very much avoidable. Apply a little vigilance, follow our suggestions, and throw in a healthy dose of common sense, and you should keep your computer healthy.

As for any viruses that may be trying to attack your body? For that, you have to call home to Mom! (And she paid us to write that.)

Chapter 9

"Help! There's a Hole in My Browser!"

Ahoy, matey! We've got some news for you: That browser you use to surf around the Internet is much less seaworthy than you think. Almost daily, experts report on new ways that your browser can be tricked, coaxed, and cajoled into squealing on you. But the real kicker is that some of the ways your browser squeals on you aren't that tricky — and some of them were put there quite deliberately!

In the first part of this chapter, we describe cookies, Web bugs, and other ways your browser springs leaks, why some of these leaks were put there on purpose, and how businesses use these techniques to keep track of your every move online.

Your browser's leaks are nothing compared to the number of privacy holes some popular software packages have — holes that are secretly sending your personal information hither and yon. Some of these capabilities are for your convenience, or so say the software manufacturers. But are they really? In the second part of this chapter, we talk about the growing problem of spyware and help you find out whether any double agents are lurking on your computer and how to stop them for good if you do!

In the last part of this chapter, we tell you about some ways to beat cyber-snoops at their own game by looking at some programs you can download that crumble cookies, swat the Web bugs, and flush the spies into the open.

Your Leaky Browser

So much of the average computer user's daily life revolves around Internet Explorer and Netscape that it's important to know the extent to which these old stand-bys sometimes turn out to be fair-weather friends. But, wait a second: You've been using your trusty browser to surf the Web for years! Sure, you've hit a few rough patches along the way, but you can trust your browser to treat you right, right? Not necessarily.

Six ways your browser can betray you

As you go about your day, your browser can play fast and loose with your privacy in many ways:

- Your browser regularly tells Web sites what kind of browser it is, when you last upgraded it, what operating system you have, and which Web site "referred" you to the current page you're visiting (so if you follow a link from an incriminating or embarrassing site, the site has a record of it).

- Many browsers capture and store your e-mail address, so certain sites can then coax your browser into revealing that information about you without your even knowing it.

- Your browser may be secretly storing little text files called *cookies* that let Web sites assign you unique electronic nametags so that they can later identify you on future visits.

- The default settings of most recent versions of popular browsers let evil Web sites send you Web pages that act like viruses and can take control of your computer and let hackers have the run of your computer and all the information on it.

- Your browser may be capturing your user IDs and passwords for Web sites you log in to, letting anyone with access to your machine log in to those sites as though they were you.

- Your browser may be keeping track of every Web site you visit — every picture and page you view — and it may even be keeping copies of all that for others to see, if they know how to find it!

Your browser's privacy controls

The most popular browsers, Internet Explorer and Netscape, have their own built-in privacy settings and controls. They vary in the level of control they allow over elements like cookies, but the choices are better than nothing. You can find near the end of this chapter some directions for accessing those privacy controls for Netscape, Internet Explorer, and a small, fast browser from

Norway, named Opera. Far and away, the most advanced settings are found in Opera, and for that reason we make the case for your giving it a try; see the sidebar "For highly refined viewing, try Opera," near the end of this chapter.

Why do browsers leak?

In the early 1990s, a fellow by the name of Tim Berners-Lee invented the data-exchange standards that make the Web possible. He did this not to become rich and famous; rather, he was just looking to find a better way of letting researchers share their data with others. So he took some time from his duties at a high-energy physics research laboratory in Switzerland, named CERN, to work on the *HyperText Transport Protocol,* or *http,* for short. The data exchange process was so useful that it caught on quickly, and the rest is history.

But when the first Web servers and Web browsers were developed, not much attention was paid to subjects like security and privacy. The developers just wanted the stuff to work, so they put in features that would let them easily get to the root of the problem when something went haywire and help them figure out whether the buggy culprit was a server or somebody's browser. That's why virtually every browser leaves a trail of its type, version, operating system, and referring page.

This amount of insecurity was perfectly fine when the only items being passed around were technical papers about smashing particles together at the speed of light. But it's not so great if you're counting on the same technology to keep your personal information secure when sending love letters or company secrets or your credit card number when you're buying a sweater online.

Connections made using the HyperText Transport Protocol are *stateless,* which doesn't mean that their home state has fallen into the ocean. It means that after your computer receives the content of that page, the connection between your computer and the faraway Web server is closed and the server forgets that the connection ever happened. Rather than maintain a constant open connection "state," each file that makes up the page (such as each of the graphics on a page) creates a new and separate connection. That's why you can sometimes receive all the text of a Web page, but not the pictures.

An on-again, off-again relationship

If you've read the preceding section, you know this fabulous new geekspeak word, *stateless.* Why would anybody want it? Why not keep the connection open?

To understand the answer to that question, think about what happens when you pick up the phone and call the operator for directory assistance. You don't have a direct line open to the operator at all times. Instead, you connect only when you need an operator's services and only for as long as it takes to get the necessary information. This process is a much more efficient way of doing things and allows one operator — or one Web server — to serve many more people at a time.

If a file server is throwing around millions of pages every day to millions of people, you occasionally may want the server to remember who you are. For example, if you log in to check your stock portfolio, you want the server to show you only your information and no one else's. By the same token, you want to be sure that other people are seeing only *their own* information and *not yours*!

On the other hand, you don't want to have to reenter your password every time you visit this site or for every individual server connection or for every image or text file that gets loaded into your browser. (Remember that every file is a new and separate connection: On one typical E*Trade account page, for example, more than a dozen individual image files are combined into one nicely formatted and readable page!)

How do you make the server remember that you're you so that it protects your data but also doesn't ask you to reenter your password every time? Or, to use geekspeak: How do you create a constant state in an otherwise stateless series of connections? Believe it or not, the answer to that is something called a cookie.

Making a case for cookies

A *cookie* works kind of like your ticket stub at the movies. If you have to run out to the bathroom or the snack bar, you can show your stub and get back in. How convenient! Just think — if you didn't have a stub, you would be stuck outside and if you wanted to see the movie, you would have to pay to start over from the beginning.

A cookie does the same thing: It makes sure that the server can remember you through many steps in a visit or even when time has passed between visits. Remember what we said about every new page being a separate Web connection? When Gregg bought a shirt online, he went through a number of pages. He had to use a separate page to

- Pick the shirt style.
- Pick the color.
- Pick the size.
- Specify the monogram.
- Enter his shipping address.

✔ Enter his credit card number.

✔ Confirm that all the information was correct.

Without cookies, that entire process would be much more complicated, probably requiring Gregg to reenter some or all of his information many times along the way. Cookies help the Web server remember that sequence of pages and entries as all belonging to you. And because you're trying to complete a business transaction with as few complications as possible, that's pretty handy.

When the server gives your browser a cookie, the browser software stores the cookie in the form of a small file on your hard drive. That's all a *cookie* really is: a small file with a little bit of data in it, called a cookie file, as shown in Figure 9-1.

Figure 9-1.
What a
cookie
really looks
like

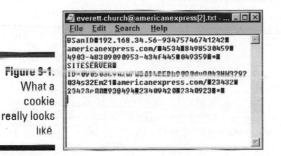

To see all the cookies you have on your machine, click the Start button and choose Search⇨Files or Folders and enter **cookies** in the Search for Files or Folders named field. The result shows you one or more (depending on the kinds of Internet software you have installed) folders and files where cookie files are stored. To see the cookies themselves, just open one of the files or documents that turns up in your cookie search.

The difference between homemade and store-bought: first- and third-party cookies

Everybody knows that homemade cookies are very different from store-bought ones and that usually the homemade ones are much yummier. As you can see in Figure 9-1, Internet cookies are uniformly bland regardless of their origin, but quite a difference can exist between those cooked up by the Web site you're visiting and those that come from a third party.

As we say elsewhere in this chapter, many sites use their own cookies to make their Web sites work better and to keep track of shopping carts, for example. But some sites also rent out space on their Web pages to third parties, often for placement of advertisements. Along with those ad banners, many third-party advertising companies also try to set their own cookie on your browser. Why? Usually for two reasons:

✔ To manage ad frequency (so that they don't show you the same ad over and over and over and over and over and over until it drives you crazy).

✔ To track your movement between the many sites on which they place advertisements so that they can learn about your interests, based on where you surf, so that they can send you ads *chosen especially for you!* (This idea is one that you either love or are totally creeped out by, so we talk more about this topic later in this chapter.)

That's the way the cookie crumbles

Cookies — are they good or bad? Far be it from us to settle any debates. What we do say is that technology, by itself, is neither good nor bad. It's how people *use* the technology that's good or bad.

Cookies are useful items. For example, when you have a password for a Web site or some kind of registration or display settings associated with a particular Web site, a cookie can come in handy. Maybe you often visit a financial Web site where you like to see price updates on your 50 favorite stocks and mutual funds. The cookie is what saves you from having to enter your password and those same 50 stock symbols every time you visit.

But some cookies aren't nearly as useful, or at least not to you. Because cookies let a server keep track of what pages you see, the cookies can be used to keep track of *any* pages you see, on any Web site, and across many Web sites. Advertisers make extensive use of cookies to track you as you surf from Web site to Web site, in the hope of building a file about which Web sites you like to visit.

We talk more about that tracking in a minute, but assume for now that you've heard horrible things about cookies and want nothing to do with them. So you've gone into your browser settings (using the instructions the last main section in this chapter, "Accessing Your Browser's Privacy Controls") and decided to turn off all cookies and get back to surfing. Brace yourself for a bumpy ride!

Why "no cookies" sometimes means "no lookies"

Many Web sites contain a great deal of frequently changing content, so the only way to operate efficiently is to use Web servers tied to databases that generate Web pages on the fly. In some of these cases, the Web servers require cookies to help determine, for example, whether it should serve up something new and fresh for you. Still other sites use cookies, as we mention earlier in this chapter, to help customize the content based on your preferences. Still more sites use cookies to help remember what language you want or to give you weather or sports scores for your local area. The MSNBC Web site asks you to supply your zip code and favorite stock symbols so that it can personalize the site for you, and it stores that data in a cookie.

If you choose to block all cookies, you cannot take advantage of these personalization features.

A special type of cookie, called a *session* cookie, resembles other cookies in every sense except that it's automatically set to delete itself within a relatively short period, usually within about 10 minutes after you leave a site. This type of cookie is typically used for remembering information over a short duration, such as what you've stored in your shopping cart while on a virtual shopping spree. (That's why, if you walk away from your computer for too long while surfing some sites, you get a message that says "Session expired.") Because session cookies are so short-lived, they don't have quite the same privacy implications. That's also why some browsers let you block regular cookies while allowing you to accept session cookies at the same time.

Shutting off all cookies may help you avoid being tracked, but it may also be throwing the baby out with the bath water.

Applying the "Peter and The Wolf" principle

Most popular Web browsers have another setting for handling cookies. Somewhere between the settings for Accept All Cookies and Reject All Cookies is one that says Notify Me. This setting causes an alert box to pop up each and every time a site tries to set a cookie. This strategy can cause several problems.

You may be surprised to see just how many cookies one Web page can send you (often, as many as 5 or 10) and it can get tiresome to click Accept or Decline for each cookie you run into across the Web. Some sites are more persistent than others, with multiple cookies attempted on each page, requiring you to make a choice multiple times.

In some cases, the cookie interception allows you to see the contents of the cookie. Unfortunately, most cookies are meaningless strings of gobbledygook that are meaningful only to the server and to the guy who programmed them. In Internet Explorer 6, you can have the browser prompt you to make a choice each time a site attempts to set a cookie.

Should you accept all cookies?

John: I mostly use Netscape and Opera, both of which can reject third-party cookies, so I set them that way and don't worry about it. Microsoft finally got with the plan in Internet Exploder 6.0, although you have to use the Advanced button on the Privacy tab from the Tools menu to find the place to turn off all third-party cookies.

Ray: If Web browsers would let you uniformly reject third-party cookies — cookies being set by somebody other than the site you're visiting — then I would say that you should accept all the other cookies. But some versions of some browsers don't allow you much ability

to fine-tune the cookie controls. As a result, rejecting cookies can be a real pain. My suggestion: Accept them all and then clear them out once a week, except those from sites you know you want to keep. An example is the cookies from sites where I've asked them to store my password. I keep those and trash the rest.

Gregg: Because I'm absent-minded, I have scheduled a weekly reminder into my desktop calendar to remind me to clean out my cookies once a week. Without the reminder, I would probably forget to clean them out for weeks or months or years.

If you aren't ready to turn cookies off completely, but aren't ready to let cookies ride roughshod over your browser, turning on cookie notification is an option. But then you run the risk of being complacent and habitually clicking Yes, Accept Cookie every time you get one without paying attention to the context in which the cookie is being set. The result is that you've accepted all cookies anyway.

As a basic security measure, cookies can be read only when a server in the same domain requests it — so only a server in the yahoo.com domain can read cookies set by a server in the yahoo.com domain. You may think that the cookie that rolled behind your refrigerator is old, but it's nothing compared to how long some Web cookies are intended to stay around. Browsers require that every cookie have an expiration date, so most Web site designers set a date a few decades from now — essentially making them permanent, or *persistent,* cookies.

Help is on the way (choosing cookie-management software)

If you long for more cookie choices than your browser offers, some cookie-management software may just be your ticket. Most of these packages are browser *plug-ins,* meaning that after they're installed, they integrate nicely into the browser, adding their own buttons to the toolbars and menus right alongside the familiar browser buttons. Some of the more popular include

✔ **iDcide Privacy Companion** (www.idcide.com): The iDcide Privacy Companion is one of the easiest-to-use cookie managers available. Although it works with only Internet Explorer, it integrates seamlessly, adding a few small icons at the top of your browser's toolbar. The icons are displayed at a glance whether the site you're visiting has set its own cookies or is setting cookies for third parties, and it lets you set the level of privacy you want, which translates into whether and what kinds of cookies it accepts on your behalf. The Privacy Companion also provides a quick and easy display of what third-party ad networks are operating on which sites you've visited, and it lets you quickly sort, read, and delete your cookies.

✔ **Cookie Pal** (www.kburra.com): Cookie Pal is a little piece of shareware that watches for cookies in browsers (including Internet Explorer, Netscape, and Opera), in Microsoft Outlook, and in a few other programs. As Web sites attempt to set cookies, Cookie Pal asks whether you want to accept or reject the cookie. More importantly, it lets you remember that choice temporarily or permanently. For example, if you go to a site that tries to set many cookies, you can permanently accept the ones that help you personalize the site and reject the ones from advertising companies you've never heard of. After you've made your choice, Cookie Pal remembers it and never bothers you again. It also provides you with a screen for reviewing earlier decisions and gives you a list of all the cookies you've accepted in case you want to dump them.

✔ **Cookie Cruncher** (www.rbaworld.com/Programs/CookieCruncher): Cookie Cruncher works much like the others discussed in this, letting you block, view, edit, and delete cookies. Its main difference is that it also works with the AOL browser, something the others either don't do or don't do as well.

✔ **HistoryKill** (www.historykill.com): HistoryKill not only lets you manage your cookie files but also helps clear out your Web histories and temporary Internet files every time you close your browser. It can be set to not only delete cookies and history files but also wipe them from your hard drive using a method that meets military and National Security Agency specifications. HistoryKill also has a Boss Key feature that quickly hides all your browser windows and a PopUp Killer that blocks additional ad windows from opening.

✔ **Cookie Crusher** (www.thelimitsoft.com/cookie.html): Cookie Crusher automates the process of refusing cookies in Netscape and Internet Explorer. Although both browsers have settings to ask before accepting cookies, Cookie Crusher takes over the tedious task of clicking OK, silently rejecting them all.

Proxies: Your own, private agent

Another category of privacy-enhancing software is a little more complex, but can offer you more alternatives. These packages don't simply attach to your browser software — they run separately and act as a *proxy,* or a kind of go-between, that filters all the data passing between your browser and the Internet sites you visit. These proxies not only intercept cookies but also even block the entire advertisement image from loading, and they can even block Web bugs. This list shows some examples of these proxy-type cookie managers:

- ✔ **Guidescope (**`www.guidescope.com`**):** Guidescope is a free software package that acts as a proxy, filtering all the data passing to and from your Web browser. It requires a few configuration changes for your Web browser, and depending on how complicated your Internet connection is (such as if you're surfing at work from behind your company's firewall or proxy), it may not work. But if you've got a standard Internet connection, Guidescope transparently reroutes all your Web browsing through its preprogrammed listing of known advertisers and blocks the ads coming from there. It also identifies and intercepts cookies, handling them according to your instructions. Guidescope automatically updates its listings regularly to keep up with advertisers that may change the way ads are served and, in case it still misses some ads, gives you the chance to quickly review images and check off missed ads for future blocking. Occasionally, Guidescope causes Web pages to look a little funny, often because advertisement graphics are used to help provide formatting for some pages.

- ✔ **AdSubtract (**`www.adsubtract.com`**):** AdSubtract is a content-filtering proxy server that passes all data to and from your Web browser, looking all the while for advertisements, pop-up windows, music files, JavaScript features, and more. The software is simple to install and easy to configure, although, like Guidescope, AdSubtract occasionally causes pages to look a little funny, and it occasionally messes with your ability to use certain snazzy Web page features, like dynamic menus and animated images. AdSubtract costs about $20.

- ✔ **Junkbusters (**`http://www.junkbusters.com/ijb.html`**):** Arguably the granddaddy of ad-blocking software, the Junkbusters software is highly configurable, but a good bit less user friendly than the Guidescope offering.

Web bugs: Cookies on steroids

Oh, those data-hungry advertisers; they always want to know more, more, more about your personal habits and interests, and a new technology called Web bugs gives them the much-needed boost that every growing ad executive needs.

Web bugs are special links in Web pages that collect much more detailed information about your online activities than a simple cookie can and then feed all that information about you directly into a database containing tons of other information about you that has been gathered and stored by other Web bugs.

As we mention earlier in this chapter, every time you load a Web page, it's an on-again, off-again relationship, with each graphic on a Web page a separate connection by Web servers and Web browsers.

When a Web bug is programmed into a Web page, its code looks similar to the code for just about any graphic image appearing on that page. In reality, though, it has three differences:

- ✔ The Web bug graphic is often called from some third-party site, just like a third-party cookie.

- ✔ The Web address used to call in the Web bug graphic is encoded with loads of extra data about you and your visit.

- ✔ The graphic image associated with the Web bug is deliberately made to be so tiny that it's invisible to the naked eye. (When somebody goes out of their way to make something invisible, you would think that something deceitful is going on, wouldn't you?)

Most Web bugs are the size of a single screen pixel. What's a pixel? If you look *really* closely at your computer screen, you see lots of tiny dots. The smallest unit of dot on your computer screen is the *pixel*. It's about the size of the period at the end of this sentence. But even a period is still visible, so they often make the Web bug pixel from a kind of graphic image called a clear GIF, or a transparent GIF, which allows the background color or image to show through it. So all you see is — nothing!

What kind of data can advertisers get when they load a Web bug into your browser?

Web bugs, like every other graphic on a Web page, have to come from somewhere. And, depending on the data that's encoded in the address used to call up the Web bug, the person who controls that bug can tell an awful lot about you.

Many sites use Web bugs to help track how many people have visited a particular Web site or to track what kinds of browsers are being used. For advertisers, the really exciting news is that Web bugs can be used to collect information — about you! — such as what sites you're visiting, the contents of the pages you read, and how long you looked at that page before clicking to another page.

Because Web bugs can be embedded in any Web page or HTML document, they can also be included in e-mail, allowing sites to track details about when you read your mail and who you may be forwarding messages to.

In fact, according to privacy expert Richard Smith, the former chief technology officer at the Privacy Foundation (www.privacyfoundation.org), Web bugs are getting so sophisticated that they can

- Count the number of times you have visited a particular Web page.

- Track the Web pages you view within a Web site.

- Track what Web pages you visit across many different Web sites.

- Count the number of times a banner ad has appeared on your screen.

- Measure the effectiveness of a banner ad campaign by matching your visits to a Web site to whichever Web sites you were on when you saw the ads.

- Match your purchase to a banner ad you viewed before making the purchase. The Web site that displayed the banner ad is typically given a percentage of the sale.

- Allow a third party to provide server logging to a Web site that cannot do logging.

- Record and report the type and configuration of your Internet browser when you're visiting Web sites. This information is typically used in aggregate form to determine what kind of content can be put on a Web site to be viewed by most visitors.

- Record and report search strings from a search engine to an Internet marketing company. The search strings are typically used to profile users — like you!

- Transfer demographic data about you (gender, age, and zip code, for example) from one Web site to an Internet marketing company. This information is typically used for online profiling purposes.

- Transfer previously entered personally identifiable information about you (name, address, phone number, and e-mail address, for example) from a Web site to an Internet marketing company. This information is typically used for online profiling purposes. It also can be combined with other offline demographic data, such as household income, number of family members, types of cars owned, and mortgage balance, for example.

- *Synchronize* cookies, which allows two companies to exchange data about you in the background. This data can be demographics or personally identifiable data, typically used for online profiling purposes.

Turning the kitchen light on Web bugs

Several of these cookie and ad blockers also block Web bugs. Only one program that we know of flushes the bugs into the open: Bugnosis. Created and distributed by the privacy gurus at the Privacy Foundation, the Bugnosis browser plug-in looks for tiny Web bugs hiding on Web pages and replaces the tiny 1-pixel image with a much larger picture of a creepy, crawly bug (see Figures 9-2 and 9-3).

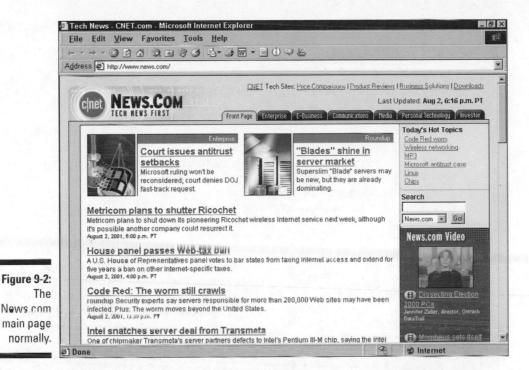

Figure 9-2:
The News.com main page normally.

Figure 9-3:
The News.com main page showing two Web bugs lurking near the navigation buttons atop the page. Do you see them?

For more information about Web bugs, visit the Privacy Foundation Web Bug FAQ: www.bugnosis.org/faq.html.

Profiling (or why cookies and bugs aren't the whole enchilada)

For folks in the advertising world, the holy grail of advertising is to be able to deliver an advertisement to you for exactly the right product at exactly the moment when you're most likely to want it. For example, nothing apparently is more exciting for an advertiser than to be able to put an ad for a cheap airline ticket to Aspen right on a page visited by people who enjoy skiing.

As you may guess, people who enjoy skiing don't spend every moment of their lives looking at Web pages for skiing equipment. So where's the best place to put an ad for cheap tickets to Aspen? Well, you could do research and find out what other Web sites are visited by skiers. But it turns out that skiers are as different as everybody else and spend a great deal of time reading all kinds of different things on the Web that you could never assume would appeal to people who like skiing.

In the beginning of Web advertising, the Aspen advertiser's only hope would have been to put ads for Aspen on as many ski pages as possible, hoping that some skiers would stumble across it. But advertising is expensive, and they yearned for some way of increasing their odds of getting the right ad in front of the right kind of viewer.

How in the world would the advertiser do that? Let's think about this one. You're visiting page after page of Web sites for who knows what — and the advertiser either needs to advertise on every page you go to or needs some way to keep track of all the places you're going as well as all the places everyone else is going. But how can the advertiser remember that you are you as you go from page to page? With cookies, of course!

Soon, somebody figured out that if you put cookies on the computers of people who visit ski-related sites and then read those cookies when they visit other Web sites, the cookie can help identify them as someone who should get ads targeted for skiers, no matter what they're looking at on the Web. And the practice of online profiling was born.

Have we got a file on you!

The idea of being able to string together a long series of page visits is exciting to online advertisers. One of the ways advertisers make sure that they get the most bang for their advertising buck is to make sure that when they pay good money to put an ad under your nose, it's likely to appeal to you. The way they do that is to try to figure out what you like.

If an advertiser sells special mittens for skiers and can find out that you're the type of person who buys lots of downhill skis and ski poles and ski wax, he knows that his money is better spent sending ads and catalogs to you than to someone who has never skied.

In the real world, the mitten people can buy up the mailing lists of downhill ski catalog companies, get the ski pole warranty registration card lists from the pole vendors, buy the skiing accessory store's customer list, and put them all together. Then, when the advertiser finds some of the same names on all the lists, he knows that he has his audience. The tricky part is that when you send out a catalog, the only way you know that people are really interested in buying is when they make a purchase.

On the Web, it's different. When you're surfing to page after page of ski equipment, a pretty good chance exists that you may be in the market to buy some ski equipment! You're exactly who the advertiser wants to reach, and, what's more, if he can get his ad in front of you at this exact moment, he's got the best chance to make a sale!

Enter the superprofilers: Ad networks

An *ad network* is a company that puts advertising banners on thousands of Web sites all over the Web. When anyone visits one of the Web sites in the network, it serves up an advertisement and, along with it, sets a cookie that lets the advertiser remember that you went to that particular site. If the next Web site you visit is also part of that ad network, it reads the cookie and its server remembers who you are.

To continue with the skiing example in the preceding section, if on Monday you visit a skiing Web site and it belongs to the XYZ ad network, you would receive a cookie that lets the server remember that you visited on a particular date and are interested in skis. On Tuesday, when you surf to the ski pole Web site — which also participates in the XYZ ad network — it reads the cookie and remembers that you're interested in skis, allowing the site to serve you ads related to skis.

Here's the really exciting part for advertisers: On Wednesday, if you go looking for reviews of new laptop computers and happen to visit a Web site that is also a client of the XYZ ad network, guess what kind of ads you may see on the laptop Web site? If you said "Skis," congratulations! Give yourself a glass of milk to go with all those cookies!

The reality of this cookie-based targeting is that it doesn't work all that well. Most of the people who are trying to target ads to you by tracking your surfing habits through cookies either can't target their way out of a paper bag or don't have the right things to target you with.

As an economics side note, this situation is to a large degree the reason that so many dot.com businesses are failing. They banked on the ability to be able to send supertargeted ads to Web surfers who would then buy vast amounts of stuff, but no one has made it work yet — and probably nobody ever will.

So what's the big deal?

For many people, the use of cookies for customizing sites and targeting advertisements is of no great concern. They think, "So what if they know that I like to ski? Big deal! If they want to use that information to give me an ad full of real bargains, go for it!" A growing number of people, though, are feeling offended and creepy to know that someone is quietly keeping tabs on them, knowing what they're looking at, and sending them ads based on that information. If you fall into this latter camp, you'll *love* (not!) the information in the next section.

More Internet Software That's Soft on Privacy

The amount of data about you that can be snagged through your Web browser is certainly cause for alarm, but equally alarming is the number of software applications you probably never thought to worry about — but that are becoming more and more of a threat to your privacy.

Spyware in your midst

An entire new category of snooping software has emerged, called spyware. Computer privacy experts have defined *spyware* as any piece of software that gathers information and uses your Internet connection to send it somewhere else on your computer, without your explicit knowledge or approval. But why does the spyware do this? In many cases, the spyware is gathering information about you and your activities on your own computer and sending that data back to the software manufacturer or some other data-collection company so that it can know more about you.

One of the first known examples of spyware was Microsoft Windows 95.

As is often the case with new software, you're asked whether you want to register your purchase with the manufacturer to obtain support and to activate your warranty. But when you installed Windows 95 and it asked you to register, the Registration Wizard did much more than send in your registration information. It also scanned your computer to compile a list of all your computer's hardware and all the software you had installed. It then bundled up that information and sent it back to Microsoft, without telling you what it was doing.

Under most state laws, companies are required to honor their warranties regardless of whether you've registered. However, many companies are now requiring registration in order to obtain customer support, a service not mandated by warranty laws.

This situation provoked a huge outcry from many corners. Privacy advocates were naturally stunned at the brazen data collection without giving consumers either notice of what data was being collected or any choice about sharing it. Legal experts were deeply suspicious of what use Microsoft might try to make of the data about which competitor's programs were being used.

Even after all the ruckus, Microsoft didn't stop collecting this data. But it did modify the Registration Wizard to make transmitting the data optional during the installation process.

Following the Microsoft lead, many other software manufacturers got the bright idea to include spyware features in their software. Here's a list of software that has been caught doing some sneaky things behind your back:

✔ **Kazaa:** The popular Napster-like file trading program Kazaa was discovered in April 2002 to be secretly installing the software of an advertising company named Brilliant Digital Entertainment, which, according to the company, could turn every computer running Kazaa into a part of a stealth network controlled by Brilliant. The company claims that it will use the network only with users' permission, but if you installed Kazaa, you already gave permission! Buried in the software usage agreement is the line "You hereby grant [Brilliant] the right to access and use the unused computing power and storage space on your computer/s and/or Internet access or bandwidth for the aggregation of content and use in distributed computing." If you decline this provision, you can't install the Kazaa software. The Brilliant software can be disabled or removed after installation, without affecting the usability of Kazaa. Instructions for doing this can be found at news.com.com/2100-1023-875274.html.

✔ **Audio Galaxy:** Another popular music sharing program, this software was discovered to quietly install a program named VX2. In reports on a spyware-tracking Web site (www.poenews.com/inhouse/vx2.htm), someone investigating mysterious browser pop-ups discovered that VX2 was the culprit responsible for generating the unwanted advertisements on users' desktops. (*Pop-ups* are small Web browser windows that appear without warning and with advertisements. When they appear beneath your main browser window, they're called *pop-unders*.) But the software apparently does more, such as capture information you enter on Web page forms, including any personal information or search terms. VX2 wants to know lots about you, but the Web site lists no address or phone number, and the domain name is registered with a post office box in Las Vegas and a Hotmail e-mail address.

- **RadLight:** RadLight is a multimedia file player, used primarily for viewing video files downloaded from the Internet. During installation, this software offers to install two "small optional programs from other companies," which includes a spyware program named SaveNow. It captures information about files you download and other information from your computer. Knowing that people are becoming savvy about spyware and using anti-spyware programs like Ad-Aware (which you can read about next, in the section on removing spyware from your computer), the folks at RadLight declared war on Ad-Aware and inserted a Trojan horse program that secretly searches for and deletes the Ad-Aware software from your computer! (Find out more about Trojan horses in Chapter 8.)

- **RealDownload, from RealNetworks:** RealNetworks, the maker of RealAudio music and video streaming software, released a spyware-infested program named RealDownload. Having been accused previously of building spyware functions into its RealJukebox software — and having to reissue, under great public pressure, a version with the spyware disabled — you would think that the company would have learned its lesson. Of course not! The Internet sleuth Steve Gibson discovered that the RealDownload software sends a unique identifier back to RealNetworks every time you use the software to download music files. And, if you had ever made a purchase from RealNetworks, personal information (including your name and e-mail address) got stored in a cookie during that transaction that gets accessed and sent back to RealNetworks. Although Gibson was threatened by lawyers from RealNetworks, he went on to reveal that RealDownload is one of several programs that incorporates spyware code from another software package named NetZip Download Demon. (According to Gibson, RealNetworks bought the NetZip company and — ta-da — also got the NetZip database of more than 14 million users and all the information NetZip had gathered about them!)

- **Comet Cursor:** Provided as an automatic download at more than 50,000 Web sites, Comet Cursor replaces your regular mouse cursor with various animated images, including cartoon characters like Garfield and Pokémon. On many of these sites, you're immediately presented with a box asking whether you want to accept "a free 10-second download." If you make the mistake of accepting the download without further investigation, you'll never know that you've just downloaded spyware that sends a unique identifier for you back to Comet, allowing it to track your visits to affiliated Web sites. All this happens without your knowing or consenting to it before it happens.

- **zBubbles:** This online shopping tool from Amazon.com, introduced in late 1999, allowed users to quickly see consumer product reviews and price comparisons while shopping online. Unfortunately, unbeknownst to those who downloaded it, zBubbles would regularly transmit data (including names, addresses, e-mail addresses, and other personal information) to Alexa, a subsidiary of Amazon. In fact, the privacy policy for zBubbles said that it absolutely didn't provide personally identifiable information. Ultimately, Amazon was sued privately, but settled the case. In a related development, the Federal Trade Commission issued a ruling in the spring of 2001 that the Amazon subsidiary Alexa had engaged in deceptive trade practices. Normally, the FTC would deal harshly with this type of violation, but because the company had already abandoned the practice, the FTC decided to go easy on poor Alexa.

✔ **GoHip.com:** This Internet search engine site distributed a version of the Microsoft Windows Video Player. Along with the video player, GoHip distributed a little piece of software that secretly modifies various settings on your computer and mysteriously adds a tagline or signature line to all your outgoing e-mail — advertising GoHip! On closer inspection, the details of the modifications were buried in the software license, but most consumers don't expect to give permission for a video player download to rewrite their e-mail software settings. No one knows whether GoHip still distributes this software (and, frankly, we're too scared to try downloading it!).

Detecting and blocking spyware

If spyware is running on your computer, you can find it in two ways:

✔ Look for programs known to have spyware capabilities.

✔ Look for suspicious attempts by a software program to "phone home" to its creator.

Incorporating the first approach, Ad-Aware, from LavaSoft (www.lavasof usa.com), searches your computer for software that is known to have spyware features. This freeware, which is simple to download and install, scans your computer, looking for known spyware applications.

As we mention in the preceding section, Ad-Aware is so effective at discovering and removing spyware that the spyware makers have declared war. For example, some versions of the Internet video-viewing software RadLight check to see whether you have Ad-Aware installed and, if so, automatically (and secretly) uninstalls it. Because this behavior is similar to that of a virus or a Trojan horse (see Chapter 8 for more talk about those nasty critters), many popular download sites removed RadLight until its makers issued a revised version that warns you in advance that Ad-Aware will be uninstalled. Thankfully, the folks at Ad-Aware have already issued their own new version of the software that RadLight can't touch.

But programs like Ad-Aware can uncover only the spyware it knows about. If you're looking for something that may discover programs Ad-Aware doesn't know about, a good tool is ZoneAlarm, from Zone Labs (www.zonelabs.com).

We talk more about ZoneAlarm in Chapter 8, when we talk about using personal firewall software to keep hackers from probing your computer for hackable weaknesses. ZoneAlarm also offers a feature that's incredibly useful for detecting spyware. Along with blocking out people who may be probing from outside, it also keeps an eye on situations in which software on your computer tries to access the Internet without your knowledge or permission.

Zone Alarm keeps tabs on *every* piece of software that tries to access the Internet, and the program asks whether you want to let it pass through the firewall. So when your e-mail program or your Web browser triggers ZoneAlarm, you can quickly click OK. But when your new screen saver or a new game of Solitaire starts asking to connect to the Internet, you can keep it quiet and uninstall it before it rats on you.

When spyware isn't spyware

As was the case with the sneaky Kazaa and GoHip software, many cases of spyware are in a gray area when it comes to being called spyware, because somewhere deep in the terms of their download agreement, the distributor explains all the devious things it does. But, saying "It was buried in the fine print, so it's your fault for not reading more carefully" doesn't usually leave consumers feeling warm and fuzzy. Because of public relations nightmares that often follow the discovery of spyware-like activities, an increasing number of companies using software that does tracking and data transmission are being more up front about it. Here are some popular shareware programs that do disclose their data-collection activities, either on the company's Web site or during the installation process:

- GO!zilla
- Free Solitaire
- GetRight
- PKZip
- CuteFTP
- SurfMonkey

Not sure whether that cool new "free" software you downloaded has something nasty lurking in it? The folks who brought you Ad-Aware have a free, downloadable database, named Ad-Search, that lists all the known bits of spyware:

www.ad-aware.net/english/lsdownloads.htm

Spyware extraordinaire?

A new kid in town isn't exactly spyware, but its functions are every bit as frightening — if not worse!

The folks from the search engine company AltaVista have begun offering a version of its Web searching software to businesses. This indexing software, AV Enterprise Search, crawls through company networks looking for stray bits of data that may be of use to a company's managers.

The search doesn't stop with network servers; it continues right on your desktop PC, indexing and archiving everything stored on your office computer. And it doesn't stop there, either: It can also search and catalog anything connected to your PC, including CDs, PDAs, cell phones, and anything else that may be attached. Storing the password to your Ameritrade account on your PDA? Have the phone number of your favorite headhunter programmed in your cell phone? Now your boss knows both those tidbits, all presented to her in keyword-searchable form.

Hiding Your Movements: Anonymous Surfing

As we discuss in Chapter 6, every computer connected to the Internet gets assigned a numerical address, called an Internet Protocol (IP) address. This address, often coupled with cookies, can often be used to uniquely identify you as you move around the Web. One of the most effective ways to foil Internet snoops who are trying to follow you around is to deny them the ability to tie a unique IP address to you.

The best way to hide your IP address is to use one of a growing number of Web-based anonymous proxy services. We talk about proxies earlier in this chapter, in the context of blocking out advertisements and filtering out cookies. Another category of third-party proxy servers, however, fetches Web pages on your behalf without revealing your IP address. Because these proxy services fetch pages for hundreds or thousands of people, Web sites that try to track you wind up with hordes of people listed in their databases, all with exactly the same IP address.

None of these techniques is foolproof, though. For example, if you accept cookies over these anonymized connections, marketers who want to track you may not be able to know your name or your IP address, but they can still build an anonymous profile of you. An *anonymous profile* means that the marketers don't know your name, but they know that one particular individual went to the tracked sites. And if they ever *do* learn your identity, such as if you make a purchase with a credit card or provide your mailing address, all your anonymized efforts are immediately destroyed because they can use your credit card information to tie your anonymized identity to your real identity.

If you want to give anonymous browsing a try, here are some popular Web-based anonymous surfing sites:

- ✔ **Anonymizer:** www.anonymizer.com
- ✔ **IDzap:** www.idzap.com
- ✔ **theCloak:** www-new.the-cloak.com/anonymous-surfing-home.html
- ✔ **Rewebber:** www.rewebber.de
- ✔ **Ponoi:** www.ponoi.com

If you want to protect your identity but still use a credit card on the Web, see Chapter 14 for information about private payments.

Accidents Happen

If you've been reading along in this chapter, that's enough about all the ways browsers are designed to intentionally rat you out. Now it's time to talk about some of their unintentional privacy and security problems.

When Web pages attack!

Hardly a week goes by in which someone doesn't uncover some new security flaw in a Web browser. Thankfully for everyone, many of these holes are fairly obscure, usually discovered only by some nerdy researcher who spends his days poking and prodding the browser like a rat in a medical experiment. Given how complex a program like Internet Explorer is, with capabilities to interpret dozens of file types, accept software plug-ins, and integrate with dozens of other programs on your computer, it's no wonder that occasionally somebody can coax the browser into doing something it shouldn't.

Sometimes the security holes discovered by these researchers are so complicated and theoretical that the alarms they sound are reminiscent of the geologists' press releases breathlessly warning us that sometime in the next 12 million years, a volcano will rise beneath San Francisco. These types of alerts are often more about the researcher getting more funding than about a real security threat.

Occasionally, though, the pocket protector crowd uncovers problems that can be quite scary. For example, in March 2001, a bug was found in the way Internet Explorer handles Web pages attached to e-mail messages. Because

Internet Explorer can be automatically launched by your e-mail software to assist in the viewing of e-mail messages, a malicious person could easily send you an e-mail that could automatically hijack Internet Explorer and have its way with your computer.

Luckily, the security hole was discovered before anyone found a way to exploit it. With the regularity of these discoveries, though, you have to give some thought to the care and feeding of your favorite Web browser.

The Microsoft red alert du jour

Our good friends in Redmond, Washington, can always be counted on to keep the privacy and security folks jumping. We could write a whole book about all the problems they have had, which isn't all that surprising considering how many different types of software they race to produce in their effort to put everyone else out of business. Yet here are some of our favorite Microsoft privacy invasions:

- ✔ **Globally Unique Identifiers (GUIDs):** It turns out that Microsoft Word, along with other Microsoft software products, embeds a unique identifier in every document you produce, identifying your computer as the source of the document. This capability was discovered during the investigation of the Melissa virus outbreak and was allegedly used to help identify the creator of the virus.

- ✔ **Microsoft Macro Viruses:** In Chapter 8 we go into great detail about how security flaws in certain versions of Word, Excel, and PowerPoint allow virus creators to hijack computers by distributing infected document files.

- ✔ **Microsoft Outlook and Outlook Express:** Numerous computer viruses have been unleashed because of security problems in the way Outlook and Outlook Express handle certain kinds of e-mail file attachments. We also talk about these security holes and how to fix them in Chapter 3.

- ✔ **ActiveX:** The GoHip software we mention earlier in this chapter uses a Microsoft scripting system named ActiveX, which can be embedded in Web pages and can, if written by someone with ill intent, seize control of your system, simply as a result of your visiting the wrong Web page.

It's time to fire up the bilge pumps and patch those leaks!

As we said, some security alerts are less urgent than others. And browser makers are usually pretty good about responding to realistic threats. As security flaws are found, most software makers work quickly to get software patches posted to their Web sites.

To download the most recent version of Internet Explorer, go to www.microsoft.com/windows/IE, where you can also get a copy of any security patches for earlier versions.

You may ask "What about Netscape and Opera?" Although Netscape and Opera are not flawless, they have had far fewer high-profile security incidents. Still, browsers are complex pieces of software, and you should be alert to security issues.

To check for recent security issues for Netscape, go to home.netscape.com/security/. To check for recent security issues for Opera, go to www.opera.com/support/service/security/.

Some Hardware That's Soft on Privacy

Lest you think that software is the only source of danger on the desktop, the hardware that you know and love has its own share of sneaky features, including

- **Intel Pentium chips:** Beginning with the Pentium III, Intel began building into every chip a unique identifier. This code could be accessed by various programs, including Web browsers, to tie you and your machine to specific activities. The idea behind it was simple enough: Electronic commerce could be more secure if a particular transaction could be positively traced to a specific computer. But this unique identifier could also be used for other purposes; for example, as a kind of supercookie that could never be deleted short of prying the processor off your motherboard. After a threatened ban of Intel chips by activist groups, Intel announced that it would ship its chips with the ID code turned off by default.

- **Network cards:** With the increased availability of high-speed connections, including DSL and cable modems, more computers are being equipped with network cards. Most network cards can transmit data at speeds hundreds of times faster than conventional telephone-based modems. To work correctly, however, each network card is equipped with its own, unique identifier, called a *MAC address.* This address ensures that when data flows through a network, if the network card sees its address in the data stream, it knows that the data traveling along with that batch is destined for your computer. MAC addresses don't lend themselves to the same kind of tracking activities as the Pentium III identifier was intended for, but the MAC address certainly can be used for tracing activity back to one specific computer.

- **Cell phones:** Although not exactly in the same category as unique identifiers embedded in your desktop computer, we should mention that with today's breed of Web-enabled cell phones and other wireless devices, your activities can be tracked to your particular device. In fact, some early Web-enabled cell phones used your phone number in cookies and other identifiers so that Web sites you visited could look in their server logs and see your phone number. In addition, with new legislative requirements that cell phones be capable of pinpointing the exact location of anyone who makes an emergency call (enhanced 911), these devices are becoming more and more convenient ways of keeping tabs on you. (We talk more about cell phones in Chapter 15.)

✔ **Wireless Ethernet:** Many companies — and many home users — are giving up on fishing wires through walls and are moving to wireless Ethernet. Using a small base station with little antennas that get plugged into the network, computers can be outfitted with a wireless network card that beams data back and forth to the base station. This system works especially well with laptops, allowing users to roam as far as 1,000 feet away from the base station. Need to go farther than 1,000 feet? Just plug in another base station, and the system automatically works like a cellular phone, allowing you to roam uninterrupted. But two major security issues have arisen. First, unless you carefully turn on network encryption features, anyone with a wireless network card (for sale at your local computer store) can access *your* internal network, including a hacker sitting with his laptop in a car outside your house. Second, like other communications signals passing through the air, the data transmitted between your computer and the base station can be intercepted and read. The makers of wireless Ethernet have embedded automatic encryption in their hardware, but in August 2001 encryption experts reported that the type being widely used was terribly easy to crack.

Accessing Your Browser's Privacy Controls

Now is the time to roll up your sleeves and take control of how much information about you is leaking out through your browser.

Internet Explorer

Internet Explorer has three menus that offer five ways of exercising some control over your privacy. You can access all of them by choosing Internet Options from the Tools menu:

✔ **Cookies:** On the General tab, in the section labeled Temporary Internet Files, you have the option of deleting all the cookies that have been stored in your browser. But be warned: Deleting all cookies may destroy any personalization you've done at Web sites you've visited.

✔ **Cache Files:** Also in the Temporary Internet Files section is a button labeled Delete Files, which deletes copies of all the Web pages and graphics for sites you've visited recently. Internet Explorer is set to keep copies of those pages so that if you click the Back button on your browser, it doesn't make you wait to reload everything again because it likely hasn't changed. But those files stick around for days or weeks, providing a detailed trail of everything you seen.

✔ **History Files:** On the General tab, in the section labeled History, is a button to clear the *history file,* which is a listing of every Web page you've visited recently. Next to the Clear History button is a setting where you can adjust how many days' worth of your surfing history it keeps.

✔ **Personal Information Settings:** On the Content tab, in the section labeled Personal Information, you can delete any passwords and personal information that the browser has stored. If data, such as your e-mail address, is stored in your browser, the browser may occasionally provide that data automatically.

Suppose that you have entered a password for a Web site and told Internet Explorer to remember it — and then promptly forgotten the password. What can you do? Some folks at iOpus Software have the solution: a free software program that extracts your passwords and tells you what they are. Unfortunately, this highly useful program also highlights just how insecure the password-storage feature in Internet Explorer really is: Anyone with access to your computer could install the iOpus software and easily retrieve all your passwords. You can find the password recovery software at `www.iopus.com/password_recovery.htm`.

✔ **Privacy Settings:** Beginning with Internet Explorer Version 6, Microsoft offers support for a new Internet protocol named Platform for Privacy Preferences Protocol (or P3P). In short, P3P allows a Web site to encode on every page of its site the details about its privacy policy. Internet Explorer 6 looks for the P3P data, also called a *compact privacy policy,* and handles the cookies in the manner shown in the following table.

Option	Meaning
Block All Cookies	Cookies from all Web sites are blocked. Existing cookies on your computer cannot be read by Web sites.
High	Blocks cookies that don't have a compact privacy policy and cookies that use personally identifiable information without your explicit consent.
Medium High	Blocks third-party cookies that don't have a compact privacy policy; third-party cookies that use personally identifiable information without your explicit consent; and first-party cookies that use personally identifiable information without implicit consent.

Option	Meaning
Medium (the default setting)	Blocks third-party cookies that don't have a compact privacy policy and third-party cookies that use personally identifiable information without your implicit consent. Restricts first-party cookies that use personally identifiable information without implicit consent.
Low	Restricts third-party cookies that don't have a compact privacy policy and third-party cookies that use personally identifiable information without your implicit consent.
Accept All Cookies	All cookies are saved on this computer. Existing cookies on this computer can be read by the Web sites that created them.

Additional settings allow you to customize cookie handling for first- and third-party cookies, including permitting *session* cookies, which we describe in the earlier section "Why 'no cookies' sometimes means 'no lookies'."

If you're just dying to learn more about the World Wide Web Consortium's P3P Project, visit its home page. Be warned: It's techno gobbledygook of the highest order.

```
www.p3p.org
```

Netscape Communicator

Like Internet Explorer, Netscape allows you to control a number of privacy-related settings. Choose Edit➪Preferences from the menu bar to access these items:

- ✔ **History:** When you choose Navigator➪History, you can clear your history file and the list of sites from your location bar's drop-down menu. You can also adjust the number of days for which history files are kept.

- ✔ **E-mail Address for FTP:** On the Advanced tab, you can choose whether to let Netscape send your e-mail address as your login for file storage (FTP) sites. Many sites permit limited access to FTP servers, but they ask you to log in using the username anonymous and giving your e-mail address as the password. Unchecking this option sends a generic e-mail address (such as user@domain).

- ✔ **Cookies:** By choosing Advanced➪Cookies, you can choose to permit or reject cookies, to accept cookies only for the site you're visiting (first-party), or to be alerted each time. You can also view (and delete) your stored cookies.

✔ **Forms:** Choose Advanced⇨Forms to have Netscape remember information you enter into data fields, such as your mailing address, e-mail address, and other personal data. You can also review and manage data that is already stored.

✔ **Passwords:** When you choose Advanced⇨Passwords, Netscape lets you store passwords for Web sites that require you to log in. It also lets you choose whether to store that data in an encrypted fashion on your hard disk.

✔ **Cache:** When you choose Advanced⇨Cache, Netscape lets you clear the cache of files for sites you've previously visited as well as define how much disk space you want to allocate to the storage of those files.

Opera

Of the three browsers we talk about in this book, Opera gives you the most detailed level of control over the amount of data your browser can share with sites. It also provides a quick-menu link to delete private data, placing you just three clicks away from clearing all your private information from the browser. Here are the Opera methods for managing your privacy:

✔ **Delete Private Data:** From the File menu at the top edge of the browser window, an option labeled Delete Private Data gives you one-click control over the deletion of nearly every bit of private data that may be stored in your browser.

In addition, when you choose File⇨Preferences, the following choices are accessible, as shown in Figure 9-4:

✔ **History and Cache:** You can both clear and limit the size of the history files, the disk cache, and the memory cache.

✔ **Personal Information:** Opera lets you store your personal information, which can be automatically pasted into forms.

✔ **Privacy:** Atop this list is a setting unique to Opera. You can choose whether to let the Web server know the *referrer* Web site, which is the site you were visiting immediately before you visited the current site. This screen also gives you an array of cookie settings and lets you automatically clear all cookies each time you close the browser.

The biggest downside to Opera is price. Yes, it has a price. You have two choices: You can buy it, or you can use it for free in sponsored (advertiser) mode. *Sponsored* mode means that part of your toolbar is taken up with an advertisement. Opera costs only $39, but in this age of Netscape and Internet Explorer being given away for free, any price seems odd. If you give Opera a try, you may come to agree that, when it comes to browsers, you really do get what you pay for. (And no, we don't get any money if you buy it!) For highly refined viewing, try Opera.

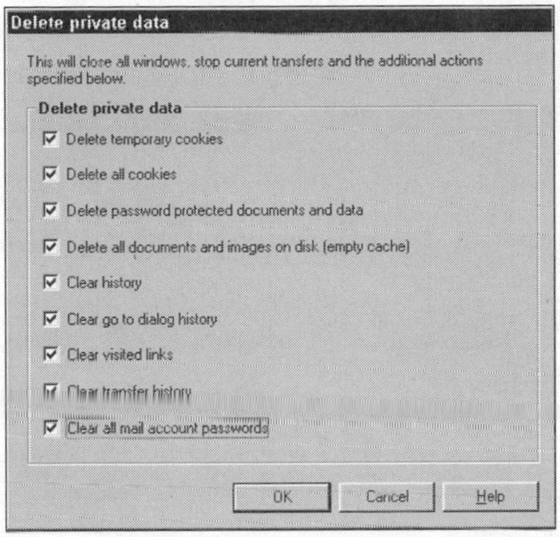

Figure 9-4:
Opera lets
you delete
private data.

For highly refined viewing, try Opera

Throughout this book, we provide a number of examples using various Web browsers, including the two most popular: Internet Explorer and Netscape. But a third choice out there is growing in popularity: Opera (www.opera.com).

Developed by some clever guys in Norway at Opera Software, Opera is advertised as "the fastest browser on earth!" If you compare it side by side with Netscape and Internet Explorer, you come away thinking that these Norwegians are right.

In addition to the excellent privacy settings we discuss in this chapter, Opera is about half the download size of Internet Explorer and Netscape. The reason is that the programmers who developed the software did so with a kind of "just the facts" mentality. The programming code is much less complicated than its competitors, and as a

result it takes less memory and runs blazingly fast. How fast? On an average modem connection, some Web sites load between one-quarter and one-third faster. Opera doesn't do anything to speed your modem; it just does much less thinking about displaying a page, and the result is that pages and images are rendered quicker — noticeably quicker.

Opera also has lots of conveniences built in. It has several search engines (including Google and AltaVista) preprogrammed into a Search field on the toolbar. It also has an e-mail client and a newsgroup browser, and it can support an instant-messaging system. Installation is a breeze, and you can configure it with many different *skins* (different-color buttons, snazzy borders, and scrollbars, for example) to give it an interesting look and feel.

(continued)

(continued)

Before you think that everything is perfect with Opera, though, it has some downsides. First, many of the interesting plug-ins and nifty entertainment googaws and gizmos on many Web sites don't always work in Opera. Although it has good support for Java, Flash, and Adobe Acrobat, other less mainstream programs sometimes balk.

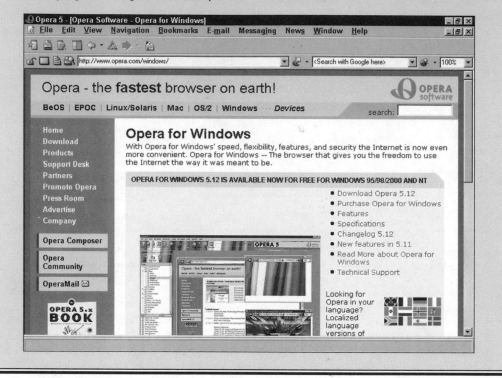

Chapter 10
Why the E in E-Mail Stands for Easy-to-Intercept

In This Chapter

▶ Unexpected places your e-mail may turn up

▶ Keeping secrets with encryption

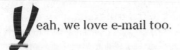eah, we love e-mail too.

But we also look at it with a rather careful eye because we know that every time we send a message, it's like we used carbon paper to make lots of duplicate copies. And we know that after we hit the Send button, we lose control of the carbons as well as the original message.

It's no big deal if you're writing to a pal about last night's game. But it may be a bigger deal if you're e-mailing someone your credit card or Social Security number or furtively using company e-mail to apply for another job.

Suddenly feeling a little nervous? Perhaps it would be wise if you were to read on.

Oh, That Elusive E-Mail Trail

When Roy Rogers hit the road, he always followed the happy trail.

When your e-mail hits the road, you have no way of telling what trail it may take, where it may stop, and who may see it along the way. That's because, let's face it, you didn't put it in an envelope and seal it like a private letter — you threw it, open-faced and exposed, into the outgoing mail bin like some picture postcard from Disney World. And when was the last time you used a postcard to say anything more significant than "Having a great time! Wish you were here!"

So now it's time to fess up and face the music; because even though we all know that e-mail is no private affair, we ignore what we know and use it to relay all kinds of personal and confidential and important information anyhow.

The frightening power of warrants and subpoenas

Let us be blunt: E-mail can come back to haunt you. Even if you've deleted a harmful message and you've convinced the recipient to delete it as well, it may live on somewhere on a server somewhere in-between. And if legal trouble occurs and it involves that e-mail, a subpoena or warrant is all that stands between that message and Perry Mason. You can read more about subpoenas in Chapter 6.

So What's the Risk?

We give you the bottom line. Two risks are associated with sending sensitive data by e-mail:

- **More copies than Kinko's:** Virtually all e-mail server software packages have some sort of log that keeps track of outgoing and incoming mail — where it came from, where it was sent, the time of the message, and maybe even the size of the message. In some cases, the servers even keep the full text of the message. But that's just the tip of the iceberg because it's not just *your* server you have to worry about. The recipient's e-mail server is involved, and all the servers your e-mail may bounce to on its way to its final destination. (If you want to find out more about the long and winding road an e-mail takes to get from your computer to its final destination, see our discussion of tracing junk e-mail in Chapter 20.) Any one of these servers can perform an archive or a backup and save a copy of your e-mail. Meanwhile, the recipient may have all his e-mail stored on his ISP's server or save all e-mail on his own hard drive. That's a bunch of copies!

- **It's an insecure medium:** E-mail travels over the Internet in packets, just like all other data. And, just like all other data, e-mail can be intercepted by the wrong person.

Does all this mean that unauthorized people are looking at every e-mail you send? No. But it does mean that someone *could* be looking at your e-mail — so think before you click so that you don't end up sending a message that can be damaging for you down the road.

At Work, E-Mail Lives Forever

At some companies, *all* e-mail is saved forever. Perhaps even in multiple locations. On company archival disks. On company backup disks. On your hard drive. On everyone else's hard drive. Meanwhile, as you find out in Chapter 16, your employer owns all the e-mail you send and receive from work, and it's also their right to read it whenever they darn well please.

When the American Management Association surveyed 2,133 mid-size to large corporations, it discovered that 38 percent of the responding companies monitored their employees' e-mail. (See Chapter 16 for more results from the survey.)

The secret shroud of free e-mail accounts

Okay, you think: "I have a job. And I have a life. Sometimes at my job I have to — or want to — handle the personal parts of my life. And I don't want those details lingering about the company e-mail servers until the end of time."

"So what am I supposed to do?"

The good news is that you can get free Web-based e-mail at a variety of places on the Internet. These accounts allow you to send and receive e-mail on your browser via the World Wide Web (rather than use a separate e-mail software program, like Eudora or the one that came with your browser) so that you can access your e-mail from any computer with Internet access. You can either adopt your new Web-based e-mail username as a permanent e-mail address, or you may be able to set up your Web-based e-mail account to go fetch e-mail for you from other e-mail accounts so that you can read it over the Web.

Yahoo! Mail is a popular, Web-based, free e-mail service. Although the default setting for reading Yahoo! Mail is via a non-encrypted connection, Yahoo! offers a secure connection, indicated by the padlock adjacent to the Sign In button.

Web-based e-mail has its pros and cons, but we don't enter into those debates other than to consider the privacy and security issues involved.

Web-mail pros and cons

What we like about Web-based e-mail is that it allows you to use e-mail to communicate with others about personal matters even while you're at work, yet without using your company's e-mail servers.

Don't let this statement lull you into a false sense of security: If your company really wants to read your Web-based e-mail (or just ferret out anyone's Web-based e-mail that contains, for example, the word *résumé*), it can use *sniffers* (software that watches all the data zipping by on a network and looks for certain words or phrases) or keystroke monitoring (software that secretly records every keystroke you make) to get to the content of Web-based e-mail. Believe it or not, programs that would enable your company to do this cost as little as $39.95. (These same risks exist for instant messenger messages, too. You can read more about workplace privacy issues in Chapter 16.)

Larger Web-based e-mail services are working hard to help you protect your privacy. For example, Yahoo! now offers all users the ability to encrypt outgoing mail as part of its free e-mail service, which is great — but the encryption service encrypts your e-mail for only part of its journey across the Internet. The e-mail travels via regular e-mail from Yahoo! to the company (SecureDelivery.com) that provides the encryption service, and only then is your message encrypted. And the service doesn't include a way to receive encrypted e-mail. However, you may be able to use an encryption program, like Pretty Good Privacy (which we talk about later in this chapter), to send and receive encrypted messages from your Web-based e-mail account.

Web-based e-mail is very common and is available from Yahoo! (`www.yahoo.com`) and Microsoft Hotmail (`www.hotmail.com`) as well as from special-interest portals, like BibleWeb.com (`www.bibleweb.com`) or the over-40s portal ThirdAge.com (`www.thirdage.com`) and many others or from companies like mail.com (`www.mail.com`), which let you pick from dozens of domain names for your e-mail address ranging from `YourName@loveable.com` or `YourName@doglover.com` or `YourName@umpire.com`.

Some ISPs, including AOL, offer their own Web-based e-mail, so you can check your existing e-mail address from any computer with Internet access without having to get a new e-mail account.

Is Web-based e-mail a good idea?

John: I'm peculiar. I collect Web-based e-mail accounts for a hobby. But I certainly agree that you want to keep your personal mail separate from your work mail, and they're as good a way to do it as any.

Ray: Sure. Using Web-based e-mail makes it just a tad harder for your employer to snoop into your private communications. It's like one of those flimsy locks on your suitcase: It doesn't stop somebody determined to root through your skivvies, but it's enough to deter the nosy Nellies.

Gregg: Absolutely. Using Web-based e-mail certainly puts you at no greater risk than using your company's e-mail system to send and receive personal e-mail — and for most of us, just getting off the company's e-mail server for personal correspondence is all we need.

Spilled Secrets in the Internet Café

One of the great things about Web-based e-mail is that it allows you to send and receive e-mail from *almost* anywhere — a friend's house or office, the copy shop or mailing store, or a public library or Internet café.

But doing so may also expose you to some privacy and security risks.

Turn off AutoComplete

Most browsers now offer a feature that automatically remembers your key-strokes as you fill in forms and passwords to make it easier for you to fill in those same forms and passwords at a later time. The danger, of course, is that after you type your username and password for your e-mail account, anyone who goes to check their mail with the same Web-based service finds that AutoComplete drops down a menu and offers them your username and password! To turn off AutoComplete before you check your mail:

In Internet Explorer 6: Choose Tools⇨Internet Options from the menu bar, select the Content tab, click the AutoComplete box in the Personal Information section, and then uncheck the boxes for using AutoComplete for Forms and User Names and Passwords on Forms.

In Opera 6: Choose File⇨Preferences⇨Accessibility and uncheck the box labeled Enable Auto Completion Dropdown.

In Netscape 8.

1. **Choose Edit⇨Preferences⇨Advanced from the menu bar and then choose Forms from the drop-down menu. Uncheck the box labeled Save form data from Web pages when completing forms.**

2. **Choose Edit⇨Preferences⇨Advanced and then choose Passwords from the drop-down menu. Uncheck the box labeled Remember passwords for sites that require me to log in.**

AutoComplete offers other dangers to people who do their computing at public terminals. We talk more about this topic in Chapter 9.

Dump your cache

As you breeze along the information superhighway, your browser tries to make your trip go faster by saving copies of the latest pages you have visited. That way, if you decide to click the Back button to go back to where you have already been, the browser can quickly pull the page from the local cache memory rather than have to go all the way back and reload it from the Web site where the page lives. That technique sounds great until you realize that after you walk away from a computer after checking your Web-based e-mail, it *may* continue to store your e-mail in the cache, where someone else can easily access it. To erase your e-mail from the cache:

In Internet Explorer 6:

1. **Choose Tools⇨Internet Options from the menu bar and select the General tab. In the Temporary Internet Files area, click the Delete Files button.**

2. **Just below the Temporary Internet Files area is the History area, where clicking the Clear History button also deletes the list of sites you've visited.**

   In that same box, you can set the Days to keep pages in history option to 0.

3. **Click Apply to finish.**

In Netscape 6:

1. **Choose Edit⇨Preferences from the menu bar. After you click the Advanced button, choose Cache from the drop-down menu.**

2. **Click the two buttons labeled Clear Memory Cache and Clear Disk Cache.**

3. **Click OK to finish.**

In Opera 6:

1. **Choose File⇨Preferences from the menu bar. Click the History & Cache button and in the Disk Cache area of the dialog box, click the Empty Now button.**

2. **If you want the cache to be dumped each time you close your browser, click to put a check mark next to the Empty on exit option.**

3. **Click Apply to finish.**

Log off

Many Web-based e-mail services offer a place to click to log off the service. This habit is a smart one to get into because if you walk away from the computer without signing off, the next person to use the computer may have access to your mail account. (If no one uses the computer, the service eventually logs you off automatically, called *auto logout.*)

In Yahoo!, log off by clicking on the Sign Out link in the upper-right corner of your screen.

In Hotmail, log off by clicking on the Passport Sign Out button in the upper-center area of your screen.

You may be tempted to just close your browser window when you're finished using an online account (any account, whether it's e-mail, banking, or shopping) rather than click the Logout or Sign Off or Exit button. The problem is that many Web-based e-mail services track your session with cookies (see the section in Chapter 9 about making a case for cookies), and just closing your browser or that particular window doesn't delete the cookies. Anyone who restarts the browser can pick up where you left off. (It would be wrong for us to say that logging out tells the server to toss your cookies, so we won't.)

Encryption: Hide That Private Message Inside an Envelope!

If you want to say something mushy or personal on the back of a postcard and you don't want anyone else to read it, the best thing to do is to stuff it into a envelope before mailing. Wouldn't it be nice if you could do the same thing with e-mail? Okay, we know that it's tough to stuff a virtual e-mail inside a real-world envelope, but fortunately you can use encryption to turn your message into a giant pile of gibberish for all except the person you intend it for. For example, after encryption, the simple phrase "Hi, Moose Lips" looks like this:

```
-----BEGIN PGP MESSAGE--- -
Version: PGPfreeware 6.5.8 for non-commercial use <http://www.
     pgp.com>
qANQR1DBwU4DG87viyLPgkoQB/408lZAhSfy4rQSuaq7ZTxu//5cj27GNRjWRFv
a7Hvc5Gerq3lHibZO6XbYt4A11I6pYwDNNjzdy/5pxA/O8WhdA2cc1E6ryJZFez8
cuqn5/LLjRJE8FwswzaR7fdC13CTRdszMu5GqlpRBth34Rkx8dwl31byMSjSOF4S
P377aSLKUsWoOWsLU5kdfLwWO/UmDY+oGsfhanGbRakuCDHXgIq7hITkNBNNylMg
gweb6isVCAOF41/1FNZ/ZIYdB/ISMam2ch7M+3qIRO3fef+5Y+GXJ7tNAYzXkQM4
SfOQ9DHwrza+ejln+KaOEisw26Fi9iCupJribQ6fDrjugxaOB/45KcubcVZMlqyl
1M2vDwzjuzjpxKMr4olhiKh93bYkQDkypnZT6t1jllYrLlR/wzj8a1TVUJ+mGs44v
6FbX2x6q9dKZJm9G5oEF1mlEmLXvDmOf+p46NhmNm1UZaZF5zDhQXadI2fbqpHrc
cwWF2/KCDVGy+IUQNbQBusnnsamjrxn3cl+j8x2Au67cw5JJNcwsKexxUcyxxCHF
i/yX9uOeADHjsj+hLfyGEBC3Q23KDObcKNz/u4AontmUh/MP3r9BX1TVGLz5c4j72
wfgnfa3Bmih8ZS8EQRFFgwiOAaaNqrayYsjqfdhc+RBO2X6J?MDWgqTMq7CmdsJO
KVnKiJWyySdZ49nKs/HXkoX4011d483GvCx8/AyXuNpPM2d2dRJEHKYHoETgPdI=
=CNkG
-----END PGP MESSAGE-----
```

The most commonly used e-mail encryption program is PGP, for *pretty good privacy*. Yes, we know: the name begs the question "Are there ways to get even more private?" Yes, there are, but they're locked in a filing cabinet in an unused bathroom in the basement of the National Security Agency with a sign on the door saying "Beware of the leopard." For most of us, the level of privacy that PGP offers is secure enough. In fact, PGP uses military-strength algorithms — with names like Diffie-Hellman, Digital Signature Standard, and RSA — to protect messages.

Just like with the lock on your front door, your security depends as much on the key as on the lock itself. Encryption strength is determined by the length of the key, and what sets PGP apart from most other encryption programs is that it's capable of generating keys up to 4096 bits, although most others use "weak" 40-bit keys that can be cracked in a matter of hours.

If you want to know more about how encryption and algorithms work so that you can show off to your friends, visit these sites:

- ✔ **A Cryptography Primer for Business Lawyers:** Good for non-lawyers too; www.pkilaw.com/primer.htm

- ✔ **Cryptography/Security Primer:** Good descriptions for laypersons; www.gemsafe.com/crypto_primer.html

- ✔ **National Academy Press — A Brief Primer on Cryptography:** A little more technical, but quite understandable; www.nap.edu/books/0309054753/html/364.html

Dpnjuio/3dsfj (Or, how to put encryption to work for you)

Want your own copy of PGP?

A commercial version of Pretty Good Privacy (PGP) used to be available, but was discontinued by its vendor, Network Associates, in mid-2002. We recommend the freeware version distributed by the Massachusetts Institute of Technology. To get it, go to web.mit.edu/network/pgp.html and download a free copy. The next thing you know, you'll be zapping personal, protected messages all over the Internet.

These steps show you how to use PGP after you've downloaded it:

1. **Keep in mind that PGP was developed by and for people who really like to roll up their sleeves and tinker around with computers and code and stuff like that.**

   This is our polite way of saying that we love PGP, but we also know that it's wildly complicated and lacking in useful help screens. "How complicated could it be?" you ask. According to one account, the PGP *readme* files are about 35,000 words long. To put that number into perspective, this book has about 100,000 words in it.

2. Follow the wizard.

In spite of the warning we just offered, PGP comes with a pretty good wizard that guides you through the installation process even if you don't quite understand what you're doing. The wizard asks you to indicate how you connect to Internet, if you have a keyring (sort of like a PGP address book) from an earlier version of PGP, and maybe some other stuff that's all Greek or encryption to you. Think of these questions as part of a multiple-choice exam from freshman English. Hey, you didn't exactly know the answers or even understand most of the questions back then, either, but you somehow muddled through it and got to where you are today. Take the same attitude while installing PGP. Take your best shot at answering the questions and if you're wrong, you can always go back and patch things up on another day.

Now that you've installed PGP, you need to create your own set of keys.

3a. Click the Start button and choose Programs➪PGP➪PGPKeys➪Keys➪ New Key. Another wizard helps you. Think "high school English class" again as you fill out the necessary blanks.

At one point, the wizard asks you to choose a pass phrase.

3b. This step is very important: Your pass phrase can be anything you want, but make sure that it's something you will remember forever because no one but you will ever know it and no one can e-mail it to you later if you ever forget it.

The Passphrase Quality meter increases with the length and complexity of your phrase. In this example, adding a question mark, capital letters, and numbers meant that the quality meter reached its limit by the word *brown,* but your passphrase can be just about as long as you want — as long as you can remember it all! (Of course, for demonstration purposes, we turned off the Hide Typing option, something you shouldn't do if there's any chance that someone is looking over your shoulder.)

3c. Here's one important box to check along the way: Send my key to the root server now.

This option adds your name to the PGP users' directory on the PGP servers so that if someone wants to send you an encrypted message, she can easily find your public key. If you don't want to be found, don't check the box.

PGP may want to reboot your computer a few times in the process of installing and getting you a set of keys. Don't be alarmed — this is normal behavior. Just play along as though you understand everything that's going on.

"Okay, so what's the difference between 40 bits and 4096 bits?"

It all has to do with extremely complicated mathematical and cryptographic principles, but think of it as the difference between a 4-digit PIN for your ATM card and a 200-digit PIN. More bits means more possible combinations, more complexity, and a few more centuries of computer time needed to crack it.

Most encryption applications are based on a public key/private key system. Together, your public and private keys make one digital ID. When someone wants to send you an encrypted message, she uses your public key to encrypt it. After you receive the message, you use your private key to decrypt it. If the message gets intercepted while it travels over the Internet or is lifted off an e-mail server, it's meaningless without your private key.

Now that you have your own set of keys, you can

✔ Have fun, fun, fun 'til your daddy takes the T-Bird away. (Oops! Sorry! That's a transgression back to Gregg's Beach Boy surfing days.)

✔ Click the Start button and choose Programs⇨PGP. Then try to figure things out on your own and get thoroughly confused.

✔ Do things the simple way, as we outline them in the following section.

In the beginning, we recommend doing things the simple way, which means doing all your PGP navigation through the PGP icon on your taskbar at the bottom right corner of your screen.

Sending an encrypted message

To send an encrypted message to someone — Bill Gates, for example — follow these steps:

1. **Put your cursor over the PGP icon on your taskbar, right-click, and choose PGPKeys.**

2. **On the PGPKeys screen, choose Server⇨Search.**

3. **Type the name of the person you want to send a message to.**

   For fun, you might do a search for yourself and then send yourself an encrypted message — something simple like "Hi, Moose Lips," works just fine — so you can see what it's like to both send and encrypt and then receive and decrypt a message.

4. **After PGP has completed your search, highlight the name of the person you were looking for, right-click, and choose Import to Local Keyring to save with your own set of keys.**

5. **Jump out of the PGP window for now and switch to your e-mail program. Address and write an e-mail to the person you just searched for — then (and this part is *very* important), make sure that your cursor is in the message window of the e-mail. Then right-click on the PGP icon on the taskbar again and choose Current Window⇨Encrypt.6**

If your cursor isn't in the message window of your outgoing e-mail, PGP gets horribly confused — and so will you. Alternatively, if you and PGP are horribly confused, odds are that the reason is that you didn't put your cursor in the message window before trying to encrypt. But that's okay. To straighten things out, just go back to Step 5a.

0. **When you choose Encrypt, PGP opens your PGPtray-key selection dialog box, which is just some programmer's fancy way of saying "address book."**

This dialog box should have two fields. The top field is a listing of all the keys on your local keyring (or your address book), and the bottom field should be empty — until you select the name of the person you want to send your e-mail to and drag it down there, under where it says Recipients.

7. **Click OK.**

Wow, what a mess! That big ball of qANQR1DBwU4DG87viyLPgk-oQB/408lZAFhSfy4rQSuaq7ZTxu//5cj27GNRjWRFv — is your message, encrypted.

8. **Click on the Send button and send your e-mail on its way.**

Decrypting a message

This answer may be obvious, but you know when you've received an encrypted message because it looks something like the encrypted "Hi, Moose Lips" message that we show you earlier in this chapter. To decrypt a message, follow these steps:

1. **Make sure that your cursor is inside the message window of the e-mail.**

2. **Right-click on the PGP icon on your taskbar. Choose Current Window⇨Decrypt & Verify from the menu bar.**

3. **Voila! qANQR1DBwU4DG87viyLPgkoQB/408lZAFhSfy4rQSuaq7ZTxu//5cj27GNRjWRFv — becomes "Hi, Moose Lips."**

Easy, right?

"Look out — he's got a PGP key!"

Did you know that the government used to consider both PGP and bazookas as weapons and that both were therefore forbidden from export outside the United States without the special approval of federal agencies? You see, the government argued, encryption could be used by enemies of the United States to conspire against us, so in its eyes PGP was no different from guns, explosives, or jet fighters. You may think that this classification is silly, but it was no laughing matter when the government accused PGP's author, Phil Zimmerman, of posting a copy of the PGP source code on a file server outside the United States. Years, and hundreds of thousands of dollars in lawyers' fees later, the government decided not to throw Phil in jail and eventually relaxed its restrictions on strong encryption.

Give the world your key

Believe it or not, your public PGP key is as unique to you as your fingerprint. The way *public key encryption* works is that the sender (Bob) uses his private key and the recipient's (Jill) public key to encode a message. The magic of encryption means that after the message is encoded, only Jill's private key can unlock it. So everybody *must* have your public key — and that's why people put them on Web pages and upload them to key servers, where anybody can access them. After all, anyone who wants to send you an encrypted message needs your public key, but only you can decrypt the message because only you have the private key.

That's a mighty big key you've got there

With all this talk of PGP keys, you may be wondering what one looks like — so for your entertainment value, we offer one of Gregg's old public keys:

```
-----BEGIN PGP PUBLIC KEY BLOCK-----
Version: PGPfreeware 6.5.8 for non-commercial use <http://www.
         pgp.com>

mQGiBDpiIbORBADBzVBcEaZBqoQHPO1rUx1xxzpJFfz41y8I9iPQ9IQXu+CS76O8
S8VYmz25UURaiLUR6zbLGOE7IYZBgmvR3JeJ1d4kFi7JHS/JePHfDlkIgcVPG6Vs
xO+9vGSJhW/Wp1qhpnMphthrUjQn4rmo+S6ag7fSzF6zWOaat4mzR9E2EwCg/+DY
vzYPcA8uwco8MdMDErHjVaUD/37fDawAWyZfmgK/OMyDQmCbo5oxHYbLmug15KDn
+KzriZRN5CPenIObsM2tje/YioyPOuLOOkEST4N/+/r3RYFhk1ud36Yr/IKQYLEr
3KdwOCc32/1an/lwn1K5k5IpoaihDQ4Dkqu9jqXVN5/7FXPcpSde3/rLhwF2FbuT
Wy3tA/kBfRMpAVJhxhCeU74vtqoQ6+YRkel7B/isCSf7U1N1gcPvZTQf9qqoOPOe
yllUew33+e8/it1p2pAXaETPkLj3YFgsq/UsHlTbdNfRYuLLdD4971xNy+SVIkZO
XNIWFibwvnH5MjgSCWJnXD7jQ9jNiuu6js9xDiGWQsK7apljZrQkR3JlZ2cgTC4g
U3RlYmJlbiA8R3JlZ2dAc3RlYmJlbi5jb20+iQBOBBARAgAOBQI6YiG9BAsDAgEC
GQEACgkQM1X7hBNB9gpxiACghSbOuFcKgf1/MejjAkhV3MFooyoAoOV6vlvbuLFa
```

```
yqkHP2D9qB2A9b5HuQINBDpiIbOQCAD2Q1e3CH8IF3KiutapQvMF6PlTETlPtvFu
uUs4INoBplajFOmPQFXzOAfGyQOplK33TGSGSfgMg71l6RfUodNQ+PVZX9x2Uk89
PY3bzpnhV5JZzf24rnRPxfx2vIPFRzBhznzJZv8V+bv9kV7HAarTW56NoKVyOtQa
8L9GAFgr5fSI/VhOSdvNILSd5JEHNmszbDgNRROPfIizHHxbLY7288kjwEPwpVsY
jY67VYy4XTjTNP18FldDox0YbN4zISy1Kv884bFpQBgRjXyEpwpy1obEAxnIByl6
ypUM2Zafq9AKUJsCRtMIPWakXUGfnHy9iUsiGSa6q6Jew1XpMgs7AAICCAC7ziOW
kIDHaaLdUur/a7hUgaKdUO5TTzWt6Yggx4SGoL+1w8u7gN2iAJU+NX/wlnyzgPse
IkQcRJKG2LaKuAGqTNwNvVkjGS3VbP1omqc5PGQHZUJf+KKyTluL+vXmTiHoXHqc
IdV037NQ3Hv7fcakHMAYhiIsUWBToz2umL1OZeRm32ptutKKbMzjVtij4cas11PR
Zu1W7TLy2uKW/DEX8/FOhDvZ8U0u2X84Qx5zWFGzrmhTp3U1k/FogP21fheSIUhu
iNIAKQm+GdaZSZzAG3vbsExo1e2+30nn9n3d4/NKS11BiTSk9EfKKU4Wme7hUQWg
zOWOqkWNGm2rTYENiQBGBBgRAgAGBQI6YiG9AAoJEDNV+4QTQfYK2mMAoLZafw25
P813uanRuW3YuLOGXYf1AKDgSjFQV3I6yvBeQrdRPqJmY3+ECg==
=Ozvr
-----END PGP PUBLIC KEY BLOCK-----
```

Don't ever tell anyone what your private key's password is. It's the key (excuse the pun) to the safety and security of all your encrypted e-mail.

Are you sending your message to the "right" Bill Gates?

All the superduper cryptography in the world doesn't do you any good if the recipient of your encrypted message isn't who you think it is. (This situation is likened in cryptocircles to a safe with a 10-ton steel door and a cardboard back wall.) PGP addresses this problem with a "Web of trust," in which people can sign the keys of other people that they know personally. If an unknown person's key is signed by someone you know, you can be quite sure that the unknown's key is legit. If you don't know the signer, but you know someone who signed the signer's key, you can be pretty sure, and so on. This process sounds complicated, but in practice it's easy enough to use — you look at the signers of the key of an incoming message and decide whether to trust it.

PGP does *lots* more than the few functions we describe a little earlier. If you really want to dig in and gets your hands (and arms and the rest of you) dirty, we suggest that you invest in a copy of *Internet Secrets,* 2nd Edition (Hungry Minds, Inc.), which has chapters on cryptography in general and PGP in particular.

Anonymous remailers and pseudonymous e-mail

Sometimes you don't want to hide the contents of what you're saying, but you want to hide your identity as the one who is saying it. Anonymous speech is a right enjoyed by all Americans, ever since our Founding Fathers defended the new Constitution in 1789 by passing out flyers written under the pseudonym Publius. But in this wired world, speaking anonymously takes a little work. As you may know from earlier in this chapter, e-mail leaves trails, and in most cases those trails point back to you. Enter anonymous remailers and pseudonymous e-mail.

Anonymous remailers work by taking your e-mail message, stripping off the information about where the message originated (this information is called the *header*, which you can find out more about in Chapter 20), and then passing it randomly through a bunch of other mail servers that exist for the sole purpose of helping you get rid of your scent by also stripping off the information in the header before sending it on to the next server, and the next server and the next server and the next server, and eventually your message gets spit out into the mailbox of your intended recipient without a trace of where it's been or where it originally came from. Voila! All message, no header, no trail.

What if you want the recipient to be able to reply to you? If you have left no trail, you have left no way for a message to get back to you. Here's where pseudonymous e-mail comes in. It works on the same principle as anonymous remailing, except that somewhere along the way, your contact information gets turned into a pseudonym that the system remembers belongs to you. That way, the recipient can reply to the pseudonym, and the process works in reverse to deliver the message back to you via a completely untraceable route

So what's the difference between a pseudonym and just using a fake name on a free e-mail service? Traceability. Most free e-mail services faithfully record things like the IP address of the computer you're connected to. In the ordinary course of sneaking around, this isn't much of an issue unless your ISP gets a subpoena with your pseudonym on it (see Chapter 6). But some of these anonymous remailers and pseudonymous e-mail services are vitally important for whistle blowers, freedom fighters in repressive countries, and people whose speech may be politically unpopular.

Here's a list of some anonymous remailer and pseudonymous e-mail services:

- **Global Internet Liberty Campaign's WWW Remailer:** www.gilc.org/ speech/anonymous/remailer.html

- **COTSE Webmail:** webmail.cotse.com/webmail/

- **AnonMailNet:** www.anonmail.net

- **Jack B. Nymble:** www.skuz.net/potatoware/jbn2/index.html

- **HushMail:** www.hushmail.com

- **SecureNym:** www.securenym.net

- **Anonymous Remailer FAQ:** www.andrebacard.com/remail.html

Comparison shopping for remailers

Don't take the choice of anonymous remailers lightly — after all, if your message is important enough to warrant using a remailer, the last thing you want to do is choose one that is sloppy about security or that spies on people's e-mail before sending it. If, for example, a remailer doesn't allow you to send messages that are encrypted, you may ask yourself why; the only reason we can imagine is that the remailer himself has an interest in reading other people's mail.

Echelon and the international conspiracy to read all your e-mail

You wouldn't think, when you sat down to write an e-mail to your sweet, dear old aunt about what you did on your summer vacation, that you would be setting the wheels of a vast international privacy invasion and conspiracy in motion.

In the mid 1970s, an industrious English journalist named Duncan Campbell stumbled across rumors and whispered stories about something that sounded way too kooky to be true: The governments of the Western world were engaged in a vast global conspiracy to listen in on every phone call and every telex message coursing through the world's telecommunications wires.

Naturally, this story sounded like an idea cooked up by the kind of guy who mutters to himself while walking down the street and wears tinfoil hats to keep spy satellites from beaming bad thoughts into his brain. But Duncan was as sane as you and us — well, you, anyway — and the more he looked into "the conspiracy," the more evidence he found that it existed.

Soon, he uncovered this global conspiracy's code number, Project P415. And then he found its name: Echelon.

Although none of the governments allegedly involved (including the United States, Britain, Australia, Germany, Japan, and, somewhat surprisingly, China) will confirm or deny anything about it, evidence of Echelon's existence is mounting. Duncan Campbell and other investigators have uncovered documents, explored mysterious antenna farms located in strategic parts of the world, and in one case posed as a real estate speculator interested in buying a decommissioned listening post on the western coast of England.

What does Echelon listen for? How do the governments intercept, store, and process as much traffic as is claimed? Who knows? But if you find out, don't call to tell us! You had better use PGP with a lo-o-o-o-o-o-o-o-o-o-o-o-o-o-o-ong key or, better yet, try smoke signals.

Get the inside story of Echelon:

- ✔ **Echelon: A ZDNet UK special report:** `www.zdnet.co.uk/news/ specials/2000/06/echelon/`
- ✔ **Duncan Campbell's first exposé on Echelon:** `jya.com/echelon-dc.htm`
- ✔ **Collected documents discussing Echelon:** `cryptome.org/cryptout. htm#Echelon`

Carnivore and the domestic conspiracy to read all your e-mail

Not content to let all those foreigners have all the fun, your friendly neighborhood Federal Bureau of Investigation (FBI) has decided that it wants the right to peek at your e-mail. And, well, viola! In 2000, it was revealed that the agency commissioned the creation of an e-mail-sniffing software program named Carnivore — except that sniffing is a gross exaggeration of Cyrano de Bergerac (or Steve Martin in the movie *Roxanne*) proportions.

According to documents obtained by the Electronic Information Privacy Center (EPIC) under the Freedom of Information Act, the world has learned a few of Carnivore's more exciting features:

- ✔ It has an easy-to-use interface and runs on Windows NT.
- ✔ With a click of the mouse, it can capture entire e-mails or just the headers.
- ✔ It captures file transfers (FTP) as well as entire Web pages (faithfully reproduced just the way the viewer saw them, according to the FBI documents).
- ✔ It can be configured to track IP addresses on any kind of network, including those run by ISPs for dial-up connections.
- ✔ It offers full-text searching of the data it captures, so if you're looking for the words *blow up the White House,* you can zip right to it.
- ✔ Upcoming versions are slated to have features for capturing voice-over IP services, like Net2Phone and FreeTel.

The Electronic Information Privacy Center sued for a copy of the Carnivore user manual. It got a copy, with most of the interesting bits blacked out. One thing that was clearly visible? A logo on the book cover, featuring a set of ferocious animal's teeth, dripping with blood, chomping down on a stream of binary data.

Using PGP or Web-based encrypted e-mail, like ZipLip, is one way to beat the FBI at its own game.

Take a bite out of Carnivore before it bites you:

- ✔ **Declassified FBI Documents and the Carnivore Specifications:**
  www.epic.org/privacy/carnivore/foia_documents.html

- ✔ **Details about Carnivore:** www.securityfocus.com/news/97

- ✔ **FBI's Official Info on Carnivore Diagnostic Tool:** www.fbi.gov/
  programs/carnivore/carnivore.htm

- ✔ **ComputerWorld tracks Carnivore:** www.computerworld.com/
  resources/carnivore/

Chapter 11

Spam: Why It's Not Just a Funny Lunch Meat Any More

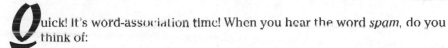

In This Chapter

▶ Why spam is a problem

▶ What you can do about it

uick! It's word-association time! When you hear the word *spam*, do you think of:

A salty, pink lunch meat that comes in a blue can?

A goofy British comedy troupe's skit with singing Viking warriors?

Annoying junk mail and other advertisements you never asked for that are sent to you via the Internet?

None of the above.

All of the above.

The best answer is —

All of the above.

As most people know, *SPAM* (with all capital letters) is a salty pink lunch meat that is made by Hormel and comes in a blue can. By the way, SPAM in all capital letters is a registered trademark of Hormel Foods (see Figure 11-1).

Hormel, the makers of SPAM (the lunch meat), say that if you want to call junk e-mail by the same name, they don't object. You just can't use all capital letters, like they appear on the can. *SPAM* is lunch meat, and *spam* is junk e-mail. Got it?

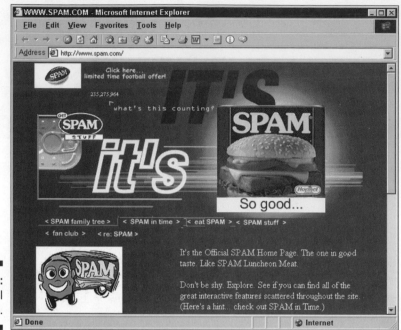

Figure 11-1:
The official
SPAM site.

Avid fans of the British comedy team Monty Python may remember the skit where a husband and wife enter a restaurant in a seaside resort town only to find that every dish on the menu features SPAM. Unfortunately, the wife is not at all fond of SPAM and searches in vain for dishes without any of the noxious substance. With SPAM appearing everywhere she turns, her frustration grows. We're not sure why, but the skit also features a large band of Viking warriors lunching at the dinette, who regularly break into a chant of "SPAM, SPAM, SPAM" every time the wife says aloud the meat's name, adding to her confusion and anger.

Everyone who uses the Internet has encountered loads and loads of junk advertisements that appear when you least expect them and usually where they're least wanted — namely, in your e-mailbox and in the newsgroups you frequent. We're talking about *spam* written in all lowercase letters (at the request of Hormel) so that people don't confuse the spam we all hate for the SPAM that some people *like*.

Spam, Spam, Spam, Spam, Spam, Spam, Spam

Spam has been around since early in the life of the Internet, long before most people had even heard of it. In fact, the sending of "junk" electronic mail was such an issue that one of the Internet's earliest pioneers, Jon Postel, posted an advisory to his fellow developers (way back in 1975!) ranting and raving and expressing all kinds of frustration over this misuse of the network.

The word *spam* appears nowhere in Postel's missive. Indeed, the exact point at which SPAM became synonymous with unsolicited advertising has been lost to the ages. Most who have investigated this mystery have tracked the term's origins to the original Internet bulletin boards, called Usenet newsgroups.

Legend has it that someone casting his eye over a menu of newsgroup discussion topics kept seeing the same ads posted in nearly every conversation thread. The continual appearance of these ads in every discussion group reminded this person of the Monty Python sketch, mainly because the sketch ends with the wife becoming so overwhelmed by the presence of SPAM in every item on the menu as well by the nearby Viking warriors' chants of "SPAM-SPAM-SPAM-SPAM, SPAM-SPAM-SPAM-SPAM" that she finally screams "I don't like SPAM!"

Yes, it's a silly comedy sketch, but if you're like us, you've spent enough time sorting through the junk e-mail in your inbox that you've found yourself screaming about spam, too.

What Does Spam Have to Do with Privacy?

First, let's ask three bigger questions: Who do you think owns your name? And your address? And your phone number?

We suspect that because you're reading this book about privacy, you agree that the answer to these three questions should be "I do."

Believe it or not, though, large and powerful groups of people out there feel differently. They think that *they* should own your name, address, phone number, and just about any other scrap of information they can scrape up about you.

Who are these people?

The people who want to own information about you are advertisers and marketers. They firmly believe that because they have gone to the trouble of collecting your personal information and stuffing it into a huge database with the personal information of millions of other people, they should they be able to use that information in any (lawful) way they choose. Even more amazingly, many of these companies have fought vicious legal battles arguing that, in essence, if it's in their database, nobody — not even you — has any right to control the data's use.

As appalling as this situation may seem to you, the law is on their side. For example, if you do business with a company, the data exchanged during the course of that transaction is part of the factual record of that transaction, with few legal restrictions on the company's use of the facts involved. And, boy, do they like to make use of those facts! (Don't believe us? Just go outside and get your mail. Did you receive any junk mail? If so, how do you think it found you?)

Marketers use circular logic to defend their actions: Because you can't legally sell what you don't own, it must also be true that you can sell only what you do own. Because marketers are already selling your name and address and phone number, it stands to reason that they must own that information.

How's that for an invasion of privacy?

Now that we've established that you don't own your own personal information, let's talk about how spam fits into the picture.

See Ray, see Ray rant — rant, Ray, rant!

Your humble co-author Ray has spent more of his life being mad about spam than just about anyone else has. In fact, because of a series of strange circumstances, he wound up on the receiving end of a flood of complaints generated by one of the most famous spamming incidents in Internet history. As a result, Ray has spent nearly a decade teed off at spammers, and he offers the following rant.

Ray: Spam is just another symptom of a marketplace whose organizing principle is that human beings are, in the words of the Internet industry analyst Jerry Michalski, little more than "A gullet whose only purpose in life is to gulp products and crap cash." To most of the direct-marketing world, you're nothing more than an entry in a database. Spam is the advertising industry's holy grail because it enables any two-bit huckster to reach global audiences for fractions of a cent.

It doesn't matter if you've never heard of the product. It doesn't matter that you couldn't possibly use a baker's dozen of wholesale tungsten-carbide oil drilling bits at any price. It doesn't matter that you're utterly offended by the offer and would never do business with them, even if they were the last company on Earth. Marketers apparently believe that they have a God-given right to jam their ad in your face.

Spam is the latest creation of people who believe that your time and attention are a resource to be mined, that your name and identity are a strategic asset that belongs to anybody but you, and that you spend your life breathlessly awaiting the perfect sales pitch. Spam has everything to do with how your privacy is viewed — or, more accurately, ignored — by the advertisers and marketers of the world.

Who hath spammed thee?

To understand the problem of spam, it helps to know who is doing it and what they're advertising. Surveying the Internet, you can quickly see a few reputable marketers using spam to advertise goods and services. To the contrary, the most commonly seen spam advertises pyramid schemes, get-rich-quick and make-money-fast scams, phone-sex lines, and pornographic Web sites. Most ironically, vast quantities of spam advertise spamming software, spamming services, and lists of millions of e-mail addresses you can buy so that you too can become a spammer.

Why spam is a bigger problem than you think

We all get postal junk mail. That's an accepted fact of life, at least in the United States. You may wonder why spam is any different.

Spam is different from the junk mail that is mailed to your house or the telemarketing calls that interrupt your dinner, for one simple reason: The people who send you that junk mail and make those phone calls have to pay for the cost of doing so, and the price can be steep. Junk mail has to be written, designed, printed, and collated, and postage must be paid. Telemarketers must rent office space, hire staff members, install phones, and pay long-distance phone charges. We don't say this to defend them, but rather to draw a distinction between the costs that traditional marketers incur and the costs that a spammer *doesn't* incur.

When a spammer sends his ad for herbal Viagra or an XXX-rated Web site or canine harmonica lessons to millions of people over the Internet, he pays almost nothing because, as we all know, e-mail is virtually free to the party who is sending it. But someone has to bear the cost of distributing those millions of e-mails to recipients all over the globe — and therein lies the difference between online unsolicited advertising and offline unsolicited advertising.

The Father of the Internet speaks out about spam

"Spamming is the scourge of electronic-mail and newsgroups on the Internet. It can seriously interfere with the operation of public services, to say nothing of the effect it may have on any individual's e-mail mail system. Spammers are, in effect, taking resources away from users and service suppliers without compensation and without authorization."

— Vint Cerf, acknowledged "Father of the Internet"

There's No Such Thing As a Free Lunch, Even on the Internet!

If you're like most people, you pay an Internet Service Provider (ISP) to get access to the Internet. (Even if your company or school pays for your access, someone is paying for it.) E-mail is one of the services your ISP provides as part of its service to you. For most people, the costs of your e-mail service are simply bundled into your service package. In reality, these costs can form a significant part of your monthly bill (as much as $3 or $4 of a standard $19.95 charge).

It wasn't long ago that ISPs charged per message for Internet e-mail. In the early days (well, 1991, which was pretty early for lots of Internet users), the service provider Prodigy used to charge 25 cents per message!

Even now, users of "free" e-mail services, like Hotmail and Yahoo!, "pay" by being subjected to advertisements all over their mailboxes, and the advertisers pay to run the servers at those sites. What seems to be free is really just costs factored into your service, and the costs related to e-mail don't stop there.

Suppose that you have a friend in Timbuktu whom you love to hear from by e-mail. The data that makes up the e-mail from your friend leaves her computer and begins a wondrous journey though any number of computers and networks on its way to you. Presumably, your friend owns her computer, so the resources used to create the message are largely hers. After that e-mail leaves her computer, though, the entire rest of its journey is spent bouncing around servers and careening down transmission lines that belong to anybody *other than* her — unless, of course, she happens to personally own her own international fiber-optic network!

Considering that most of us don't have a spare data network lying around, when that e-mail is sent, you and your friend are both depending on every service provider and communications network between you and Timbuktu to let that e-mail pass through their networks. In this way, virtually every e-mail is, to one extent or another, sent "postage due," with the postage being paid by everybody along the way.

Spam Is a Bad Deal for Everybody (Except the Spammer)

If you think about it, sending bulk e-mail to millions of people is just as cheap for a spammer as it is for a faraway friend in Timbuktu, especially when it's compared to the cost of sending junk ads by postal mail or telemarketing. After all, a spammer has no printing costs, no stamps to buy, no phones to install, no telemarketers to hire, and no long-distance calls to pay for. Instead, a spammer sends hundreds or thousands of messages per hour for just a fraction of a penny per spam.

Just because a spammer doesn't pay much for sending his spam, though, doesn't mean that someone isn't paying — and you would never guess who's at the head of the list: You.

Just like a friend you may have in Timbuktu, when a spammer decides to send the latest get-rich-quick scheme to 25 million of his closest friends, he can get an account at a local ISP and begin sending mail. After those 25 million messages leave his computer, though, the vast majority of the "postage" for delivering his mail is paid for by the 25 million recipients, their ISPs, and all the other networks, servers, and ISPs in between.

How big of a problem is spam? A study commissioned by the European parliament discovered that spam costs about $9.4 billion each year — a huge bill that is being footed by everyone except the spammers themselves.

More Ways You Pay for Spam

For your ISP, the costs associated with processing e-mail are the same, whether or not it's e-mail that its customers want. The more e-mail your ISP processes, the higher those costs. As spam volumes increase, It begins to clog Internet bandwidth and begins to fill up the storage disks on your ISP's servers. Whenever you're trying to surf the Web, therefore, you're competing with spam for the use of your ISP's Internet connection, slowing you down when you're surfing.

With overworked servers receiving and storing spam for hundreds of thousands of users, your access to your own e-mail can also slow down. E-mail servers are powerful machines, capable of doing thousands of tasks at one time. Even those big machines can get bogged down, though, and when you're eager to read your e-mail, the last thing you want is to have to compete with some spammer for access to your ISP's mail servers.

Every once in a while, an ISP gets so overloaded with spam that its servers crash. This situation causes everybody who was depending on that server to be inconvenienced. It may also be more than an inconvenience if, for example, your company's e-commerce Web site was on that same server or a bunch of customers' orders were in the e-mails that got scrambled when the server gave up the ghost. Calculating the cost in terms of lost business opportunities when customers can't reach you or think that you're ignoring them is almost impossible, but those are more costs you bear, thanks to spammers.

Eventually, if the service quality gets too bad, to keep subscribers from jumping to a competitor, an ISP begins buying more Internet bandwidth and more servers. Of course, it needs to be hiring more staff members to install that equipment and to keep everything running. At some point, those costs get passed back to you — perhaps in the form of rate hikes or longer hold times when you call your ISP for customer service.

The number of unsolicited messages sent out each day is truly remarkable. The spam-filtering company Brightmail claims that its research has shown more than 25 million unsolicited messages being sent per day in 1998, with the number steadily increasing every year since then, as shown in Figure 11-2. Antispam expert Michael Rathbun tracks the average volume of spam sent to an e-mail account. His statistics are available at www.tesp.com/tespUBErate.htm. Numerous court cases are under way between spammers and innocent victims who have been subjected to these types of floods. Unfortunately, although major corporations can afford to fight these cutting-edge cyberlaw battles, small mom-and-pop ISPs and their customers are left to suffer the floods.

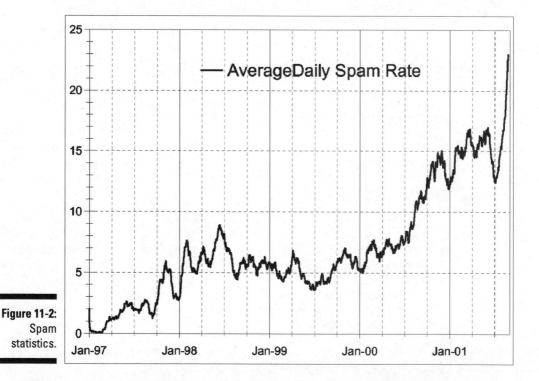

Figure 11-2: Spam statistics.

Here's another cost you may not have thought of: your time. Because of the volume of spam zipping around the Internet, downloading your e-mail takes longer. Although you may call a local number to connect with the Internet, lots of other people pay by the minute for the time they spend online. Because of spam, it takes them longer to get their e-mail, and spam costs them money in connection charges every month.

Calling Erin Brockovich!

If you saw the movie *Erin Brockovich* (which was based on a true story), you know that the sassy heroine does battle with a polluting power company that has dumped nasty gunk into the groundwater, which is causing the citizens in the nearby town to become very sick. Oddly enough, noxious floods of spam have a similar effect on the health of the Internet and all the Netizens who use it.

The reason that companies dump toxic waste into lakes and rivers is that they've done the math. It may cost them many millions of dollars a year to properly dispose of the waste from one plant. Or they could just dump it into the river for free.

Economists call the toxic waste an *externality*, which is their word for something that gets generated as a by-product of someone's moneymaking activity, the cost of which gets "paid for" by all the citizens who now have a greater risk of disease.

If the pollution levels stay relatively low, some people may never notice that they're slowly being poisoned and may eventually die of something else. Occasionally, though, somebody does get sick and for them the cost of that pollution suddenly becomes great. As in the movie, companies gamble that the amount they may have to pay for an occasional illness is less than the amount they would have had to pay to dispose of the waste properly.

Just like polluters, spammers try to spread the costs of their spam across wider and wider populations of Internet users, knowing that as long as they don't give a "fatal" dose to any ISPs, they can continue their spamming relatively unnoticed and everyone pays their little portion, never being the wiser or bothering to fight back.

Why "Just Hit the Delete Key!" Is No Answer

Although spammers love to say "Just hit the Delete key," when they do so, it totally misses the point. By the time the spam hits the fan (well, all of our mailboxes), so many costs have been incurred by so many people other than the spammer that it is either naïve or an utter act of denial to pretend that those costs can be undone with the pressing of one key.

A Throng of Things to Thwart Thpammers — er, Spammers

BOMBSHELL

✔ **Know where your e-mail address can be found (white pages and Web pages, for example):** Do you know who has your e-mail address? Do you participate in chat rooms? Message boards? Newsgroups? Do you have your e-mail address posted on your Web page?

Try putting your e-mail address into a search engine and seeing what pops up. The answer to the age-old question of "How did those #*@%#$ get my e-mail address" may be that you gave it to them!

✔ **Guard your primary e-mail address:** When somebody asks for your e-mail address, think twice before giving it to them. Or shield yourself behind an e-mail alias. For more information on e-mail aliases, see the following bullet about establishing secondary screen names for chat rooms.

✔ **Use stand-alone e-mail software:** Most Internet browsers come bundled with an e-mail program. The problem is that by bundling the two, you may be making it easy for hackers, spammers, and unscrupulous Webmasters to get your e-mail address from your browser. For that reason, we suggest using a stand-alone e-mail product, like Eudora (www.eudora.com), Outlook Express (www.microsoft.com/ie, installed with the Internet Explorer package), or Pegasus (www.pmail.com).

✔ **Play hide-and-seek with your browser:** Even if you're using a stand-alone e-mail program, you may have at some time recorded your e-mail address somewhere within your browser, or your browser may have even grabbed it and given it away for you in an attempt to be helpful. Because the whole purpose of a browser is to share information between computers, it may be giving away that information about you to others whenever they know the right way to ask for it. If you think that your browser may be blowing the whistle on you, here's how to shut down the little snitch:

  • *In Netscape:* Choose Edit➪Preferences from the menu bar atop the browser window. In the list along the left side of the Preferences dialog box, click on the plus sign (+) next to Mail & Newsgroups. Then select Identity, which appears just below the plus sign. On the right side of the dialog box appears any of your personal information that the browser has stored. Erase all the personal information you see there and click OK to accept the changes.

- *In Internet Explorer:* Choose Tools⇨Internet Options from the menu bar atop the browser window. In the Internet Options dialog box, select the Content tab and click on the My Profile button. Erase all personal information that appears on this form. Click OK to accept the changes.

- *In Opera:* Choose E-mail⇨Edit Active Account from the menu bar atop the browser window. Erase all personal information that appears on the right side of the dialog box.

(For more information about managing the personal information stored in your browser, see Chapter 9.)

✔ **Choose an ISP that actively blocks spam:** Several of the large national ISPs — like AOL, Earthlink, and AT&T — have some spam-blocking features, so if yours has it, make sure that you use it. Although you'll have more difficulty finding a local ISP that blocks spam, many are run by system administrators who are veterans of the spam wars and know how to offer spam protection that makes nuclear missile silos look poorly defended, so it's always worth asking around.

✔ **Find out how to filter your own e-mail:** Some e-mail software programs have filtering features that, if you take the time to read the instructions, can be useful in helping you manage your mailbox in many ways, including helping you filter spam directly into the trash. Be ready to experiment with those settings, and don't autodelete anything until you're absolutely certain that your filters are working right. If your filter eats that e-mail from Aunt Ethel, you may get a cold reception (and dinner) when you head for her house next Thanksgiving.

✔ **Never — *never* — click on Reply:** Most return addresses in spam are faked to deflect complaints. However, some spammers use real addresses because they really do want to hear from you — but not for the reason you may think. Why would they want to hear your angry diatribe? When you click on Reply, you have just confirmed that your e-mail address is a "live one," which is like waving a big red flag and screaming "This e-mail address is real! I really read this stuff! If you're smart, you'll send me more spam!"

✔ **Establish secondary screen names for chat rooms and message boards:** Chat rooms and message boards are among the most appealing places for spammers to gather e-mail addresses. Protect your primary e-mail address by creating other "throwaway" e-mail addresses for posting on message boards and for giving out to people and sites you're not sure you can trust. Many ISPs — like AOL, AT&T, and others — allow you to create secondary screen names or additional e-mail addresses at little or no cost, or you can get free e-mail addresses from Yahoo!, Hotmail, and other free-e-mail services. If spam comes flooding into those accounts, you can always delete them and make a new one, all the while shielding your primary address from the flood. For more on free e-mail accounts, see Chapter 10.

A free e-mail service, Mailshell (`www.mailshell.com`), allows you to create and manage a virtually unlimited number of e-mail accounts, all while keeping your primary e-mail address hidden from potential spammers.

✔ **Give and use false e-mail addresses:** This advice is quite controversial. Many people know that spammers troll through chat rooms and message boards looking for e-mail addresses, so they use fake or altered — sometimes called *munged* (rhymes with "lunged") — e-mail addresses. For example, `JohnDoe123@hotmail.com` may give out his address as `JohnDoe123@I-hate-spam.hotmail.com` and then give written or verbal instructions to friends and associates to remove the `I-hate-spam.` part before sending him e-mail. This strategy tends to confound many spammers because they often use automated e-mail "harvesting" programs that gather anything with an @ sign in the middle; because they're too lazy to sort the millions of addresses by hand, they usually end up sending their spam to the altered address. Why munging is controversial is that, depending on how you munge the address, when the spammer sends the mail, it may still end up in somebody's mailbox, most likely that of the already overworked and spam-flooded administrator of your ISP or free e-mail provider. The other reason is that many people use mail programs that don't show the e-mail address of people they're writing to, so they don't notice the munge and real mail gets lost. Please think twice before trying this one at home.

✔ **Use unique e-mail account names not found in a dictionary:** A growing number of spammers have found that going out and gathering e-mail addresses from chat rooms is just too tedious for their busy little lives. One day, a clever spammer looked at his mailing lists and saw that when he sorted them, `JohnDoe123@hotmail.com` was right below `JohnDoe122@hotmail.com`, and just above `JohnDoe124@hotmail.com`. He even had a `JohnDoe125`, `JohnDoe126`, and so on. This order held true for a whole gaggle of JohnDoes at earthlink.net and JohnDoes at aol.com and JaneDoes and JohnSmiths and on and on. The smart spammer thought, "Why don't I just skip all this gathering and just grab names out of dictionaries, randomly stick numbers in there, and then paste on an `@hotmail` or `@aol` or `@wherever` at the end and be done with this task in time to watch professional wrestling?" Thus was born the dictionary spamming attack, and that's why you may want to pick an e-mail address like `sdfj4kl6@hotmail.com` or `qw2eru9@Yahoo.com` so that spammers are less likely to pull your e-mail address out of a hat, thin air, or the dictionary.

✔ **Find out how and where to complain to get spammers shut down:** The best defense is a good offense. When spammers are offending you, offend them right back by finding out how to get them booted off their ISPs. How can you do that, you ask? Keep reading.

What More Can You Do?

Among our suggestions, the last one in the preceding section is the hardest, but it can be the most rewarding. Among your three authors, we've helped shut down hundreds of spammers' accounts and kept these privacy thieves on the run. If you're ready to put a few notches in your antispam holster, turn to Chapter 22, where we teach you how to trace Internet e-mail back to its source, to find out where spammers are operating from and how to get them shut down!

Chapter 12

Safely Shopping Online

*I*t happens. It's one o'clock in the morning, you really need a widget, and you've got your eye on one with some special features.

But you also have a problem: You know that if you go down to the local WidgetWorld in the morning, it will have a limited supply and a limited selection. You won't find the *exact* widget you need, and, to boot, you'll deal with some sleazy widget salesperson who doesn't want to let you out of the store until you buy *something*.

Suddenly, shopping on the Internet looks very attractive. You know that you can search and search and search the Web for the widget of your dreams, put your favorite models side-by-side on your screen, and make all kinds of financial arrangements to pay for your new widget from the privacy of your own home. Wait a minute! What if the widget Web site you're shopping at turns out to be just as sleazy as the widget salesperson a few miles down the road?

Privacy and Security: Is It Safe to Shop on the Web?

Shopping the Web is probably not as dangerous as trying to find a parking space at the local mall 45 minutes before closing time on Christmas Eve, and not nearly as life-threatening as hand-to-hand combat with blue-haired old ladies at the 2-for-1 bargain table at a BeanieBaby bazaar. You could wear a hard hat and safety boots. You could attach a seat belt to your desk chair. Or you could simply follow a few common-sense rules.

Be safe

Look around and be choosy. If you walked into a restaurant and saw a dirty floor and signs of mice or you were assaulted by an unpleasant odor, we hope that you would turn around and walk out. If you're smart, you apply the same principle when you're shopping on the Web. Look around before you whip out your credit card, at the two stores shown in Figures 12-1 and 12-2, for example. Ask yourself, "Does this site look like somebody put it up over a weekend? Or does it look like someone worked really hard to make my shopping experience a positive one? After exploring the site, has the company successfully instilled in me a sense of confidence and trust?" If not, it's time to go shopping someplace else.

Just as you can't judge a book by its cover, the legitimacy of a Web site is hard to gauge just by looking. If you see telltale signs of poor quality, you may want to consider moving along.

If it sounds too good to be true — you already know what we're going to say.

Use the power of the Internet to investigate: Just because you've never heard of a Web site doesn't mean that it isn't a good company. What's the best way to know whether a Web site is trustworthy? Go to Epinions (www.epinions. com) or PlanetFeedback (www.planetfeedback.com) or another online consumer rating site and see what others are saying.

Figure 12-1:
A real
Web store.

Figure 12-2:
A not-so-real Web store.

Protect your privacy

Remember that shopping is not buying. It's hard to buy something over the Internet without revealing some personal information, like your name and a credit card number. Why should you divulge personal information just to look around? If a site requires you to register just to browse, It's time to move on.

Read the privacy policy, too. Oh? The site doesn't have one? That certainly should serve as a red flag. If it does have a privacy policy, do you need three law degrees to understand it? Is the privacy policy certified by a third-party seal program? (We talk more about seals in Chapter 2.) See Figure 12-3 for a policy we like — because we wrote it.

Be sure to always use a secure server. We talk more about this subject too, later in this chapter.

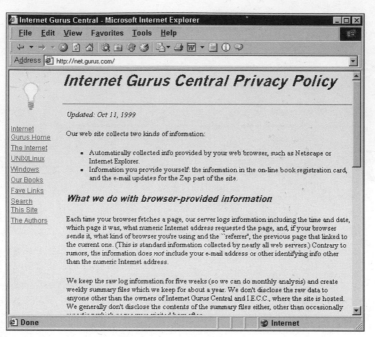

Figure 12-3:
The privacy
policy at
Internet
Gurus
Central is a
clear and
concise
policy
statement.

Is It Safe to Use a Credit Card on the Web?

Before we talk about using credit cards *on the Web,* let's talk about credit cards. Are they safe *off* the Web? While we're at it, let's talk about good old-fashioned cash.

No form of payment you may choose for making purchases is absolutely risk-free. Even cash has its dangers. For example, if you lose it or it's stolen, it's lost for good.

Like cash, some risk is associated with using credit cards — online or off. We generally don't think about those risks, however, because the convenience of a credit card far outweighs those risks.

When you use a credit card *offline,* you run the risk of someone running your physical card through the credit card machine a few times before giving it back to you or of stealing away with your carbons or a photocopy of your credit card receipt — with your signature on it. Ouch! *Online,* you run the risk of someone intercepting your credit card number while it's on its way to the vendor or of someone hacking into the vendor's database and getting your credit card number there. Ouch again!

What about Using Credit Cards Online?

Have you ever wondered, "Is using a credit card *online* any more dangerous or costly than using a credit card *offline?*"

Uh-oh — from credit card theft to identity theft

Don't worry: We have the solution.

One of the greatest dangers associated with using a credit card online is that your credit card number ends up stored in the databases of all the companies where you shop, and that's bad news when one of those databases gets hacked.

Under this scenario, the hacker steals away with your card number along with millions of other credit card numbers — and lots of additional personal information about you and all the other people whose card numbers are in the database. Now, rather than worry about someone doing bad things with your credit card number, you have to worry about them doing bad things with your *identity!*

Fortunately, some credit card issuers now offer single-use credit card numbers that can't be traced back to you, the cardholder, and they can be used only once, so you don't have to worry about database hackers *or* the fraudulent use of your card.

To date, Citibank, Discover, MBNA, and American Express now offer to their cardholders some version of this single-use card-number technology. Meanwhile, VISA offers its cardholders its Verified by VISA service as a different

solution to the same problem. After VISA cardholders register qualifying cards into the Verified by VISA program, they're prompted for a password every time they use their card to make a purchase from participating online stores.

If your credit card company doesn't offer this kind of protection, you owe it to yourself to call up and ask why!

To find out more about single-use card numbers and the Verified by VISA program, visit the information Web site at www.shopfearlessly.com.

Citibank: www.accountonline.com/CB/integrity/IntLearnMore.jsp

MBNA: www.mbnashopsafe.com

Discover Card: www2.discovercard.com/shopcenter/deskshop/main.shtml

American Express: www.americanexpress.com/privatepayments

Verified by Visa: www.shopfearlessly.com

MBNA Bank gives you a one-time-use credit card number, so if your number falls into the wrong hands after your transaction, it can't be traced back to you or used for more purchases.

Should you use a credit card online?

John: I do all the time. The worst problem I find is that a surprising number of e-commerce sites — even from familiar companies — are zombies: The lights are on, but nobody's home, and your order is never filled.

Ray: Let's be practical. What's the alternative? If you want to shop on the Internet, there aren't really any other ways to pay from afar that involve less risk. Go for it.

Gregg: If you feel comfortable using a credit card anywhere, you should feel comfortable using one online, considering the increased protection that most credit card companies are extending to users who make online purchases. Of course, if you really want to maximize your security, you get a credit card from a bank that offers single-use card numbers and use one of those single-use numbers for every online purchase you make.

The answer may surprise you. U.S. law says that you can be held liable for only the first $50 of unauthorized charges to your credit card — regardless of whether those charges are made online or offline. VISA, MasterCard, American Express, and the Discover card now offer 100 percent fraud protection on all online purchases, so if your card is used for unauthorized online purchases, you're free of liability.

Shopping with a credit card *offline* is getting safer, too: Discover, VISA, and MasterCard all offer 100 percent fraud protection against unauthorized offline shopping. (Gee, maybe someone should let American Express know about this!)

The danger of one-click shopping

Some e-commerce sites offer one-click shopping to make it even easier for you to buy. To take advantage of one-click shopping, you enter your name, credit card number, billing address, and most frequent shipping address and have the Web site save that information for you on its server. Then, when you're ready to buy, you just click once — all your personal information is automatically entered into your order. The problem with this strategy, of course, is that if you order something from a Web site using one-click shopping and then walk away from your computer without logging off, anyone can buy anything they want at the site — in your name and billed to your credit card. This statement is also true if you use one-click shopping at a public terminal and then forget to log off before walking away.

Internet Credit Cards and Credit Cards for the Net

At one time (a year ago), an *Internet credit card* was a regular old credit card, issued by an online bank and offering a host of Web-based services, such as online access to your account and increased buyer protection for online purchases. Of course, you could use the card offline too.

A credit card for the Net, on the other hand, may have been issued by either a traditional bricks-and-mortar bank or an online bank. The card was intended only for online purchases, so you often got an account number but no physical credit card. One major benefit of these cards was that they came with a separate, very low credit line to limit your liability if the card was misused.

Of course, neither of these cards makes any sense now because most other credit cards now offer exactly the same benefits.

Should you use an Internet credit card or credit card for the Net?

John: To me, it's more hassle than it's worth. I use one credit card for everything because it gives me frequent-flyer miles on the only airline that serves my one-horse hometown, but I do check my statement every month.

Ray: If you have several credit cards and you're not terribly vigilant about checking your monthly statements for unauthorized charges, getting any kind of special credit card — whether it's an Internet bank card or from some traditional offline credit provider — may be a good idea. Some folks have a credit card they use for only Internet-related purchases, so that if anything goes awry, isolating the source of the trouble is a little easier. If somebody offers a good deal on an Internet credit card, go for it. Remember, though, that nothing about an Internet card justifies higher interest rates or fees. In fact, online banks that don't have the expense of maintaining branches should, by all accounts, be cheaper. Don't leave your financial common sense behind just because it's the Internet.

Gregg: I suggest that you use one only if you get an offer for one that offers significantly better services or rates than the credit cards you've already got. Don't let yourself be rushed into making a decision: After all, whatever new perks one credit card offers today, all the rest are sure to offer tomorrow.

E-Wallets: A Place for Your Stuff

"All you need in life is a place for your stuff," the comedian George Carlin once observed in a now-famous comedy routine. "That's all your house is: a place for your stuff. If you didn't have so much stuff, you wouldn't need a house. Sometimes, you gotta move, gotta get a bigger house. Why? No room for your stuff any more."

But what about all your online stuff? Usernames. Passwords. Credit card numbers. Home address. Work address. Billing address. Phone number. Member number. Expiration dates. Verification codes.

Gee, George Carlin, do you have any advice about that?

Let's face it: Keeping track of all the info you need to go shopping online takes something much bigger than a house. It takes an *e-wallet* that not only holds all your stuff but also is easy to use and safer than Fort Knox.

A few years ago, the e-wallet concept was all the rage. It would make your browsing easier by remembering all your user IDs and passwords. It would make your shopping easier by remembering all your credit card numbers. It would make everything else easier by filling out Web forms on command with your name and address and phone number and all that other stuff you're always asked while surfing the Web.

Weave some privacy and security protection into the concept, and it sounds pretty darn appealing, so how come we're not all using e-wallets?

Because it turns out that they didn't always work so well.

Should you use an e-wallet?

John: I'm a pretty fast typist, I don't bother with anything fancy. My favorite Web browser, Opera, has an option to speed-type info, which I use for my name, address, and phone number, but the credit card numbers and passwords stay in my head or in the wallet in my pocket.

Ray: I don't like to store passwords in applications like this. Why? Because if I don't keep using my passwords regularly, I tend to forget them. Then, if your computer crashes and you lose your e-wallet, you get locked out of your own life because you let your e-wallet

remember your passwords rather than your having to remember them for yourself.

Gregg: One rule of privacy is that convenience breeds invasion. The problem with RoboForm is that if someone gets your RoboForm password, it's similar to opening the Pandora's box to *all* your most important information, all in one place. I do use RoboForm to store some of my less-sensitive passwords, but I keep the important passwords, like the one for my bank, in my head.

Microsoft, for example, has an e-wallet named Passport — but it works only on participating sites. Gee, we thought that the idea of shopping on the World Wide Web was to take advantage of shopping all over the place — not just on "participating sites." Other companies have had other e-wallet ideas, but for the most part taking the time to enter all your personal information turned out to be so much trouble that most people never bothered.

But let's not give up on the idea — particularly because e-wallet applications, like RoboForm, take a novel approach to marrying privacy and security with the best of convenience

A host of tools on the market act as e-wallets by saving your passwords, credit card numbers, and other personal information for you on the e-wallet's secure servers, ready for you when you need them. It's the part about your personal information being stored on *their* servers that bothers us, and it's why we like RoboForm so much. RoboForm collects the same personal information, but stores it as encrypted, password-protected data on your own computer so that you don't have to worry about it being hijacked from a third party's network or database. The way in which RoboForm collects your data is also unique — and effortless. The application is essentially invisible until you need it: You don't see RoboForm until you're filling out a form or field, at which point a RoboForm window pops up and asks whether you want to save the information you've just entered. The next time you visit that site, RoboForm pops up and asks whether you want it to fill the same fields for you. Every time you put your cursor in a name or address or credit card field, RoboForm knows and asks whether you want help filling in the field. In a nutshell, RoboForm makes it easy to collect your relevant personal information for later use and to fill out forms, and it does it in a way that lets you be the safeguard of your own info.

You can find RoboForm at `www.roboform.com`. For other e-wallets, visit your bank or credit card company's Web site.

Are Smart Cards Really All That Smart?

Just the name *smart card* makes you think that it knows it all: your Social Security number, your frequent-flyer-miles account number, your credit card numbers, your bank balance, and the password for your Internet Service Provider. Indeed, if tech-industry leaders have their way, your smart card will know all this information about you and more.

At first glance, this plan sounds great. After all, rather than carry a bunch of credit cards, a debit or ATM card, a supermarket discount card, a library card, an auto insurance card, a health insurance card, a work ID, three frequent-flyer cards, a video rental card, and more, you can cut your wallet some slack and carry all this stuff on just one card.

But what happens if you lose the card? Or if it's stolen? Or if the waiter at your favorite bistro stumbles onto your stock portfolio on the card while squaring up your bill and decides that he wants to make a few trades for himself?

Smart-card advocates like to point out that the cards are not just for storing information, but also for increasing security. For example, American Express markets a smart card named Blue. When you get a Blue card, you also get a free card reader to attach to your computer. When you use your Blue card at a store or restaurant, it works just like a regular credit card. When you use the card online, you must swipe the card through the reader *and* type your PIN before you can complete a transaction.

The beauty of this system is that you must meet two criteria before making an online purchase:

- ✔ **Something you have:** The card
- ✔ **Something you *know*:** Your PIN

The privacy and security advantages of this system are clear: Unlike with a credit card or debit card, if someone gets either your PIN or your card, it doesn't do them any good. Let's face it: When you stop and consider how slim the odds are that you could do something so-o-o-o-o stupid that it would result in the same person getting *both* your card and your PIN, the benefits of the American Express Blue card become obvious.

Should you use a smart card?

John: It seems to me that if I want a card that needs a PIN, I can use my bank ATM card at most places where I can use a credit card or a smart card. But I don't want that kind of card, so I don't really want a smart card either. But that little chip built into the card certainly looks cool.

Ray: Again, I'm a very practical guy. As long as the smart cards aren't too complicated to set up and use, the added security benefits are probably worth it. Unless you're the sort they call an "early adopter," one of those people who likes to ride the leading (and sometimes bleeding) edge of technology, you may want to keep an eye out and wait until all the kinks are worked out and smart cards get more widely adopted so

that you're not the one who's dying of hunger but can't buy a meal because his only credit card — a smart card — doesn't seem to be interfacing correctly with the network.

Gregg: I suppose that smart cards are inevitable, but I think that you have to control the amount and types of information that go on your card. It will be awhile before smart cards are unleashed on the world in any great numbers, so as you read and refer to this book over time, think about the kinds of information that require the greatest degree of protection — like your Social Security number — and keep that info off your card and out of your wallet!

You can find a smart card at

- ✔ **American Express Blue:** `www.americanexpress.com/blue`
- ✔ **VISA Smart Card:** `www.visa.com/pd/smart/`

Are Secure Servers Really Secure?

What is a secure server, anyway?

Using secure socket layer, or SSL, technology, late-model browsers can encrypt information as it leaves your computer, making it nearly impossible for anyone other than the intended recipient to decrypt it. Just like sending any other data over the Internet, others can still capture your encrypted information, but what they see is so much gobbledygook that it would take them centuries to decipher it.

SSL requires additional processing time on both the sending and receiving ends (in other words, it makes pages load even more slowly than normal), so it's typically used only on pages where sensitive data is being transmitted. After all, encrypting the pages of the sweaters you're browsing through makes no sense when you really need the protection only when you're ready to buy.

You can tell whether you're using a secure server, in two ways:

- ✔ **When you're using a secure server, you see a small locked padlock somewhere on your browser:**

  In Internet Explorer, the padlock appears in the lower right corner of the status bar, at the bottom of the screen.

  Netscape always shows an *unlocked* padlock in the lower-left corner of the taskbar, at the bottom of the screen. When you use a secure server, the padlock is locked.

  Opera always has an *unlocked* padlock in the upper-left corner of your browser window. When you use a secure server, the padlock is locked. If you move your cursor over the padlock, Opera even gives you the technical details of the server's encryption.

- ✔ **Look at the Web address or URL of the page you're visiting:** If it begins with the letters *https,* you know that the page is secure. (A normal Web page may contain the letters *http,* but it's the addition of the *s* which signifies that the page is secure.)

Should you use a secure server? And when should you demand it?

John: If one is available, I use it. But because I just don't hear of credit card numbers being stolen in transit over the Net — the main risk that SSL protects against — if a site doesn't have one, that's okay too.

Ray: There was a time when not every Web browsing software package could handle SSL encryption. That's really less of an issue now, and there's absolutely no good reason that any reputable e-commerce site shouldn't be running SSL for all its sensitive transactions. Although the chances of interception aren't really that huge, a secure server is such a trivial feature for e-commerce sites to offer that not having it smacks of poor management. Chances are

good any site offering a great deal but no secure server either is shadier than I would want to do business with or probably has plenty of competitors offering the same price and is concerned enough about inspiring my confidence that it uses SSL.

Gregg: If you're going to spend money on the Web, using secure servers is a must. If you're about to buy something online and the Web site doesn't offer a secure server, that should send up a huge red flag about the company. When should you use one? Use one whenever you're transmitting sensitive data, like a credit card number, over the Net.

Where's the Money?

You can't have commerce without money, and the Net offers lots of ways to handle this crucial ingredient.

Online payment alternatives

The choice used to be "Paper or plastic?" — as in cash or check or credit card — and after you made your choice, you picked up your goods and took them home.

But the Internet has changed the way we do business, pay for things, and take delivery of them. We visit companies we've never heard of on the Internet. We buy stuff from garage sales a thousand miles away. We never get to look at the other guy in the eye. We never get to talk to a soul. We just fork over our money to perfect strangers — and (gulp!) hope that they ship us a box (or a file) in return. The truth is that the new economy and its anonymous form of commerce leave a great deal to chance and luck and karma when it comes to paying and receiving. Here's how some bright minds are trying to cover the e-commerce bases for everyone.

Shopping by Web, paying by phone

Still a little nervous about giving out your credit card information over the Web? Some Web sites, like Amazon.com, let you shop online and then call in your credit card number by phone.

Sounds almost foolproof, right?

Well, it is. Almost — unless, of course, you make your call to the Web site to give your credit card with a cordless or cellular phone, which as you can read in Chapter 15, are really just radios, so your credit card number may be intercepted by others.

We bring this point up for two reasons: First, we want to make you aware that you have an alternative to giving out your credit card number over the Internet and, second, to demonstrate how easy it is to take risks with credit cards offline, too, without thinking about the potential hazards involved.

Peer-to-peer pay, PrivateBuy, and micropay

New ways to shop call for new ways to pay.

Suppose that you collect antique spying equipment. On your favorite auction site, you find some items you've been trying to locate for years — some creepy but nifty high-surveillance items. Now it's time to pay up, but do you really want to fork over your credit card number to someone who has as much interest in being a snoop as you do?

Fortunately, you have a few privacy-enhancing alternatives.

Peer-to-peer pay

If you use a free PayPal.com, Yahoo!, PayDirect, or ecount account, you can *e-mail* the seller your payment without revealing any other information about yourself other than your name and e-mail address. (The e-mail address, of course, can be bogus; for more info on how to get set up a cloaked e-mail address, refer to Chapter 10.)

Here's how it works: When you open your peer-to-peer pay account, you fund it by transferring money into the account from a credit card or bank account. When you want to pay someone, you simply go to your peer-to-peer pay account to arrange the payment, and the seller receives an e-mail with instructions on how to receive the money.

From a privacy perspective, we find the implications of this arrangement to be exciting because it enables you to create a shield around yourself and some of your most sensitive financial data — namely, credit card numbers and bank account numbers (which appear on every check your write).

You can find peer-to peer pay services at `www.paypal.com`, `paydirect.yahoo.com`, and `www.ecount.com`.

PrivateBuy.com

Suppose that you *really* want to keep your identity a secret: no name, no e-mail address, no nothing. It's time to pay a visit to PrivateBuy.com.

As with peer-to-peer pay, you open an account and fund it from an existing credit card or bank account. In return, you get a PrivateBuy account number that works online like a MasterCard but allows you to completely hide all your personal information from others.

Brought to you by the same folks who offer the ecount peer-to-peer pay accounts, here's how it works: Normally, when you're shopping online, you're required to provide your name, address, and credit card number when you're checking out. When you open a PrivateBuy account, you get a PrivateBuy account number that works just like a MasterCard account. You're also assigned a fictitious name and address to use in filling out forms when you make purchases online, so only PrivateBuy knows who you are.

If you're thinking of using PrivateBuy to buy something illegal or to buy something so that you can do something illegal, forget it. If the PrivateBuy folks are subpoenaed, they can decrypt your purchase records and will do so if required by law.

You can find PrivateBuy at `www.privatebuy.com`.

Microbreweries, microbakeries, and micropay

First, there were microbreweries, and then there were microbakeries, and now, like all things that must eventually come to the dot.com world, it's time for micropay.

For most of us, our first experience with micropay comes as a way of paying a small amount of money for something of small value, like a song on Napster; an archived news article on your local newspaper's Web site; a recipe you saw on a cooking show; OR a tiny little software application that performs a tiny little task.

At the time this book was written, businesses faced a hurdle in trying to collect these small sums of money because the only real mechanism they can use is a credit card. The minimum charge for a merchant to process a single credit card charge can run as high as a dollar, which is a problem if you want to sell something that's worth only a penny or a nickel or a dime.

Micropay is the solution, although no one yet knows exactly how it can work. Regardless of the mechanics, however, you can bet that to participate in the micropay economy, you will open some sort of account with a micropay company and have any micropayments you incur debited from that account. Most likely, your micropay account will work much like the peer-to-peer and PrivateBuy accounts we just described.

Don't worry about where to find micropay services. When the time is right and you're ready to buy, the seller makes sure that you know micropay is the best way to pay.

Here's a minority viewpoint: John thinks that micropayments will never happen and that sites are much more likely to sell monthly subscriptions than to try to collect .073 cents every time you click.

Gregg offers a rebuttal: Subscriptions are just another way to collect micropayments.

Private Payments Revisited: Are They Really As Private As They Seem?

To paraphrase a favorite line of Forrest Gump's, "Private is as private does."

The three forms of online payments that we discuss in the preceding section are *pretty* private, although the degree of privacy protection each one promises varies. You have to consider another factor: You. It wouldn't take much of a slip on your end to compromise whatever privacy each method provides.

Here are a few tips for assessing and enhancing your privacy protection while using those alternative payment plans:

✔ **Read the privacy policy:** Do you have to worry about them selling your name, address, phone, and e-mail address as part of a mailing list or customer database? Do you have to worry about them giving access to your personal buying habits to other merchants? Do you have to worry about them giving third-party vendors and contractors access to your personal information? For more information on privacy policies, refer to Chapter 2.

Should you use online payment alternatives?

John: I use PayPal all the time because I know who it is (a company in California) and it has a reasonable privacy policy. It really is a handy way to make irregular payments to other people with online access — easier than writing a check and mailing it.

Ray: They can be much handier, particularly if you do a great deal of online buying and selling, such as on eBay. You really need to look carefully at whether these companies offer any insurance against fraud and whether they limit the size of transactions you can make and then keep those issues in mind when you're engaging in transactions. If you're looking at

transactions that regularly go beyond the company's insurable limits, for example, consider using a third-party escrow service, which we talk about next.

Gregg: One's demand for privacy and a sense of security is a private matter. Personally, I'm not concerned about paying with a credit card over the Internet when I can use a secure server, and to date I've never felt the need to hide or cloak my identity from someone I was doing business with over the Web. On the other hand, I'm glad that services such as peer-to-peer and PrivateBuy are available if the need were to arise.

✔ **Consider using cash:** If you really want to ensure your privacy, find a way to fund your peer-to-peer, PrivateBuy, or micropay account with cash. After all, if you make deposits into your account with a debit or credit card, you have just created a paper trail that leads to the account itself.

✔ **Take the free insurance:** What do you suppose would happen if you were to fund one of these accounts — and then the company went belly-up? Although we're just speculating here, it seems to us that if you fund the account with a credit card that offers a buyer protection plan, your credit card company *may* just cover the loss. Check with your own credit card company before making any assumptions.

✔ **Go for the miles:** Finally, we remind you that if you make deposits into your peer-to-peer pay, PrivateBuy, or micropay account with a credit or debit card, you're creating a paper trail with the credit or debit card company, which it too can turn around and profit from by selling information about you (see Chapter 1). For that reason, we suggest that you consider profiting from the relationship too. For example, if you fund your account from a frequent-flyer mileage-bearing credit card, you may be able to earn miles on every peer-to-peer pay, PrivateBuy, or micropay dollar you spend.

Online Escrow Sites

Want to remove the faith factor from Internet transactions?

Should you use an online escrow service?

John: I've never bought anything at an online auction that cost more than $35, so it hasn't been an issue, but I would use one if I bought something expensive from someone I didn't know.

Ray: If the amount of money at stake is greater than the insurance amount provided by the auction site, alternative payment scheme, or other guarantor, you absolutely should use an escrow service. The couple of bucks you spend over a year on escrowed purchases or sales will probably never equal the amount you would lose on any one purchase that goes awry. Most escrow services would still be cheap at twice the price, so go for it.

Gregg: An escrow service undoubtedly gives added security and may also provide privacy protection. The problem with these services is that they violate the bargain-shopping mentality of many online shoppers because *someone* — buyer or seller — has to pay for the escrow service; the use of one of these services delays the arrival of the money and goods; and they violate the spirit of the adventure that often attracts people to online shopping and auctions.

One way to do it is to use an *escrow* site, which acts an intermediary between buyer and seller while removing all risk for both parties.

It works like this: You agree to buy a Liberace candelabra from a seller at GaudyAuction.com. You send your money to the escrow company. No risk is involved here for you because you know that the escrow company will hold on to the money until you receive, inspect, and accept the merchandise. Meanwhile, the seller has no risk in sending you the merchandise because he knows that you've already sent the money to the escrow company. If you accept the merchandise, the escrow company sends your money to the seller. If you reject the merchandise, you return it to the seller and the escrow company gives you back your money.

You can find online escrow services at www.escrow.com and www.i-escrow.com.

Chapter 13

Safe Banking and Investing Online

- -

In This Chapter

▶ An introduction to online banking

▶ Is your bank's Web site safe?

▶ Online bill payment systems

▶ Online brokerages and stock trading

▶ Organizing your bills with account aggregators

▶ Digital signatures

- -

Long before there was an Internet (we're talking hundreds and hundreds of years ago), people longed for more convenient ways to move their money around. Early Man didn't have credit, credit cards, or bank accounts. He didn't have investment accounts. In fact, considering what we now generally consider to be "money," he didn't have much of anything. Rather than use coin and currency and credit cards, his medium of exchange was the fruit of this year's harvest, which he had to make last all winter. When a fisherman needed some grain, he would throw a couple of dried, stinky fish over his shoulder and head toward the nearest village. After he traded his fish, he threw the heavy grain over his shoulder and made the long trek back home again.

Not much convenience there — and not much privacy, either. Today, we're lucky. Our money is so small that it fits right into our pockets, and if you don't want a wad of dough to ruin your trouser crease lines, you can still move your money around in lots of other ways. Yes, when it comes to convenience, we've come along way since Early Man.

When it comes to privacy, on the other hand. . . .

Banking Online, Defined

You have money. You keep it someplace other than under your mattress: a bank, a credit union, a savings and loan. When you want access to your cash, you may get that access in a variety of ways. The old-fashioned way, which includes a trip to the bank, is always an option, or you can write a check or use your debit card at the grocery store. Or, you may want to access your money electronically; which you can do with your ATM card (which we talk about in Chapter 14), by telephone (which we deal with in this chapter), or by using the Web.

For the sake of this conversation, let's call *online* banking the process of moving your money around electronically using the Web. This definition seems kind of simple and obvious until you start splitting hairs. For example, if you use a cell phone to access your bank account, is that online banking or telephone banking?

In this case, the answer depends on the phone. A Web-enabled phone may access online banking either way: by dialing an access number for telephone banking or by using the phone's browser to access the bank via the Web. Meanwhile, we suspect that over time the lines between your telephone, your cell phone, your Palm, your pager, and your Web browser will blur so that in the future it becomes less and less clear to even you how you're accessing your money other than those few times when you find yourself in a bank (or bank branch at your supermarket or some other strange but physical location) and chatting with a real, live teller.

Your Bank's Web Site: How Safe Is It?

Don't look at us. We surely don't know. A number of people in the technology department of your bank really don't know either. In fact, it's probably the case that a company never really knows whether its Web site is safe until it has been hacked into — and then, of course, you know that it *isn't*.

That's the bad news.

The good news is that you can do lots of things today to make sure that your online banking transactions are as safe as possible:

> ✔ **Tales from the (en)Crypt:** Browse around your browser and then your bank's Web site and make sure that both use 128-bit encryption, which, by some estimates, is so safe that it would take more than a trillion years for a hacker to crack using current technologies. How will you know if your browser offers 128-bit encryption? Most browsers tell you.

For example, Microsoft Internet Explorer has a menu option named About Internet Explorer on the Help menu. Choosing that option tells you what version of the browser you're using and in most cases includes *Cipher strength,* indicating the number of bits used for encryption.

✔ **Look for a secure server**: This advice goes hand in hand with ensuring 128-bit encryption, but the secure server gives you a visual clue that it's working. Look for the locked padlock on your browser and the addition of the letter *s* to the *http* (as in *https*) at beginning of your bank's URL. (For more information on secure servers, see Chapter 12.)

✔ **Get a second opinion:** Visit the online banking-review site Gomez.com to find out how other consumers rate your bank.

www.gomez.com

✔ **Get some insurance:** Is this bank insured by the Federal Deposit Insurance Corporation (FDIC)? To be sure, check out the FDIC Web site at FDIC.gov:

www2.fdic.gov/structur/search/findoneinst.cfm

✔ **Get it in writing, Part I:** Check your bank's Web site for a written guarantee that protects you from losses from fraud that may result from online banking.

✔ **Get it in writing, Part II:** Hey, you never know when trouble may occur. You get into much less trouble, though, if you have printed copies of all your online transaction records to prove that what you say is true.

What about telephono and wireless banking?

If you haven't noticed yet, we're biased when it comes to transmitting sensitive data (like a bank account number!) by phone and wireless device. Here are our reasons:

Our wireless-banking bias

A wireless device, like a cell phone or Palm, is really just a high-tech radio. If someone really wants to intercept your call or banking transmission, he can and will be able to do so. Does this mean that you shouldn't use a wireless device to do your banking? No, it just means that you should be aware of the risks and be comfortable with the level of risk you're willing to take.

Our telephone-banking biases

Keep in mind that your cordless phone is, like a cell phone, really just a radio. It's worse, though, because it's easier to intercept a call on a cordless phone than on a cell phone. If you want to do your banking by phone, consider how easy it would be to increase your privacy by simply picking up that good old-fashioned landline telephone.

Overall, our problem with telephone banking is that you have no way to document your transactions. If trouble happens down the road, it's their word against yours — unless you find out that the neighbor kid just happened to be listening in.

AUTHOR SURVEY SEZ

Should you use online banking?

John: I use it for transfers among accounts and looking at checks I've written, but I trust my bank to behave responsibly. (It's a small bank.)

Ray: If you're comfortable with the risk, the level of convenience in being able to manage your bank account online is great. You're probably at greater risk that somebody will steal your checkbook than intercept your banking records while accessing them online. Even then, unless you're embarrassed by how much (or little) money is in your account, not much telling

information can be gained from "Check 473 in the amount of $37.54 cleared on June 17."

Gregg: It's a matter of personal preference and comfort with the potential hazards involved. Personally, I have followed the advice we give to protect my privacy, and now I'm willing to take the risk in exchange for the convenience that online banking brings me. When it comes to banking by phone or wireless device, however, I pass.

Paying Bills Online

Paying bills online is terribly seductive. You have no need to write out checks; no need to hunt for stamps; no need to race to the post office. All this, and at an estimated savings of $85 per year in postage and $30 per year in printed checks.

We admit it: We like paying our bills online a whole lot. Before you jump on the wagon and do the same, though, you need to know a few things.

You get a choice. You can pay your bills online through your own bank, or you can choose a third-party vendor.

A strong privacy policy counts (for a lot). Keep in mind that by paying your bills online, you're building a collection of personal information about yourself that is *valuable* — and your bank or online bill-paying service may be interested in profiting from it. Make sure that you read your own bank's privacy policy for online bill paying and read the privacy policies for some third-party vendors before choosing a company to handle your online bill payments.

Reliability counts (for a lot). Don't assume that your bank will necessarily get your bills paid more reliably than a third-party vendor — or the post office. Gregg, for one, has had a terrible time with the reliability of his own bank's online bill-paying service, although others he has talked with have had excellent luck with their own banks and independent companies.

A written guarantee counts (for a lot). Will you be held liable if fraud is associated with your account? Will your bill-paying service accept responsibility for any bills it's late in paying? After you find your company's policy on these issues, make sure that you read it carefully and print a hard copy for your records. These policies can change, so a hard copy from the company's Web site enables you to prove that the guarantee you expect was in force when you opened your account.

Longevity counts (for a lot). Although Gregg has had some trouble with his own bank's online bill-paying service, the one thing he knows he can count on is that his bank will stay in business. Before you get started with a third-party bill-paying service, you should use the Web to check out the company's health and credentials. A good place to start is at online news sites and consumer ratings sites, like epinions.com, deja.com, and Planet Feedback.

What about Bill-Management Services?

Many online bill-paying services are betting that you hate getting bills in the mail just as much as you hate paying them. And, gee, guess what? If this describes you, they have a solution, too.

It's called *bill management,* or *bill presentment,* and it works like this: You change your own billing address to the address of your bill-paying service. Under this system, all your bills get sent to the bill-pay company rather than to you. Regardless of whether your bill-paying service receives your bills electronically or in hard copy, it digitizes them and e-mails copies to you. You, of course, then use the company's bill-paying service to do your bill paying. At the end of the year, you can buy a CD with copies of all your bills for your records.

From a privacy perspective, a bill-management system potentially exposes even more of your personal information than a bill-paying service because your bills can contain information about you (like account numbers, account balances, Social Security number) that you would not need to disclose to a bill-paying service.

Here are some places where you can find online bill-paying and bill-management services:

- Start with your existing bank.

- Most portals and online services, like Yahoo! and America Online, offer online bill paying.

- Online bill paying and bill management are also available from www.paytrust.com, www.checkfree.com, www.Quicken.com, and www.Yahoo.com.

Should you use online bill paying? What about bill-management services?

John: I don't pay bills online. I don't have enough that the time savings are worth the hassles and possible screw-ups. I definitely don't use a bill-management service. I have arranged for a few regular bills (credit card, electric, and gas) to be paid regularly from my bank account, but I did that through the mail.

Ray: I put many of my charges on just one or two credit cards, one of which presents me with an annual summary of my charges, sorted into categories suitable for tax preparation. Although this system means that many of my life's activities are wrapped into a neat little bundle, it's not like this information isn't already in the credit card company's database. So I say take advantage of the time savings and convenience of consolidation. If you're that concerned about somebody having access to that much information about your monthly bills, no amount of convenience can make it attractive.

Gregg: I pay my bills online, but I'm careful about my recordkeeping. It's a good thing too because my bank lost several payments over a two-month period. Because I had hard copies of the payments, which included bank-issued confirmation numbers, the bank wrote letters of apology to each of the creditors involved and paid all late fees that were incurred. As for bill management, I pass. You may be willing to give up the control and additional information for the convenience, but it's an exchange I'm not willing to make.

Trading Online

When we talk about trading online, we aren't talking about trading curios over eBay or songs over Napster.

If you're going to put your net worth and retirement nest egg on the Web, you want to make sure that you do it with a reputable, safe company. We tell you what to look for.

Your brokerage's Web site: How safe is it?

We all know about the site outages and other technical problems that have at times made it hard for online traders to trade. That's the bad news.

The good news is that brokerage houses to date have been relatively immune to security and privacy problems. As you already know, past performance is no indication of future results. Therefore, smart traders like you anticipate problems and do everything possible today to minimize future dangers and risk:

✔ **Do your homework:** Use the Web to read about the health and reliability of online brokerages:

Online Investment Complaint Center (www.investingcomplaints.com) aggregates news and information about all online brokerages, including an up-to-date directory of brokerage rankings done by such well-known publications as *Forbes, Money,* and *Barron's.*

For more of the same, visit the Investing Online Resource Center (www.investingonline.org), which is run as a public service of the Washington State Department of Financial Institutions and Securities. This site offers brokerage rankings from a variety of reputable sources (like *Kiplinger's, Gomez.com,* and *CNNfn*) as well as a wealth of other useful information for online traders and wannabe online traders.

✔ **Use a browser with 128-bit encryption:** After all, who wants to turn her back on a trillion years of privacy protection? To find out whether your browser uses 128-bit encryption, you can follow the same tip in the earlier section, "Your bank's Web site: How safe is it?"

✔ **Use a secure server:** We say it again, just in case you didn't hear it the other trillion times we say it in this book: Use a secure server for all trades and to review your account.

✔ **Keep accurate records:** We're talking hard copies, so if a problem ever occurs, you can prove that what you say is true.

✔ **Look for SIPC:** Much like the FIDC protects the money you put in the bank if the bank should ever fail, the Securities Investor Protection Corporation (SIPC) protects customers of registered securities brokers and dealers if the brokerage should ever fail. If your online broker isn't a member, it's time to move on.

✔ **Read the privacy policy:** You just never know what you may find in there, especially if you're trading with a deep-discount brokerage or even a free-trade brokerage, which have to make money somehow. How they make money — perhaps even from your personal information — may just be found in their privacy statement.

What about wireless trading?

Yeah, we know how cool you feel sitting in Starbucks and trading shares of Cisco on your cell phone or Palm. We might do the same thing if only we made enough money as authors to afford to buy our coffee at Starbucks. On the other hand, we may not because we know that a wireless device is really just a radio and we may not want to be broadcasting our trades and account numbers out to anyone with a scanner who wants to listen. For more on privacy and wireless devices, see Chapter 15.

Should you use online trading?

John: Sure. It's cheaper, faster, and less prone to errors than calling a broker on the phone. I did check out my brokers thoroughly first.

Ray: The biggest danger is not in the security of the online trading system you use — most of them use strong encryption and are backed by reputable brokerage firms. Your biggest risk is that trading is so easy and fast that you may do stupid things. If you're a day trader, you probably need a higher level of performance than some of the more basic online brokerage services, and you pay handsomely for it. If you're a true investor, in for the long haul, just about any of the online brokerage services should meet your needs, from both performance to security.

Gregg: If you're making your own trading decisions, then, of course.

Privacy and the Put-It-All-on-One-Page Movement

Ever wonder what the future of online banking and trading will look like? Or, have you ever just wished that you could look at all your financial information — a checking account with one bank, a savings account with another bank, a money market account with a brokerage house, credit cards, frequent-flyer miles, and a stock portfolio — all at one time without having to jump from Web site to Web site of one financial institution after another?

The good news is that financial aggregator sites allow you to take *all* your online financial information and post it on one updated, personalized Web page. To make this happen, you sign up with a Web site offering financial aggregation. The main two aggregators are Yodlee and Vertical One; they also offer their services to AOL, Quicken.com, and loads of other companies — and maybe even to your own bank.

After you open an account, you enter all your account numbers and passwords. This information is then stored on the aggregation company's secure servers so that when you call up your account, the aggregator can run off to all the banks and brokers and credit card companies with which you do business, gather up all your account information, and then put it on one personalized account page made especially for you. Eventually, you will be able to do all your online banking — and maybe even trading — right there from the same page.

Sounds great, right?

Of course, with all this convenience come the same old problems. First, you have to consider the security issues: The password to your aggregation account unlocks every door in your financial kingdom. What if someone steals that key or password? Or breaks into the aggregator's database and steals all your financial information in one grand heist?

Then you have to consider the privacy issues: What if your aggregator decides to gather all that information about you and sell it? For example, when your aggregator notices that you have three maxed-out credit cards, will it sell your name and phone number (which it likely can find attached to at least one of your aggregated accounts) to a credit card company so that it can call and offer you a better credit card deal while you're trying to enjoy your dinner? Or, what if your aggregator notices that you've sold lots of stock from your brokerage account? Gee, we wonder whether your phone number might be worth something to one of those cold-calling boiler-room securities salespeople who are always calling from Florida with all those valuable stock tips?

Here's the bottom line: As we say many times in this book, convenience has its price. If you decide to use an aggregator, follow these tips to make sure that your personal information and personal wealth remain as safe as possible:

- ✓ **Look for the magic number:** As with online banking and trading and bill-paying, you want to make sure that both your aggregator and your own browser use 128-bit encryption.

- ✓ **Look for a secure server:** Make this the trillion *and first* time we've said it. Demand the use of a secure server for all transactions you make over the Web that involve sensitive data.

- ✓ **Read the privacy policy:** For more on what to look for, see Chapter 2.

- ✓ **Do your due diligence:** Will your aggregation company be around in three months? Three weeks? What do others who use the company's services have to say about it? To find out, use the power of the Web. Search for recent news items about the company, and visit consumer rating sites, like epinions.com or deja.com or PlanetFeedback, to see what others have to say.

Financial aggregator services are available from many portals, like AOL and Yahoo!; Web sites, like SmartMoney.com and CNBC; and maybe even your own bank — so the best thing to do is visit the sites of the financial-services companies you already do business with to see which offer aggregator services.

If that search leaves you empty-handed, visit the site of Yodlee, the clear leader in the account aggregator business, and click on the Sign Up button to see a list of companies that offer its services:

www.Yodlee.com

AUTHOR SURVEY SEZ

Should you use an account aggregator?

John: I've played with them, particularly My Yahoo, which uses Vertical One, but I really don't want a third party knowing where to find every dime I own.

Ray: Interesting idea, but a little too creepy for me. You can do most of the things an account aggregator can do with a tool like Quicken or Microsoft Money, without having all the

information sitting on the server of somebody whose need for revenue will forever drive them to make use of that info.

Gregg: I love the idea, but I'm terrified by the possible negative consequences. Can I get back to you on this in six months, after these sites have had a chance to prove themselves and work out the kinks?

Electronic Signatures: Signing Your Life Away the 21st Century Way

Signatures are a vital part of today's business transactions, whether you're buying a loaf of bread with a credit card at the grocery store, leasing a brand new Mercedes, or the President agreeing not to invade Canada. Signatures are an important symbol of your willingness to be bound by some set of circumstances.

Fans of the television show "Star Trek: Deep Space Nine" are all too familiar with how contracts, treaties, and other agreements are signed in the 24th century: Just affix your thumbprint and the deal is sealed. But in our modern, high-tech world of the 21st century, we're still in love with squiggles of ink on paper.

Whether it's a space-age thumbprint or flowing script from an ancient quill pen, stop for a moment and think about what a signature does:

 ✔ It's a symbol unique to one individual.

 ✔ It's not easy to make a credible forgery.

 ✔ After a signature is given, denying that it was given is difficult.

A few advancements have been made along the way. For example, at many Macy's department stores and Best Buy electronics stores, the cash registers have been equipped for the past few years with one form of an "electronic" signature, where you scrawl your John Hancock on an LCD panel and it's translated into printed form on the bottom of your receipt, looking a bit like something produced on a Etch-A-Sketch.

But this isn't really an "electronic signature" of the form that is of greatest interest to the global business community. Those folks are really interested in something that is more than a digitized version of the same old signature: Global commerce is really interested in speeding transactions, reducing paperwork, and being even more confident that when somebody says Yes, you can hold them to it.

Enter Digital Signatures

Digital signatures don't look anything like their handwritten counterparts. Most people won't ever see a digital signature, in part because it's largely a string of gobbledygook numbers and letters, the product of a series of complex mathematical calculations, combined with a password, creating something that is

✔ Unique

✔ Difficult to forge

✔ Not easily denied

In June 2000, President Clinton signed into law (using a ballpoint pen, of course) the first federal law aimed at making digital signatures carry the weight of physical signatures. He did use a mocked-up version of a *smart card* to authenticate his signature. (For more information about smart cards, refer to Chapter 12.) It was just a mock-up of a digital signature system, though, because at the time of the signing ceremony, no commercially available, widely accepted system existed for easily creating and verifying digital signatures.

At the time this chapter is being written in 2002, we still don't have such a system. That's the problem. If you want people to use something as complicated and confusing as digital signatures, they have to be easy, available, and foolproof.

How soon will we all be affixing our digital signature to our documents? The answer is "no time soon." The battles are still raging between competing standards, with some companies saying that thumbprints or a laser scanning your retinas are the only way to be assured of authentication. Others are promoting voice prints as the end-all in security, and others are using biometrics, with systems that measure the features and geometry of your face or even your body odor (yes, body odor). Until these battles are sorted out, stick to your trusty fountain pen.

Part IV
Beyond the PC: Offline Electronic Privacy

The 5th Wave
By Rich Tennant

"Someone want to look at this manuscript
I received on email called, 'The Embedded
Virus That Destroyed the Publisher's Servers
When the Manuscript was Rejected.'?"

In this part . . .

We take a deep breath and remind ourselves that even before most of us ever plugged a phone cord into our computers to log on to the Internet, we had reasons to be concerned about electronic privacy. So let's go back in time and pay tribute to the things we considered potentially dangerous back then and then fast-forward to the latest in offline privacy concerns.

Chapter 14

Protecting Your E-Money, E-Credit, and E-Dentity

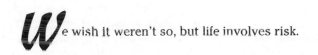e wish it weren't so, but life involves risk.

Some people get a thrill by jumping out of airplanes, and others live dangerously by buying things with a credit card over their cellular phones or dropping their receipts on the ground as they walk away from an ATM. It's our job to tell you the risks. It's your job to decide how much of a risk you're willing to take.

Paper or Plastic? The Risks of "Paperless" Money

"Who knows what evil lurks in the hearts of men?" asked a popular 1940s radio show.

Back then, the answer was "The Shadow knows." Today, the right answer is "Your bank and your credit card company know!" because they have an electronic record of most everywhere you go and everything you buy:

Call it convenience or call it an invasion of privacy, few of us have stopped to consider *just how much* information about us is being gathered about us as we go through our daily lives:

- ✔ **Credit cards and debit cards:** It seems obvious to us, but if everything you buy on your credit card and debit card shows up on your credit card bill and bank statement at the end of the month, someone is clearly keeping tabs on you. If you're planning a little shopping spree that you don't want the rest of the world to know about, we suggest that you leave your little plastic friends at home. Meanwhile, the data that is collected about you (from both your credit card and debit card) is of great interest to marketing people who spend billions of dollars every year buying this information about us and our personal shopping habits so that they can send well-targeted ads to our mailboxes and e-mailboxes and interrupt us with phone calls at dinner.

  If you want your bank and credit card companies to stop selling you out, see the sidebar "GLB for you and me," later in this chapter.

- ✔ **ATM and debit cards:** Some people use cash because it enables them to spend without leaving a paper trail. If you aren't careful, how and where you get that cash can be just as revealing. Consider, for example, that every time you use your ATM or debit card, you're creating a record of where you have physically been (or at least where your card has been) as well as a paper trail of cash withdrawals — information that may be of interest, for example, to a soon-to-be former spouse, the Internal Revenue Service (IRS), or law enforcement personnel.

- ✔ **Privacy and ATMs:** What if, after every time you use an ATM, an employee from the bank would come running out to grab your greasy fingerprints off the even-greasier ATM touch-screen? "What a horrible way to gather information about customers," you may think — but here's a scenario that's even worse: Look closely and you can see that most ATMs are closely guarded by videocameras. When you use an ATM, your mug is recorded. Thanks to the power of digital technology, companies can now do a search for your cute little button nose or your bright, beautiful eyes as easily as they can search their transaction records for your debit card number or the date of your last visit. For this reason, ATM could stand for Anonymity Taken from Me.

We know that that this statement is obvious, but we're amazed at the number of people who leave behind receipts and transaction records when they're using credit, debit, and ATM cards and ATMs. In case you're one of those people we stare at in disbelief, let us make the point here: What you're doing is dumb, dumb, dumb! If you look at your various credit card, debit and ATM receipts, you see that although they're inconsistent about how much information about you they reveal, they all contain some information you don't want other people to have.

GLB for you and me

On November 13, 2000, a new law governing the banking and financial services industry took effect. The Financial Services Modernization Act has become better known by the names of its three primary sponsors: Senator Phil Gramm, Congressperson James Leach, and Congressperson Thomas Bliley. The Gramm-Leach-Bliley Act (GLB) revamped the way banks, insurance companies, and other financial services firms do business. It also has some specific things to say about what companies can and cannot do with your personal and financial information.

Specifically, several provisions restrict when and how much of your private information they can disclose to nonaffiliated third parties, such as marketing companies. Financial institutions are also required to provide detailed notices to their customers about their information-collection and information-sharing practices. (That's why, around July 2001, when that part of the law took effect, everybody got a stack of privacy policies crammed in with their credit card statements.)

Most important for the average consumer, GLB requires that companies allow consumers to "opt out" if they don't want their information shared with nonaffiliated third parties. GLB also provides specific exceptions under which a financial institution may share customer information with a third party and the consumer may not opt out, such as for fraud investigations or credit bureau reporting.

For more information about your rights under GLB, you can check out these useful sites:

FTC Bureau of Consumer Protection — GLB Facts:
www.ftc.gov/privacy/glbact/glboutline.htm

Federal Reserve Bank of San Francisco:
www.frbsf.org/publications/banking/gramm

Financial Privacy: How to read your "opt-out" notices:
www.privacyrights.org/fs/fs24a-optout.htm

FDIC Guide to Financial Privacy:
www.fdic.gov/consumers/consumer/news/cnwin0001/NewRights.html

Direct deposit

Of all the ways you can *safely* move money around without having to touch it, direct deposit is the best. In case you haven't been gainfully employed in the past 25 years, *direct deposit* is a method of having your paycheck (or other regular payments, like annuities, bonuses, commission dividends, interest payments, and pensions) transferred directly to your bank or savings and loan without your having to dirty your hands with it or take the time to drive it all the way to the bank to make the deposit.

You have many good reasons to use direct deposit:

✔ **It's more confidential than a check:** No physical paper check is processed. From your place of work to your bank to the Federal Reserve where checks are processed and on to your company's bank, fewer people have access to information about you, where you work, and how much you earn.

✔ **Direct deposit has a proven track record of safety:** According to the Direct Deposit and Direct Payment Coalition, more than one billion direct deposit transactions worth $1.1 trillion dollars were made in the first half of 1998 alone, yet the organization claims that no payments made by direct deposit have ever been lost in the program's 25-year history. (If only we could say the same thing for our ability to keep track of our tickets for the dry cleaning.)

✔ **It's fast:** When you use direct deposit, you get access to the money on the same day — payday — which may be as many as four days sooner than if you were to take the check to the bank yourself.

For more information on direct deposit, see your employer or browser to www.directdeposit.org.

Direct payment

Otherwise known as automatic bill payment, automatic debit, electronic bill payment, or direct debit, *direct payment* (sometimes called ACH transfer) is the country cousin of direct deposit and is run and endorsed by the same folks. This method is different from paying by credit card, and even a little different from paying by your ATM card that has a credit card logo on it.

Should you use direct deposit?

John: I would if I could, but because I'm a free-lancing author rather than a normally employed guy, I have to look enviously at those who can use direct deposit.

Ray: Absolutely. In fact, some banks waive certain bank account fees if you have at least one payment per month directly deposited to your account. In years of getting paychecks deposited directly, I've never had a problem. I do recommend keeping your pay stubs or other direct deposit receipts in a safe place in case a problem arises.

Gregg: You bet. I buy into the notion that along with the convenience and faster access to my money, I also get some increased privacy protection. Meanwhile, for those who have concerns about electronic transfers in general: Get over it because this is just one — and certainly not the only — example of where your money is winging around the world electronically, whether you like it or not. Of course, you *must* keep your own paper trail (in a safe place, of course!) in case an error ever occurs.

AUTHOR SURVEY SEZ

"Should I use ATM, debit, and credit cards? Should I use ATMs?"

John: I use my ATM card as an ATM card at branches of my bank because it already knows who I am (but I know who it is too because it's a small bank), and at other banks when I travel (to avoid carrying lots of cash), and otherwise not at all. When I buy stuff, I use my credit card for the same reason Ray and Gregg do: I want those frequent-flyer miles.

Ray: I worry less about using my credit cards and ATM cards than I do about carrying around lots of cash on city streets. I seldom use my ATM and debit cards, though, preferring not to give anybody a direct line into my bank account. If somebody steals my credit card number and runs up a big charge, at least my car payment doesn't bounce! Besides, my credit card gives me frequent-flyer points. Woo-hoo!

Gregg: Because I'm deliberately a law abiding citizen and have nothing to hide, I don't worry about using an ATM card or ATM. Because I always pay my bills on time, I use a credit card and get an interest-free loan from my credit card company every month. I also get a free vacation every year because my credit card company gives me frequent-flyer miles every time I make a purchase. I recognize that I'm paying a price with my privacy for the "free" vacation and interest-free loan because my credit card company sells the information it gathers about me based on the purchases I make with my card, but I see the trade-off of my personal information for the loan and the miles as a fair economic trade-off. With all this in mind, however, I refuse to use a debit card. Again, it's a matter of economics. Why should I expose information about my personal shopping habits to my bank for nothing, when I can use a credit card to expose the same information and get the loan and the miles in return?

Direct payments are probably best described as check payments, but without the hassle of the paper. Direct payment systems usually make use of all the little numbers on the bottom of your check, including your account number and something called a *routing number,* which uniquely identifies which bank has your account.

Because a little paperwork is usually involved in setting up direct payments — which often includes providing a copy of a voided check (a blank check with the word *VOID* written all over it) — this method is most suitable for bills you pay at the same time every month and that are always for the same amount.

In Chapter 13, we talk about online bill-payment systems, services that help you organize your bills. Some even help you write and mail out checks when the time comes to pay. More and more are striking deals with companies to permit direct payments, but not everybody you send checks to each month is capable of accepting direct payments.

Should you use direct payment?

John: I do for three specific bills: VISA, cell phone, and electric. For the VISA bill, the reason is that they charge my account on the bill's due date so that I get the maximum float; the other two bills are small ones that I always forget to pay on time otherwise. It does help that I'm a compulsive sort of guy who always balances his checkbook and that my bank has a handy Web site where I can check to see what checks have cleared and *exactly* what my balance is.

Ray: I'm not a big fan of direct payments. I joined a health club back during law school, and they required it. As a poor law student, it was sometimes quite a struggle to keep enough balance

to cover the scheduled payments. Inevitably, I ended up spending at least one sleepless night balancing my checkbook and making sure that everything would clear. I don't like that pressure.

Gregg: Nope. In many ways, privacy is about control, and I refuse to give away control over how and when I spend my money. Every time I pay a bill, I am voting with my dollars — and I can withhold or delay my payment if I'm unhappy with the product or service I have received. I take the voting power of my dollars seriously and wouldn't want to lose sight or control of my economic vote.

Direct payment systems offer many of the same benefits as direct deposit — most notably, convenience and increased privacy because no paper trail and fewer humans are involved in the transaction.

The upside is that after you make arrangements to have your payment deducted from your bank account each month, you never have to think about it again. Naturally, we assume that you're vigilant about balancing your checkbook and keeping faithfully to your budget, never overspending. For those poor folks — with the emphasis on *poor* — who must ride their account balances like a knife edge, automatic debits can be the bane of their existence.

The bottom line: The convenience-versus-security debate

In the digital age, added convenience almost always brings with it increased security risks. Does that mean you shouldn't take advantage of the added convenience? That is a choice that only you can make after you understand and acknowledge the increased risk and accept it as part of the cost of the new convenience.

Using a wireless device to manage your money is riskier than using a standard landline to make those same transactions over the Internet, which is riskier than making the same transaction by telephone using a standard landline. In fact, no matter how you manage your money, some risk is involved. For example, you could lose your wallet on your way to the bank or be taken hostage by bank robbers while waiting in line for the next teller. It's really up to you to decide.

Banking By Phone

If Dick Tracy were a modern-day hero, would he be using his watch to transfer money from checking to savings? Or, would he play it safe and wait until he got back to headquarters so that he could use a good old-fashioned landline to call his bank?

If Dick were here, you know that he would be the first guy to consider the safety of his bank-by-phone options:

- ✔ **Cellular phone:** Rather than ask us whether banking via your cell phone is safe, ask poor Newt Gingrich what he thinks. As you may recall, in 1997 he was on a conference call in which another member of Congress, John Boehner, joined in by cell phone. The call was picked up by some Democrats with a scanner and released to the press. Could the same thing happen with your next call to the bank? That depends on how secure your cell phone is, how secure your wireless provider is, and whether you happen to be driving through an area with a high crime rate at the time you make the call. Although the cellular phone industry may tell you that, thanks to digital and PCS technology, security is no longer an issue, we disagree for this simple reason: What is secure today will be hacked or cracked tomorrow. Security is always an issue.

- ✔ **Cordless phone:** While you wander around the house, chatting with your best friend or your local banker on your cordless phone, others could be listening. A cordless phone is, after all, really just a glorified radio that sends a signal from the handset to the base unit, much like a radio tower sends a signal to the radio in your car. As with the cell phone industry, experts in the telephone industry can tell you that every year cordless phones get more and more secure. Of course, it's helpful for you only if you buy a new cordless phone every year. Meanwhile, it's only a matter of time before someone with enough technological know-how and motivation cracks the latest and greatest device of the day, which means that it's time to go shopping again!

- ✔ **Traditional landline telephone:** Now you're talking. If you have to do your banking over the phone, your safest bet is to cast all new gadgets aside and grab your old pink Princess phone.

What about Wireless? Managing Your Money By Cell Phone, Palm, and Pager

Sure, you can buy and sell stock, pay bills, and transfer money between accounts on your cell phone, Palm, or pager — but is it a smart thing to do?

Privacy is an issue because your wireless device is really just a radio. That's why no matter how hard the wireless industry tries to make its radio devices and services secure, the pirate mentality assures us that bad guys will always find a way to crack the code. The good news is, of course, that companies in the wireless industry are as motivated to continue keeping the wireless world safe as bad guys are motivated to figure out how to keep breaking in, so a delicate balance is continually being maintained between industry experts making new advances in privacy and security and bad guys trying to break the walls down.

If you decide to use wireless technology to manage your money, make sure that you follow these tips for the highest level of safety and security:

  ✔ **Check out the security of your wireless provider.** Start at its Web site, call its customer service line and ask lots of questions, and use the Web to find recent privacy stories about your provider.

  ✔ **Read up on your wireless device.** Start by asking about ratings at the store or Web site where you bought the device. Visit consumer rating Web sites, like `www.epinions.com`. Use the Web to do further searches.

  ✔ **Don't forget to look into the security of your bank and brokerage.** Again, a call to its customer service line and a search of the Web can tell you a great deal.

For additional information, you can also visit the Cellular Telecommunications Industry Association (CTIA) at `www.wow-com.com` and the Personal Communications Industry Association at `www.pcia.com`.

Credit Reporting in the Electronic Age

Thanks to the wonders of digital data collection and electronic communications, it's easier than ever for accurate and up-to-date information about your credit to make the rounds to all the folks who have a bona fide reason for wanting it, including creditors, landlords, and anyone else with a "legitimate business need." It's also easier than ever for incorrect information about you to make the rounds and for that same information to fall into the wrong hands.

What is a credit bureau?

Each of the three major credit bureaus (Experian, Equifax, and TransUnion) does the same thing: Collect financial information about consumers and make that information available to lenders and others with "legitimate business needs" to help them decide whether an applicant is a good credit risk.

They know who you are (or, "I see deadbeats")

When a credit bureau issues a report, it's a personal financial history of — guess who?

If you pay your bills on time, that information is in your credit report. If you don't pay your bills on time, that information is in your credit report. If someone at one of the credit agencies slips up and confuses you, the always-pay-your-bills-on-time John Smyth with John Smith who doesn't ever pay his bills on time, guess where it shows up?

Wait — we have more! Your credit report contains more than just your bill-paying history. It may also contain your Social Security number and your employment history, where you live, as well as the past and present balances of your bank and credit card accounts. It may even include information about liens, bankruptcies, and delinquent child-support payments.

"I want my rights!"

According to the Fair Credit Reporting Act (FCRA), certain information cannot be included in your credit report:

- ✔ Medical information unless you have given previous consent
- ✔ Negative credit information from more than ten years ago
- ✔ Information about debts more than seven years old

We don't dig into many of the specifics of FCRA (but you can find out more at www.ftc.gov/os/statutes/fcra.htm), although you have certain rights when it comes to reviewing and correcting the information in your credit report:

✔ **You have the right to know what's in your file:** In some states, you're legally entitled to a free copy of your credit report from each of the three big credit bureaus. Even if you're not entitled to a free copy, FCRA says that each bureau must provide you with a copy of your report for a minimal charge (usually about $8.50). You can find contact information for the three major credit bureaus in the following section.

✔ **You must be told if information in your report is being used against you:** In other words, if you're being denied credit because of something in your credit report, the person or organization denying you credit must tell why they're denying you and which bureau they used to check your credit. This rule allows you to follow up with the appropriate bureau to get a copy of your credit report and make corrections to the report, if necessary. If you're requesting your credit report because you've been denied credit, the bureau gives you the report for free.

✔ **You have the right to dispute information in your credit report:** Inaccurate information must be corrected or deleted, but lots of laws and loopholes exist to sometimes make it difficult to get credit bureaus to follow through with these corrections. Mistakes can happen — and re-happen — over and over again. For example, if the company that filed inaccurate information about you resubmits it to the credit bureau, you may wind up going through the entire correction process again. Of course, if a credit bureau violates your FCRA rights, you can sue the bureau in state or federal court. For more information on your rights, contact the Federal Trade Commission Consumer Response Center at www.ftc.gov/ftc/complaint.htm or 202-326-3761.

✔ **You have the right to opt out of, or remove yourself from, credit bureau mailing lists:** When credit bureaus aren't selling information about you in the form of credit reports to creditors, they're selling info about you in the form of mailing lists to marketers. You have the right to be removed from these lists for two years by contacting each of the three bureaus below at their toll-free numbers, or you can be removed from their mailing lists for life by calling the same number and requesting, and then returning, the appropriate written form.

Here's an ironic twist: If you get reams of preapproved credit card applications in the mail, it's sometimes a sign that you have good credit. In many cases, the banks that send these preapproved applications have bought lists of consumers with excellent credit from the same credit bureaus.

Here's an even more ironic twist: Several credit card companies specialize in offering high-interest credit cards to people whose credit is a little shaky. If you think that you've got good credit but you get lots of offers from Providian, a credit card company that specializes in high-interest cards, you may want to check your credit record to see what's going on there.

Checking your credit

Use the contact information at the end of this section to contact all three credit bureaus and order a copy of your credit report at least once a year.

Avoid services that offer to quickly "fix" your credit for a fee. If you have bad credit, you have no quick fixes. In many cases, these companies charge you money to contact the Big Three credit bureaus to notify them of any errors in your credit report, which you can do yourself and save your money.

In some cases, the "services" these companies provide aren't only things you can do yourself — they're *illegal*. For example, some companies recommend that you request a new Social Security number or an alternative tax ID number as the means to "repair" your credit. The problem is that trying to dodge your credit record by getting new numbers like these is illegal.

If you find that you still need help fixing your credit, contact a member agency of the nonprofit group National Foundation for Consumer Credit. To find the office nearest you, call 800-388-2227.

Be wary of services advertising on the radio and in newspapers that offer to provide you with all three credit reports for free. As you may have already read, however, nothing is truly for free, so a catch must be involved. In many cases, it's a way to hook you into an annual credit-watch service that is billed to your credit card 30 days after you get your free credit reports. The great minds running these services are assuming that by the time you get your credit card bill, you will have forgotten about signing up for the service and probably won't notice the charge there, anyway. Ironically, these services typically cost $39 to $69 per year, whereas you can get the same credit reports for about $25 by calling the Big Three credit bureaus yourself or visiting their Web sites for yourself.

Here's how to contact the big three credit bureaus:

- ✔ **Equifax:** 1-800-997-2493; www.equifax.com
- ✔ **Experian:** 1-888-EXPERIAN (888-397-3742); www.experian.com
- ✔ **Trans Union:** 1-800-888-4213; www.transunion.com

"I have my credit reports — now what?"

Take the time look over your credit reports carefully. At first, as Figure 14-1 shows (it's big!), a report may look like a jumble, but as you study it, it begins to make sense. You see information like your name and address, Social Security number, and employer. The report also lists all your credit accounts — from a car loan to a home mortgage or apartment lease to credit cards and bank accounts — as well as your payment history with each organization.

Confirm that each of the accounts listed in the report is legitimate. If you find accounts you have forgotten about or no longer use or never belonged to you, notify the credit bureau immediately so that it can correct your file.

Figure 14-1:
Part of a
sample
online credit
report.

Public Records ❓HELP

The information in this section comes from federal district bankruptcy records, state and county court records, tax liens and monetary judgments, and in some states, overdue child support records. Public records remain on your credit report for 7-10 years.

Plaintiff: **A-1 Home Loan**   Court: SF Muni Dist

Type of Record: Judgement	Reference Number: 436653
Amount: $ 1200	File Date: N/A
Asset: $ 0	Last Updated: Wed, Feb 19, 1992
Liability: $ 0	

Your Accounts ❓HELP

This section contains specific information on each account you've opened in the past. Positive information about your accounts remains on your report indefinitely.

Payment Legend

OK	30	60	90	120	PP	RF	CO
Current	30 Days Late	60 Days Late	90 Days Late	120+ Days Late	Payment Plan	Repossession or Foreclosure	Chargeoff or Collection

QUICKSORT Sort your Accounts by: [Select Your Inquires ▾] [SORT ◇] [SORT ◇]

There are 3 accounts on your report.

MOUNTAIN BK `ACCOUNT OPEN`

Account Number: 3562A0197325346R123453562A01973****		Balance Date:	May 17, 1996
Type of Business: Unknown		Balance:	$ 19330
Type of Account: Installment		Credit Limit:	$ 43225
Date Opened: Mar 1, 1993		Monthly Payment:	$ 956
		Past Due:	$ 956

24 Month Payment History ⊙ SHOW LEGEND

OK OK OK OK OK OK OK OK OK OK OK OK OK OK OK OK 30 OK PP RF 120 90 30
JUN JUL AUG SEP OCT NOV DEC JAN FEB MAR APR MAY JUN JUL AUG SEP OCT NOV DEC JAN FEB MAR APR MAY
1994 ▶   1995 ▶   1996 ▶

7 Year Payment History

30 30 Days Delinquent: 5 Times

BAY COMPANY `ACCOUNT OPEN`

Account Number:	65RR8****	Balance Date:	May 16, 1996
Type of Business:	Unknown	Balance:	$ 55
Type of Account:	Revolving	Credit Limit:	$ 1400
Date Opened:	Jan 1, 1968	Monthly Payment:	$ 10
		Past Due:	$ 0

24 Month Payment History ⊙ SHOW LEGEND

OK OK RF PP OK PP OK OK OK OK 30 60 OK OK OK RF OK OK OK PP RF PP RF OK
JUN JUL AUG SEP OCT NOV DEC JAN FEB MAR APR MAY JUN JUL AUG SEP OCT NOV DEC JAN FEB MAR APR MAY
1994 ▶   1995 ▶   1996 ▶

7 Year Payment History

30 30 Days Delinquent: 1 Time
60 60 Days Delinquent: 1 Time
90 90+ Days Delinquent: 1 Time

CREDIT AND COLLECTION `ACCOUNT CLOSED`

Account Number:	98E54318****	Balance Date:	Apr 5, 1996
Type of Business:	Unknown	Balance:	$ 050
Type of Account:	Installment	Credit Limit:	$ 500
Date Opened:	Sep 1, 1994	Monthly Payment:	$ 0
		Past Due:	$ 0

24 Month Payment History ⊙ SHOW LEGEND

OK OK OK OK OK OK OK OK OK OK OK OK OK OK OK OK OK OK OK OK OK OK OK OK
MAY JUN JUL AUG SEP OCT NOV DEC JAN FEB MAR APR MAY JUN JUL AUG SEP OCT NOV DEC JAN FEB MAR APR
1994 ▶   1995 ▶   1996 ▶

7 Year Payment History

OK Nothing Delinquent or Derogatory Reported

[Buy It Now!]

Secured by VeriSign   QUICK TO TRUST WEB

Home • **Credit Reports** • **Loans** • **Help** • **Security**
About Us • **Affiliate Program** • **Business Solutions** • **Sitemap**

© QSpace, Inc. 1996-2000 all rights reserved

If you find errors and report them to the bureau, be sure to create a paper trail of all your communications with it (follow up all telephone conversations, for example, with a letter sent by certified mail) so that if the bureau doesn't act on your request, you have a way to prove that you've already made the request. If a credit bureau doesn't amend its records, you can file a complaint with the Federal Trade Commission (FTC). If the situation is bad enough, you can even sue the credit bureau. (Don't hold your breath, though. The FTC has had ongoing suits against the credit bureaus for most of the past decade. Even in the midst of this situation, a commissioner of the FTC had trouble getting a home loan — because of errors on his credit file that one of the bureaus kept refusing to correct!)

Still, you should summon all your persistence and courage before tackling this list:

✔ Ask the bureau to notify everyone who has requested your credit report of this correction.

✔ If you find an error on one bureau's report, check the other two to see whether they've made the same error.

✔ Wait 60 days and then order another copy of your credit report to make sure that the correction was made.

✔ In six months, order *another* copy of your credit report to make sure that the same error hasn't slipped back into your file.

Here's an ironic twist: At least one credit bureau, Equifax, lets you pay $39.95 per year for the right to have it notify you every time an inquiry about your credit is made or a change in your file occurs. It's a nice idea, but one that gives you a false sense of security because you still don't know what's going on with your credit at the other two credit bureaus.

Try this smart move: Check your credit reports before you go out to buy a new house or car, or to rent a new apartment. That way, you can report to the credit bureaus any errors you find before they prevent you from getting the car or house or apartment of your dreams.

The Sam Spade connection

Just when you thought that you had heard enough bad news about credit reports and credit bureaus, a creepy new wrinkle gets tossed into the mix: Some companies that operate credit bureaus (for example, Equifax) also operate their own detective-like agencies that offer "investigative consumer reports." These reports include information about you that could be collected only by interviewing your neighbors, friends, and co-workers and by doing deep searches of public records databases that hold information about your driving record, education, court, and criminal records. Although these reports are governed by the same laws and rules as credit reports, they're clearly more invasive. Ironically, you have the right to correct misinformation about you in an investigative consumer report, but you don't necessarily have the right to know that the report exists.

The Identity Theft and Assumption Deterrence Act of 1998

The Identity Theft and Assumption Deterrence Act makes it a federal crime when someone "knowingly transfers or uses, without lawful authority, a means of identification of another person with the intent to commit, or to aid or abet, any unlawful activity that constitutes a violation of federal law, or that constitutes a felony under any applicable state or local law."

Note that under the Act, a name or Social Security number is considered a "means of identification" — and so is a credit card number, a cellular telephone electronic serial number, or any other piece of information that may be used alone or in conjunction with other information to identify a specific individual.

Your credit score and how one dot.com hero fought for your right to see it!

Or, "Who is Isaac, and who said he's Fair?"

Just when you thought that the system could get no more tipped against you, it's time to find out about credit scores (which are not to be confused with credit reports).

When you apply for a new loan or credit card or apartment lease, your would-be creditor gets a credit report about you, and that credit report includes a credit score that is a measurement of the probability that you will make your payments regularly and on time. As you can imagine, your credit score is the single most important piece of information contained in your credit report.

More often than not, your credit score, or *FICO* score, comes from a company named Fair Isaac. After you hear this story, though, we think that you will agree that Fair Isaac is anything but fair.

Because these Fair Isaac credit scores play such a significant role in one's ability to get a home loan, the online mortgage broker E-Loan decided in February 2000 to make these credit scores available to its customers and for free.

Everyone thought that this idea was a good one, except for Fair Isaac, which shut down E-Loan and refused to provide it with any more credit scores until it stopped giving the scores away to its customers. After a great deal of outcry, E-Loan led a successful lobbying effort in California to pass a state law requiring Fair Isaac to allow California consumers to see their FICO score.

You can find out more by visiting the E-Loan home page at www.eloan.com and clicking the Free Credit Reports Now Available button.

Equifax saw the handwriting on the wall and recently introduced Score Power, a service that permits consumers to purchase access to their FICO credit scores for $12.95. The other major credit bureaus are bitterly resisting efforts to force them to show you your FICO score.

Identity Theft: I Am Me — and So Are You

In one of the *Beverly Hills Cop* movies, Eddie Murphy lets go with a big laugh when he's accused of stealing a house: "A house? How can you steal a house?" he asks with a broad grin. Yet, to a thief who is accustomed to stealing cars and cameras and purses and wallets, a house must seem like the ultimate prize. After all, it's jam-packed full of valuable stuff he can sell, and it will keep him in business for a long, long time.

To the electronic thief, who is accustomed to stealing Social Security numbers and credit cards and cell phone numbers, your identity is similarly the grand prize. After all, it's also jam-packed full of valuable stuff he can fence and it will sustain him for a long, long time.

In most cases, identify theft begins with a single stolen piece of information: perhaps a credit card number, a Social Security number, or a driver's license number. The thief then uses that piece of ID to uncover other pieces of your identity and to create new pieces of ID and accounts in your name, including possibly a new driver's license, new credit cards, and a new cell phone.

If someone were to steal your house tomorrow, you would probably notice by tomorrow night that it was gone. Unfortunately, when someone steals your identity, it may not become obvious to you until most of the bills for your existing credit cards roll in, you start getting bills for new credit cards, and you're suddenly swamped with calls from creditors — new and old — who want to know why you aren't making your payments.

What are the odds?

The bad news is that identity theft is on the rise, and an estimated 500,000 victims are subjected to identity theft every year. The good news is that if you follow these guidelines, you can diminish the odds that it will happen to you.

Cop an attitude

The most valuable lesson you can learn about identity theft is that it's almost never personal. If you're a victim, it's not because someone was out to get *you*.

Instead, identity theft is often a crime of opportunity, and the perpetrator is out to find an easy mark — and for some reason or another, you looked like easy prey. The best way to avoid becoming a victim of identity theft is to develop the attitude that your personal information is too valuable to leave lying around everywhere, and certainly too valuable to be giving to every person who asks for it. If you keep the right attitude and have taken all the necessary precautions (like those listed in this section), you can reduce your chances of being taken for a ride.

Protect your driver's license number

No matter what the nice lady at the bank behind the new-accounts desk says, you should not have your driver's license printed on your personal checks.

Protect your Social Security number

Don't carry your Social Security card in your wallet. In fact, the best thing to do is to memorize your number and destroy (shred, burn, or eat) the card.

Don't include your Social Security number on your printed checks.

If your state offers the option of not making your driver's license number your Social Security number, take them up on it.

If your school or employer insists on using Social Security numbers as ID numbers or on identity badges, explain to them the danger of their policy and request that you be given a different ID number.

When asked for your Social Security number, question authority. Ask whether and why it's necessary. Resist giving your number, whenever possible. Except in the case of banks (which are required to file documents with the IRS), you have no obligation to disclose your Social Security number to any private company. John has made a point of not knowing it; "Duh?" as an answer to "What's your Social Security number?" is hard to argue with.

If your Social Security number is listed on your insurance and or other ID cards, carry a photocopy of the IDs with your Social Security number blacked out.

Protect your outgoing and incoming mail

Make sure that your mail is delivered to a locked post-office box or mailbox.

Don't leave outgoing mail in unlocked or unsecured mail drops.

Don't assume that your junk mail is junk to an identity thief. Shred all credit card offers and other junk mail that may contain sensitive information about you.

If you notice that you're not receiving as much mail as usual or you stop receiving your normal monthly bills, contact your post office immediately to make sure that someone hasn't filed a change of address card in your name.

Spy on yourself

Order and carefully examine copies of your credit report from the three major credit bureaus at least once a year (see the section "Checking your credit," earlier in this chapter).

If Identity Theft Happens to You

Act immediately!

- After you identify which pieces of your ID have been hijacked, contact the issuers immediately.

- Contact the three major credit bureaus:

  - Tell each bureau that you're the victim of identity theft and report your ID as stolen. Because you're the victim of identity theft, the three bureaus will each give you a copy of your credit report for free.

  - Ask all three credit bureaus to flag your file with a fraud alert and add a victim's statement to your file. This statement can be as simple as "Someone is using my ID to fraudulently apply for credit. Before new accounts can be opened, I must be contacted at <your phone number.>"

  - Ask all three credit bureaus to tell you the names and phone numbers of all creditors with whom fraudulent accounts have been opened. Contact each of these creditors to report the identity theft.

  - Ask each credit bureau to clear your file of all inquiries that have been generated as a result of the fraudulent use of your information.

  - Be sure to request and check your credit reports every few months to watch for new incidents of fraud.

- Report the identity theft to your local law enforcement agency. Insist on filing a written report.

- Monitor all other financial records (incoming mail, phone bills, credit card bills, and bank statements, for example) for signs of other fraud.

For the most up-to-date information on how to protect yourself against identity theft or what to do if it happens to you, visit www.privacyrights.org
and www.ftc.gov/bcp/conline/pubs/credit/idtheft.htm.

"What are my rights?"

Although the thought of Eddie Murphy stealing a house may be funny, nothing is funny about identity theft. In fact, it's against federal law as well as the
laws of many states to assume someone else's identity for the purpose of
committing fraud.

If you're a victim of identity theft, you may have to fight just as hard with
creditors and credit bureaus and law enforcement personnel as you have to
fight with the actual thief.

No matter what anyone may tell you, you have the following rights:

- As a victim of identity theft, you're entitled to receive free copies of your
  credit report on a regular basis from each of three large credit bureaus
  as the means to watch for new and ongoing incidents of fraud.

- Although some law enforcement agencies are reluctant to write reports
  about identity theft, you have the right as a victim of theft to get the
  crime on the books. In some rare cases, enough of a paper trail exists for
  police to track down the crook — but don't count on it.

- You're not required to pay any bills or cover any checks that have
  resulted from fraudulent use of your personal information. If any creditor,
  merchant, bank, or collection agency tries to coerce you into paying for
  something that you didn't buy or order, you should report the incident to
  1-877-FTC-HELP.

"Do I need a shredder?"

You know that privacy has gone mainstream when you walk into your local
Mega-Office-World-Warehouse-Superstore and you're greeted by wall of multi-
color, multifunction shedding machines, all priced at $19.99 or less.

But do you *really* need one?

Some may say that it depends on where you live, what kind of mail you get,
and what kinds of other paper cross your desk. Gregg, for example, lives a
simple life out in the country, and most of the mail he receives is addressed
to Occupant. He has difficulty imagining someone climbing the big ol' hill to
his house to sift through his garbage, and he has equal difficulty imagining a
stranger going down to his quaint little local dump (which they call an "envi-
ronmental park" in his part of the country) without being shooed away by a
big guy with a mean dog and a shotgun. Ray, on the other hand, lives in a

more dense urban setting and, as a lawyer, is always careful about destroying sensitive documents. John is the sewer commissioner in the village he lives in, so if he needs to shred something, he can always just take it along on his weekly rounds and throw it into the sludge.

Shredding the case against shredders (or, why you may never look at your junk mail the same way again)

What you don't know really can hurt you, especially when it's contained in those annoying preapproved credit card offers you get in the mail every day — which you always toss in the trash unopened. The problem is that almost one billion of these credit card applications were mailed to U.S. consumers during the second quarter of 2000 — and nothing can stop a bad person from digging the ones with your name on them out of the trash and submitting them *in your name but with the bad person's signature and address on the application.* Suddenly, someone else is walking around with a wallet full of credit cards in your name and with no intention of ever paying them off. Whose credit rating do you think will take the hit? Discarded credit card applications are a favorite tool for identity thieves, so don't make it any easier for them. The moral of the story: *Think before you toss, and when in doubt, shred it out.*

Lots of people get their mail sent to a post office box because they value their privacy, and then what do they do? They stand in the lobby of the post office and throw their junk mail into the official USPO recycling bin, where anyone who wants to can dig it out and put it to bad use.

Should you use a shredder?

John: Take it from the sewer commish: No matter where you live and how safe you think it is, you never know where the effluent of modern life — with your name and other important info — will end up. I shred stuff with personal info.

Ray: Of course. I even paid extra and got one of those fancy "crosscut" shredders that makes everything into tiny little flakes of paper. It's also handy for making confetti for surprise parties.

Gregg: Yup. If you're worried enough to want one, don't settle for the cheapest one in the store. Ask any professional snoop, and he'll tell you that the only shredder to buy is one that shreds your paper into little pieces rather than long, thin strips because those long, thin strips are a cinch to piece back together. The same professional snoop can also tell you that shredding stuff is the surest way to attract a professional snoop's attention. After all, if you went to the trouble to shred it, it *must* have been important, right?

Chapter 15

Your Telephone and Your Privacy

*I*f you're like us, you just love those old black-and-white movies that are on TV every Sunday afternoon, especially when they get to the part where the hero of the story is shouting over the phone, struggling to be heard over two old ladies gossiping on the town's only party line.

Most of us laugh when we see this stuff because we've never suffered the indignation of having a personal phone call monitored by everyone in town. Still, if those black-and-white movies leave you pining for the good old days, you'll be happy to know that many of your phone calls may not be as private as you think.

And You Thought That You Were Making a Personal Call?

Personal, schmersonal. The odds that your next phone call will be a purely personal affair between you and the party on the other end are diminishing. Why? Because hardly anyone uses a traditional landline telephone any more when we have so many other, more convenient or economical options — a cordless phone, a cellular phone, Internet telephony. We generally don't think about privacy when we pick up the phone because we've grown accustomed to thinking of a phone call (before cordless and cellular and Internet telephony came along) as a pretty safe bet. Meanwhile, even when you use a landline to make sure that the content of your call is private, the mere fact that you're using the phone reveals loads of personal information about you.

When it comes to privacy, how do the various telephones in your life stack up?

"How private is my cordless phone?"

Your cordless phone isn't private at all. In fact, it's not even a phone. It's a radio, and you're the DJ. For all you know, the entire world may be tuning in.

When you make a call, the handset you're holding up to your ear sends radio waves to the base unit, which is the telephone part of the deal. Depending on what type of cordless phone you have (analog, digital, 900MHz, 2.4 MHz, or some newfangled thing that has shown up in stores since we wrote this book), your conversation may be heard in a variety of ways (scanner, other cordless phones, interrupting the ballgame on your neighbor Grandpa Jones's radio, or pumped through the baby monitor to entertain the little Jones kids).

"How private is my cellular phone?"

Can your cell phone calls be heard over Grandpa Jones's radio? Probably not. On Baby Jones's baby monitor? Probably not. On a scanner from Radio Shack? You bet. Just ask Former Speaker of the House Newt Gingrich, who got in an awful lot of hot water after a conference call he was on that included another Congressperson on a cell phone was picked up by some Democrats with a scanner. Modern digital phones are considerably harder to snoop on than older analog phones, but it's still not out of the question.

"How private is my landline phone?"

Although a landline may be the best thing going when it comes to protecting the content of your calls, as a by-product they dish up a bunch of useful personal information about you for your local and long-distance phone companies; such as who you call, when you call, and who calls you. Oh, and those smart phone companies, they not only get to collect loads of information about you, but they're also always on the lookout for ways to make you pay them for that information or ways to make you pay to keep that information about yourself a secret from someone else.

Here are a few examples of products that demonstrate the phone company's ability to keep tabs on you and turn the information it collects into profit:

✔ You can pay for *Caller ID* and, like the phone company, you know who is calling you even before you pick up the phone — unless, of course, the person calling is smart enough to pay to use _Caller ID Blocking_ — which shouldn't bother you if you pay to have _Anonymous Call Rejection,_ which blocks anyone with Caller ID Blocking from reaching you.

✔ If the same annoying person keeps calling you but slips through the cracks of Caller ID, you can always pay for Call Screen, which allows you to manually block ten phone numbers from ever reaching you again. Before you get too excited about the prospect of blocking calls from annoying Aunt Martha in Florida for the rest of your life, you should know that at least with one California phone carrier, you can block only calls that originate from within your local service area.

Although Aunt Martha may be bad, she can't hold a candle to the human barker (who you suspect is really Uncle Albert, who looks just like a Chihuahua) who keeps calling you and growling like a dog. Even with Caller ID, Anonymous Call Rejection, and Call Screen, some calls (from some cell phones and from some businesses with multiple lines) _still_ slip through, and your heavy barker seems to be one of them. If you order Call Trace, it can immediately trace a call and report it to the appropriate law enforcement agency. Here are two little ironic twists, though: Call Trace works only if your barker is calling from a phone line that's able to send Caller ID and, even though you have to pay for Call Trace, neither the phone company nor your local law-enforcement official gives you the phone number from which these barking calls are being made. After all, for them to give you the number would be a violation of the human barker's privacy.

✔ If you want to know that it's your sweetie calling without having to run all the way across the room to cop a look at the Caller ID box, you can pay for _Priority Ringing,_ which gives a special ring every time she and nine of your other favorite people call.

What about Internet telephony?

Considering the popularity of anything that's _free,_ you're sure to hear more and more about Internet telephony in the years to come. As you may have read earlier in this book, free is often at the expense of your privacy.

Your phone records and the law

Bottom line: If your phone records (long distance, local phone service, cellular) are subpoenaed, you have nowhere to hide. This statement doesn't apply to just the al Qaida terrorists and the Oklahoma City bomber, but also to people involved in divorce, child custody, and other civil matters.

Should you use cordless and cellular phones and Internet telephony?

John: I'm with Gregg (see his opinion at the end of this sidebar). Most of what I say on the phone isn't particularly secret. For the stuff that is, I use a real phone.

Ray: I spent a little extra money and bought a cordless phone for home that has encryption between the handset and the base unit. It even has a Test button I can press to hear what you sound like encrypted. (It sounds like a human voice but garbled, a little like a George W. Bush press conference.) It won't stop somebody who really wants to hear your conversation (like the National Security Agency, which may be listening to me after that last crack), but it's more than enough to foil a snoopy neighbor. Unfortunately, you don't have many options for encrypting your cell phone conversations; although many cell phones are capable of it, most cellular systems in the United States don't use it. Still, the convenience of cellular phones outweighs the slight possibility that somebody may be listening when my other half calls me to remind me to pick up milk at the grocery store. As for Internet telephony, privacy issues aside, it's an awful lot of trouble to go to just to get a cheap phone call with sound quality only slightly better than soup cans and string. Unless you're making lots of calls internationally, you're better off getting a good "one-rate" cell phone plan or low-cost long-distance landline plan.

Gregg: Sure, why not? They're all wonderful tools for talking about last night's baseball game or what groceries you need to pick up on the way home from work or little Suzie's homework. When it's time to discuss your financial future with your accountant or use a credit card to order a bouquet of flowers for someone you love, your best bet is to use that good old-fashioned telephone that plugs directly into the wall.

Internet telephony now works something like this: You hook up a sound card and microphone to your computer and use special software to make free or nearly free calls to others. When you make a call using a landline, you get the whole line to yourself. When you make a call over the Internet, your voice is encoded digitally. Like all other things that travel over the Net, it's broken up into packets and sent on its way across a vast network where it can, theoretically, be intercepted and fall into the wrong hands.

Of course, the crazy, mixed-up jumble of connections that make up the Internet also works in your favor, making it difficult for all but the most determined people to sniff out the packets that comprise your call, assemble them, and intercept your treasured secrets. In fact, in some ways digital telephony is a little more complicated to intercept than plain old telephone service over copper wires. It used to be that all an eavesdropper needed was a pair of alligator clips. Now that person needs a double major in electrical engineering and computer science, a great deal of time and money, and a fair amount of luck. Even when you access the Internet and talk on the phone over the same line — like those lucky folks we know who live close enough to a telephone switching station to get DSL, it's all just packets of data moving across the wires.

Cellular Nightmares of the Near Future

As we say many times in this book, convenience often comes with privacy trade-offs. When it comes to the conveniences of a cellular phone, those trade-offs are multiplying quickly.

Because mobile phones are, by design, intended to be mobile, they're often the first on the scene of accidents, crimes, and other emergencies. Therefore, the federal government has mandated that by 2004 wireless providers must be able to pinpoint the location of a wireless 011 call to within 100 feet so that emergency calls can be immediately directed to the closest emergency call center. That plan is great when someone is trying to run you off the road, but the idea of your cell phone acting like a homing beacon creates the potential for a horrible invasion of your privacy during the other 99.9999999 percent of your life.

A cell phone that knows exactly where you are and everywhere you go has really become an annoying personal handheld homing device that is tracking and logging your every move as you wander through life. That's the *good* news. The bad news is that someone will get access to that data. "Who will that likely be?" you ask. Law enforcement, definitely. Advertisers, probably. Criminals, maybe. Take our word for it: Lots of people would do anything to get their hands on that information about you.

"Help! I'm being attacked by advertisers!"

For most of us law-abiding citizens, the worst part of the deal will be the assault by advertisers. As you drive into town around lunchtime, the local Italian restaurant may beep you to remind you that it's there. As you walk through a department store, a competing store may beep you to remind you that it's there. *Everywhere* you go, someone may be beeping you to tell you would be better off shopping or eating or buying or spending somewhere else. Is that really why you bought a cell phone and pay through the nose every month to use it?

Of course, advertising is relatively harmless. But there is an even darker side for a population that is being tracked. For example, if access to the tracking data falls into the wrong hands, criminals would know when you're away from your house. A stalker would always know where to find you. Your boss would know when you went to the ballpark rather than pitch a new client over lunch. Take a few moments to let your mind wander, and you will realize that the possibilities are grim — and endless.

Peek-a-boo, we see you

At the time this book was written, cell service providers were looking at providing the mandated E911 (Enhanced 911) service in one of two ways:

- **The good way:** Your service provider can install tracking software inside its own network, which relies on signal strength and mathematical formulae to pinpoint your location. From the consumer's perspective, this option is a safer alternative if you want to avoid walking through your day carrying a homing device and advertising channel in your pocket or purse.
- **The bad way:** Your provider can meet the E911 mandate by having GPS (global positioning system) technology put inside its phones. This technique is bad because it means that they will soon bombard you with ads trying to convince you that you need to upgrade to one of these new phones *and* tracking you and selling real-time geographic data about your whereabouts to advertisers or sending you ads themselves.

What can you do about it? We suggest that you check with your own provider to find out which method it uses. If the answer is the GPS-based system, it's time to scream loudly, slam down the phone, and change cellular providers.

Cell phone viruses

Here's some bad news: The first cell phone virus was unleashed in Spain in the summer of 2000. First, it attacked PCs and then ordered the infected computers to dial all the cell phone numbers in their address books to deliver a flaming text message about the Spanish telephone company Telefonica. So, really, it was a computer virus that just affected cell phones, and as far as computer viruses go, it was relatively harmless. It clearly raises the specter, though, of what a virus *could* do to your phone, like rack up thousands of dollars in fraudulent phone calls.

Now, the good news: It has happened only once, and the folks who make antivirus software aren't waiting for it to happen again. They're already developing products to combat future cell-phone viruses with the hope of getting them in stores before a real cell virus hits.

Yum! It's wireless spam!

Want to fight back? Let Congressman Rush Holt (D-New Jersey; www.house.gov/rholt; 202-225-5801) know that you support his efforts to make the sending of unsolicited advertising to cell phones against the law. Better yet, says Holt, let your own representatives in Congress know that you support the Holt bill so that everyone in Congress knows how important the bill is. If Holt has his way, offenders will be hit with a $500 fine for each piece of unsolicited mail they send.

Find your Congressperson: clerkweb.house.gov/mbrcmtee/members/housemem.htm

Find your Senator: www.senate.gov/senators/senator_by_state.cfm

Luckily, the people who run your cell phone service are concerned about spam as well, as are the people who want to make sure that you get ads and notices you're interested in seeing. The newly formed Mobile Marketing Association (www.mmaglobal.com) is hard at work on the problems. As its mission statement says: "Wireless advertising raises a whole new set of questions about privacy, spamming, location, revenue streams, media buying, sales training, and consumer awareness." Although no easy answers exist just yet, the good news is that folks like the Mobile Marketing Association know that if they annoy consumers too much, they lose any hope of making wireless advertising successful.

Short message service (SMS)

Think of SMS as an Instant Messenger or ICQ system for cell phone users; in other words, it lets you use your cell phone to send text messages to the cell phones of others. Of course, it won't be long until you can use SMS to send programs too, and that's where the potential for trouble lies because what's to stop someone from using SMS to spread a virus throughout the cellular world? The answer lies in the laws of economics: As SMS becomes more and more popular, antivirus companies will have an increased incentive to get an effective cell phone antivirus program on the market — hopefully, before an outbreak occurs.

We settle the debate: Is it safe to talk while driving under an overpass?

There was a time when, as you drove along the freeway talking on your phone, someone on the overpass above you could be stealing access to your cell phone account by grabbing your phone's mobile number and electronic serial number out of the air with a scanner or specially configured cell phone. These numbers could then be programmed into another cell phone, known as a *clone*.

If your phone was cloned, someone else would be making calls on your account and you wouldn't realize it until you got your next bill.

In 1996, more than $850 million worth of cloned phone calls were made. By 1999, the value of cloned phone calls in the United States dropped to $166 million because new technology made it harder to clone phones and easier for law enforcement to trace them.

But don't let yourself be lulled into a false sense of security. You should check your cell phone bill every month to make sure that all the calls are yours. If they're not, report to your cell phone provider, which should be willing to eliminate all legitimately fraudulent calls from your account without charge.

How to get a private hearing

Listen, we know that it happens: For whatever the reason, you've got to make (or take) a *private* phone call. You don't want anyone listening in — not your mother, your brother, your spouse, your boss, your best friend, your roommate, or your neighbor. You don't want the phone company to know whom you're talking to either!

What can you do? Stand at a pay phone and feed it quarters all night? Or go to the phone of your choice (pay phone, private phone — even your own phone) and make your phone call untraceable by paying for it with a disposable long-distance phone card, like the beautiful ones shown in Figure 15-1?

You can find these calling cards almost *anywhere,* from book stores to convenience stores, and as long as you don't pay for the card with a check, debit, or credit card, you can call anyone you want without leaving a telltale trail behind you. Remember that although nobody knows who buys a particular card, the card's vendor logs the calls and can identify all the calls made with a particular card, so if it can figure out that you made one of the calls, it knows that you made the rest of them. This strategy is one of the ways in which the FBI tracked down the Oklahoma City bombers.

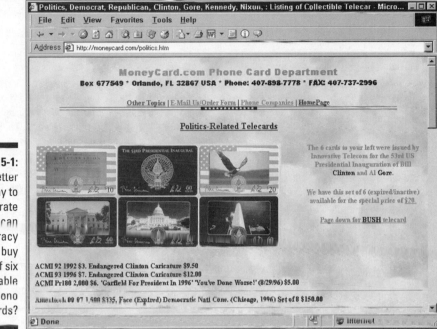

Figure 15-1:
What better way to celebrate American democracy than to buy a set of six collectable phono cards?

"But I Thought My Number Was Unlisted"

You may wonder why you continue to receive unsolicited telephone calls even though you have an unlisted number. One way those grubby telemarketers get your number is by using autodialers to call all numbers in a telephone exchange, or in a particular neighborhood. Those numbers are usually called in numerical order (555-0000, 555-0001, 555-0002, and so on), so they generally have no idea whether the number is listed, unlisted, or unpublished.

Unlisted? Unpublished? Or undecipherable?

Technically speaking, the Federal Communications Commission (FCC) distinguishes between unlisted and unpublished numbers. Unlisted and unpublished numbers are not listed in telephone directories; how-ever, unlisted numbers can be obtained from a directory assistance operator.

Unpublished numbers, however, cannot be obtained from a directory assistance operator. If the reason for the distinction makes any sense to you, please let us know — that is, if you can figure out how to get our phone numbers.

Privacy — and antiprivacy — laws you should know about

Many laws regulate telephone privacy, some more effectively than others.

Electronics Communications Privacy Act: If the Feds want to tap your phone, they can do it only after they demonstrate "probable cause" to a judge that certain specified felonies have been committed. If they receive a court order to tap a phone line, it's for a specified period (usually 30 days) and limits the surveillance to only communication that is related to the specified crimes. (In other words, they can record your calls to your bookie if that's relevant, but they can't write down what kind of pizza you ordered Saturday night.) On the state level, laws relating to wiretapping vary from state to state, but are fairly consistent with the federal law.

One-party consent provision: It may take two to tango, but it takes only one to agree to let the Feds listen in and tape a phone call. This law comes in particularly handy in cases where an informant has already squealed but none of the bad guys knows it yet. What's good for the Feds, though, is not good for the gander — just because they need the permission of only one party to monitor or tape a call doesn't mean that the same provision works for you.

Communications Assistance for Law Enforcement Act (CALEA): "If the FBI has its way, the only communications medium invulnerable to government snooping will consist of two soup cans and some string — and even then, I'd be careful."

Barry Steinhardt, the associate director of the ACLU, says:

"In the good old days, there was only one way to spy on someone's phone calls and that was to use a wiretap. Thanks to modern technology, though, all that has changed, and our friends the Feds want to be able to keep abreast of technology and not be limited to just wiretaps when it comes to monitoring phone calls. This law is controversial because the Feds want to not only expand their legal powers but also expand the definition of who, when, and where they can eavesdrop since digital technology will now let them do all kinds of things they couldn't do in the past. For example: In recent years, law enforcement agencies nationwide had court approval to wiretap about 850 phone lines a year. For you math wizards out there, that's about one wiretap for every 174,000 phone lines. Following the passage of CALEA, the FBI proposed a plan to Congress that would it allow the agency to eavesdrop on as many as 1,479,000 telephone conversations *at the same time*. Later developments under CALEA included the controversial Clipper chip, which, had it been approved, would have required manufacturers and service providers of any digital communication systems (telephone, fax, e-mail, Internet access, cell phones, wireless Internet access, wireless e-mail, and forms of communication that folks like us haven't even seen yet) to design all their equipment in such a way that the government could easily intercept, record, and read every digital communication (yes, that includes all phone calls, faxes, e-mails, and anything else you can think of that involves some form of electronic equipment), the idea of which strikes a devastating blow to personal privacy. Fortunately, Clipper went nowhere, but the snoops haven't given up."

As with any hot issue, CALEA always has late-breaking news. To keep abreast of the most recent developments, visit www.epic.org/privacy/wiretap.

How unlisted do you want your unlisted number to be?

Or, thank goodness for the power of voice-mail.

Here's one of life's little ironies that we love: You pay the phone company a couple of dollars every month to keep your phone number *out* of the phone book, and then what happens? You run around town dropping off laundry and ordering a cake and getting your shoes repaired, and the first thing they ask is "What's your phone number?" Without thinking about it, you give it to them, thus defeating the whole purpose of having it unlisted.

That's where the power of voice-mail comes in. It doesn't matter where or how you get it, as long as you get it with a separate number that people can call to leave you a message. You get to keep your privacy while the dry cleaner and the baker and the shoe-repair shop still have a way to reach you.

You can now get a *free* voice-mail number and account right over the Net. For more information, visit www.j2.com.

What it costs you to call toll-free numbers

When you call an 800, 888, 877, or 866 number, you think that it's free. Although it's true that you don't have to dip into your wallet or change purse to make the call, a toll-free call costs you a little bit of your privacy instead.

The downside of voice-mail

When you leave a message (duh!), you're leaving a message that is *recorded* somewhere — in your own voice and probably beginning with the phrase "Hi, this is <insert your name here>." In many cases, voice-mail systems allow one recipient to forward messages to one or every other voice-mail recipient on the system. At the least, when you leave someone a phone message, you make it easy for that person to hold a tape recorder to the phone and create a permanent record of the call. If you have something to say to someone that is personal, private, intimate, angry, stupid, or otherwise incriminating, say it to the person's face or say it while you have the person live and breathing at the other end of the phone, but don't leave it as a voice-mail message.

Party line at the phone company

Phone company employees can listen in to your phone calls just about whenever they want, as long as they're smart enough to claim when they're caught that they were doing it to monitor the quality of service or taking care of other official phone company business.

When you make a long-distance call from your own phone, you pay for the call. You're entitled and expect to see an itemized bill from the phone company at the end of every month detailing every call for which you're being charged. When you make a call to a tollfree number, *someone has to pay for the call,* even if it's not you. Whoever foots the bill for that call is, likewise, entitled to see a list of all charges and all numbers from which calls were received. Therefore, every time you call a tollfree number, your number gets recorded and reported to the company you called — and you have no way to stop it from happening. If you're concerned about keeping your private phone number private, you had better hoof it over to the nearest pay phone when it's time to make a tollfree call.

Could this phone line be tapped?

Sure, your phone line could be tapped. Anyone's line could be tapped, but most of us aren't running for office, don't wear polyester pinstripe suits with wide collars and hang out in New York's Little Italy, and don't manage a shady financial empire worth billions of dollars. For most of us, the reality is "Why would anyone bother?"

On the other hand, if you have a legitimate reason to be concerned, read on.

First of all, in Movieland the presence of clicking or noise on the line causes people to assume that their line is being tapped. Those movies are usually 30 or 40 years old. People don't dress like that any more, and they don't tap phones like that any more either. In reality, modern wiretapping technology is silent — so if you hear lots of noise on the line, you're better off pointing your finger at your local phone company and telling someone there to find you some phone wires not infested by squirrels.

Next, you have to understand that if your calls are being monitored, a wiretap is just one of two ways it can be done. Therefore, before we go any further, let's draw a distinction between wiretapping and electronic eavesdropping:

✔ Wiretapping, as you may guess, involves tapping into your telephone wire to listen to what is being said.

✔ Electronic eavesdropping, on the other hand, is a high-tech affair that uses an electronic transmitting device — and it has nothing to do with the phone wire that runs into your house — or what you do on the phone, for that matter.

If you think that your calls are being monitored (see how slick we are? — we said it in a way that includes both wiretaps and electronic eavesdropping), you want to take the following steps:

Call your local phone company and ask to have your line or lines inspected. In most cases, the company makes this inspection for free, so the only cost to you is the loss of pride as the service person looks at you funny and talks about you behind your back. If the person finds a wiretap, he checks to see whether it has been placed there *legally* — in other words, with the permission of the courts. (We talk about the legality of wiretaps in Chapter 17.) Of course, if it's a legal wiretap, the phone company probably helped put it there in the first place, and it probably is tapped at the phone company's central office, not at your house, so you're not much better informed. If the wiretap is *illegal,* someone will tell you what was found, notify the proper law enforcement personnel, and have it removed.

If, after you have had the phone company check your line, you still think that someone is monitoring your calls, it's time to call an electronics expert or private investigator who specializes in electronic surveillance. A good one probably can sweep (search) your house for listening devices that aren't necessarily connected to your phone.

Chapter 16

Protecting Your Privacy at Work

. . . .

In This Chapter

▶ How much privacy you have at work

▶ What you can keep private

▶ Workplace privacy in the real world

. . . .

*B*race yourself! This chapter is not intended for the happy-go-lucky or faint-of-heart. In fact, we probably even have stuck some things in here that are downright depressing.

Why?

Because the same laws and regulations that protect you against invasions of privacy by complete strangers barely do you any good when it comes to protecting your privacy at work. In fact, most work-related privacy issues end like most other job-related conflicts: The boss wins, and you lose. Meanwhile, short of strikes, worker rebellions, and Bolshevik revolutions, your company probably will continue to have the upper hand because, well, until we all get together and start screaming louder about our right to privacy at work, your company definitely has the legal upper hand.

Wait — there's still hope!

The good news is that as advances in technology make it easier and easier for *them* to monitor *you*, other advances make it easier for you to take back some control over your personal privacy, keeping your employer from listening to and watching your every move. In this chapter, we tell you about what companies are doing to take away your privacy and how you can use technology to get some of it back.

We even have some more good news for you: As you see in many cases, employers aren't half as sneaky as they want to think they are. If you follow our recommendations — and use some good old-fashioned common sense — you can run circles around those who think that *they have you* under their thumb.

Workplace Privacy? What Workplace Privacy?

"When it comes to privacy in the workplace, you don't have any." So says a recent story in *Business Week* magazine. And the writer of this article offers plenty of statistics to back his assertion. As he notes, an American Management Association survey of 2,133 corporations completed in 2000 reveals that

- 54 percent monitor employee Internet use.

- 38 percent monitor employee e-mail.

- 34 percent monitor employees using video surveillance.

- 30 percent monitor employee computer files.

- 11 percent monitor employee phone conversations.

- 7 percent monitor employee voice mail.

A follow-up study done by the American Management Association in 2001 shows that these numbers are dramatically on the rise; for example, the percentage of companies monitoring Internet use rose to 63 percent and the monitoring of e-mail rose to 47 percent.

If it's a privacy issue at work, it's probably not the *only* place where the issue arises. For that reason, almost all the privacy topics covered in this chapter appear in other chapters too.

Why employers do it

Believe it or not, you're not being monitored because your life is so much more interesting than your boss's (although we're certain that that's also true). Mostly, companies have three reasons that they listen, watch, and read over your shoulder all day long:

- They don't want anyone to steal from them (and we mean company secrets, not paperclips).

- They don't want to get sued (because, for example, if you get accused of sexual harassment for sending naughty e-mails or visiting naughty Web sites, the company gets into trouble too).

- They think that you should be working when you're at work.

Your company: Villain or victim?

In providing Internet access and services like e-mail, chat rooms, and bulletin boards, companies have also opened themselves up for a host of legal troubles. Along with the ability to work more efficiently — and to goof around a little — companies are now finding themselves blamed when nasty stuff comes pouring in over the wires. A case in point: sexual harassment.

In a landmark legal case, a female pilot for a major airline had complained about pornography posted in aircraft cockpits by her male colleagues. When word of her complaints got out, she was subjected to a great deal of harassment over the airline's employer-sponsored, private computer message boards. When she finally sued, a court in New Jersey held that although an employer isn't required to monitor what its employees say and do via a company-sponsored electronic forum, if it finds out about a pattern of harassment, it has a duty to crack down on the harassers.

In other cases, employees have complained that their co-workers sometimes leave pornographic images on their Web browsers or pass around sexually explicit jokes through office e-mail, creating a "hostile work environment" in violation of sexual harassment and gender discrimination laws.

However, some companies have chosen the "an ounce of prevention is worth a pound of cure" approach and have taken steps to stop the dirty stuff before it starts. Many companies have put filtering mechanisms on their e-mail to look for dirty words, and other companies have taken to blocking known pornographic Web sites. Still others haven't gone to such technological extremes, but have issued zero-tolerance policies regarding the use of office computers for anything inappropriate.

Unfortunately, some of these measures have resulted in confusion and in some cases have wound up creating problems for both innocent and not-so-innocent people. For example, in 1999, 23 employees of the *New York Times* were fired for trading dirty jokes over the office e-mail system. In numerous cases, innocent employees who were the unwilling recipients of pornographic junk e-mail have been accused of violating company policies about viewing these types of materials.

One particular case shows how zero-tolerance policies, combined with the workplace monitoring of Internet activity and some overzealous managers, can result in making the lives of innocent people miserable. In this all-too-typical example, a federal government employee in Texas received a piece of unsolicited e-mail that, when he opened the e-mail, launched a Web page. The page was filled with not only dirty pictures but also hidden programming code that caused new Web pages to be launched whenever you closed the browser window. This technique, called *mousetrapping,* can cause dozens of Web pages to open in rapid succession, sometimes requiring you to shut off the computer to be rid of it all. That's exactly what occurred in the case of the government employee in Texas. By the time he restarted his computer, though, his superiors already had in their hot little hands the logs of the dozens of Web pages he had allegedly been viewing.

The story does end happily, sort of. After weeks of the man having to fear for his job, the union representing employees in his office demanded a hearing and was able to demonstrate that the employee was a victim and not a porn-surfing pervert. Still, similar stories are pouring in from offices all over the world, and not everyone has the benefit of being defended by a union or even having the opportunity to defend themselves before zero tolerance sends them packing.

Be careful where you click because someone may be watching!

How employers do it

If you can think of it, companies are already out there doing it. They can archive all e-mail, actively monitor it in real-time, and block or flag messages that may contain inappropriate language.

They can also watch where you go on the Web, and use filters to prevent you from surfing to naughty or other "outlawed" sites (see Figure 16-1). Companies can listen in on your phone calls, log your phone use, listen to and record your voice-mail, and read your faxes.

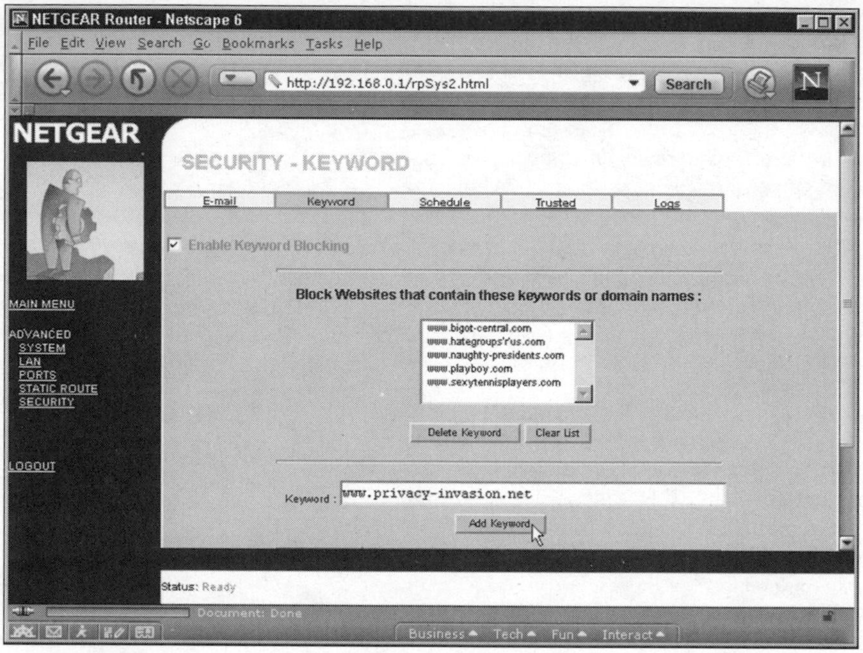

Figure 16-1:
A firewall/
router can
block
domains or
keywords
in domain
names.

Companies can even — and this should *really* frighten you — log how much time you spend working at your computer and even monitor your keystrokes as you make them so that if you write a foolishly furious and flaming e-mail to your boss — and then wisely decide not to send it — they could still have a record of it even though you clicked Delete rather than Send.

If you think that this scenario sounds frighteningly familiar to a spy program the FBI has been calling Magic Lantern, you're right. But one major difference exists between the FBI's Magic lantern program and a program an employer may use to monitor your keystrokes: The FBI is using its program to snoop on bad guys, but your employer is using its program to snoop on you.

Filtering follies

Some companies are so concerned about protecting themselves — and protecting their employees — that they do some goofy things. For example, Ray runs several e-mail discussion lists on Internet-related legal issues. After signing up for one of the lists, an attorney complained that the list was malfunctioning because he was getting only about one of every five messages being distributed. After some investigation, it turned out that the lawyer's firm was blocking all e-mail containing "bad words." Because no bad words were being used on the mailing list, what was triggering the filters? Further investigation revealed that this lawyer was missing out on almost every message concerning a controversial anti-pornography law because the firm had decided that even the word *pornography* was too racy for the eyes of its tender employees.

Your employer can also watch you with hidden cameras or cameras that are in full view or hide microphones around the office to eavesdrop on you.

Here's another point to ponder: How much information do you think that ID tag hanging around your neck is telling your employer about where you go and what you do all day long? Some ID tags are equipped with radio transponders that allow companies to track workers' movements around the office like biologists tracking herds of wildebeests on the Serengeti.

Privacy Rights — and Wrongs — at Work

When it comes to your privacy at work, you have certain rights — and so does your employer.

Their rights: Few laws on the books protect your privacy when it comes to employee monitoring, so your company can do pretty much anything it wants.

Your rights: Here are two you can count on, sort of:

- When employers monitor phone calls, they must stop listening at the point at which they realize it's a personal call. Watch out for this loophole, though: If you've been told not to make personal calls from work and then do it anyway, you're on your own.

- Employers can videotape you while you're in the bathroom, but not while you're in the stall.

Their right: Companies can make up the monitoring rules by which you, as an employee, must play. They also have the right to publicize those rules, or to keep them a secret so that you don't find out what the rules are until you get dressed down for violating them at your next annual review.

Your right: After an employer states the company's monitoring policy, you have the right to hold the company to it.

Know the Rules — and Play By Them

Even when the odds are stacked in the other guy's favor, you still get to choose between two options: Either give in or play to win!

We are absolutely *not* encouraging you to take advantage of your employer in any improper or illegal way. But we are encouraging you to

- ✔ Educate yourself about your general rights with respect to privacy at work and your employer's privacy policies, in particular.
- ✔ Educate yourself about your employer's right to, well, legally invade your privacy at work.
- ✔ Aggressively take full advantage of all privacy laws and regulations to protect your privacy at work.

 If your employer has well-established policies against tasks like using your office computer for certain activities or making personal calls from your desk, we recommend that you follow those policies. Like it or not, you're on the company's clock and using its resources, so you really do need to follow its rules, even when those policies treat you like a 3-year-old.

Our goal in this chapter is to help you deal with your employer if the company is monitoring you unfairly, if it hasn't been forthcoming about its privacy policy, or if the policy is so vaguely worded that you can't figure out what you can and cannot do without running the risk of violating the policy. Ultimately, like much of this book, this chapter is about preventing trouble before it happens.

Protecting Personal Employment Information

You go to work, you do your job, you go home. You know what you know about your company based on what you do in your job, gossip you hear from co-workers, and maybe what you read in the newspaper. But have you ever thought about what your employer knows about you?

Of course, your employer knows where you live. And it knows your phone number. And, if you use direct deposit, the company knows where you bank and your bank account number. Have you ever stopped to consider what else it knows about you? For example, your employer knows

- What kind of car you drive and your license plate number, if you have a parking permit. Depending on how your local department of motor vehicles is run, someone can get an awful lot of information about you with just your license plate number.

- All about your past jobs and where you went to school. Your company may even know your grades from high school or college.

- Your salary, Social Security number, marital status, number of dependents (and their ages and the gender of each one), and other Internal Revenue Service information.

- The name of your doctors and, depending on your health insurance provider, possibly even detailed information about the state of your health, your spouse's health, your children's health, and the health of your forebears.

- When you'll be going on vacation.

- Where you like to shop and eat if you submit an expense account report, particularly if you submit your credit card bill and don't mark out charges that don't pertain to the company.

- What you've been smoking or drinking, possibly, thanks to urine samples and drug testing.

Your company may even have some idea about what you're thinking and how your mind works from psychological, performance, and skills-assessment testing.

That's an awful lot of personal information — and we could even list much more, but our publisher doesn't want this book to look any more like the yellow pages than it already does.

The important thing to realize is that even though your company has all this personal information about you, few laws are in place to make sure that the company doesn't release information about you in a way that is sloppy or careless or simply violates your privacy.

To quote the book *Your Right To Privacy,* an American Civil Liberties Union handbook:

"Employers routinely disclose information about their employees to other employers, unions, law-enforcement agencies, and various other government agencies, banks and creditors, insurance companies, and private individuals. Some of these disclosures may be legally mandated or in compliance with the employee's own wishes; others may be offensive to his sense of privacy or may even cause him actual harm. Although most of the information disclosed by employers is job-related, some disclosures may reveal aspects of the employee's personal life, such as sexual orientation, political associations, or family problems. *Yet unless the circumstances are unusual, the private employer cannot be legally penalized for violating the employee's privacy.*"

We added the italics to the last sentence to make the point that your privacy at work now is anywhere other than in your own hands. You can't stop your company from doing what it's dead set on doing, and you can't force it to treat your personal information with greater care.

Ultimately, if your employer has taken its workplace-monitoring policies from the Stalin-era KGB or is storing employees' personal records in cardboard boxes out in an unlocked, dilapidated shed in the back parking lot, it's your decision about whether you would rather go on working for a company that treats your personal information in that way or start looking for a new job.

Real-World Privacy at Work

Yeah, we know that this is a book about electronic privacy, but in the case of workplace privacy, we think that it's important to address some offline issues too.

After reading about all the liberties employers can legally take with your electronic privacy, you may be left wondering about your privacy rights when it comes to your real-world existence at work: the inside of your office, cubicle, or workstation; the top of your desk; inside your desk drawers; or inside your briefcase. Here goes:

- **The inside of your office, cubicle, or workstation:** Excuse us, but who ever said that your office-cubicle-workstation is *yours?* Think again. It belongs to your employer; therefore, it's the employer's right to search it whenever it pleases.

- **The top of your desk:** Ditto. It's the company's desk, so it's the company's right to look at or search through those papers you've got piled up there.

- **The drawers of your desk:** Yup. The same concept applies, even if you keep your desk drawers locked. Who owns those drawers and the lock, after all?

- **Your appointment book or work log, in the drawer of your desk:** It's the company's desk, drawers, and even lock, so it's the company's right to read all work-related items you keep in your desk.

✔ **Your company locker:** This one is a hair more complicated, but only if you have the permission of your employer to put your *own* lock on the locker. Otherwise:

- An unlocked locker is the company's to search.

- A locker with a company-provided lock is the company's to search.

- A locker with your lock on it . . . changes the rules, based on the precedent set in the case *K-Mart Corporation Store No. 7441 v. Trotti*. Trotti worked at K-Mart. She was given a locker and, with the blessings of the company, locked her locker using her own lock. When some goods went missing from the store, someone from the company searched many of the employees' lockers (Trotti's included, although she wasn't a suspect), and Trotti sued. She won $8,000 in actual damages and $100,000 in exemplary damages for the invasion of her privacy; for, as the court ruled, she had the consent of the company to put her own lock on the locker and the company didn't ask for a copy of the key, so Trotti had a legitimate expectation of privacy with respect to her workplace locker.

Here's the moral of the story: If your company doesn't give you a locker, doesn't let you use your own lock, or lets you use your own lock only if you provide it with a key (which, we agree, is pointless), the best place to keep things you want to keep private is in the trunk of your car or in your briefcase, as we describe next.

✔ **Your briefcase:** If it's a company-provided briefcase or backpack or purse, you're on shaky ground. If it's a briefcase or backpack or purse that you can legitimately claim as your own and that contains your personal items, you may have a greater expectation of privacy. This situation can vary, however, based on state law and can also depend on whether you've already been informed that personal items are subject to search. You may also be subject to a search under other special circumstances. For example, if you're being fired or laid off, the company may also reasonably do a cursory search to make sure that you're not walking out with a boxload of office supplies or company secrets — but it probably isn't reasonable for someone to examine every shred of paper in your possession.

Now Is the Time: Take Back Your Privacy at Work

Let's be fair: Lots of companies recognize that their employees work long, hard hours and don't deserve to be watched like caged animals. If you're lucky, you work for one of those companies. If you don't, it's time to take action.

Be in the know

Before you can guard your privacy, you have to know what you're guarding it against. In other words, if you don't know your company's privacy policy, you had better find out.

The best way to find out if — and how — your company is monitoring you is to ask. Start with your boss, and if she doesn't give you a satisfactory answer (because she won't do it or doesn't know the answer), ask someone in human resources.

Watch out for vague or useless language in the monitoring policy. As Lewis Maltby, the president of the National Workrights Institute, points out: "A company that uses terms like 'reasonable' or 'inappropriate' may as well have no policy at all." If your company's policy doesn't make explicitly clear what is and isn't "reasonable" and "inappropriate," you should ask that it be more explicit and detailed and, if you can, get it in writing.

If you don't feel that your boss or the folks in human resources are sufficiently forthcoming about your company's privacy policy, do a little monitoring of your own, by asking the techies who manage your company's phone and computer systems what kind of monitoring is going on.

Take charge of your personal communications at work

Technology has made it easier for you to communicate with the outside world from work. Here are some tools you can arm yourself with:

✔ **A cell phone and a pack of cigarettes or a cup of coffee:** Get a phone with a vibrating alert so that the ring of incoming calls doesn't disturb your co-workers. Consider getting a phone and a cellular plan that includes caller ID so that you can see who is calling before answering the phone. Likewise, consider getting a phone that comes with voice-mail so that if you're away from your desk or can't take a call, the caller can leave you a message. If you receive a call and it's important that you take it — but you feel awkward about talking on a cell phone in the workplace — answer the phone by saying "Please hold" and press the phone's Mute button (if it has one). Then grab a cup of coffee and go outside for a little coffee break (as long you're allowed to take a break). After you're in a safe place, take the call. Gregg and Ray once worked together at a company in Silicon Valley where it was common to see five or ten people at a time pacing around the parking lot with cell phones held up to their ears.

✔ **A pager:** Today's pagers offer you the ability to receive as little or as much information as you need. Some simply relay the phone number of a caller, and others notify you that you have received a voice-mail message on your personal (not an employer-owned or -monitored) voice-mail system. Even more sophisticated pagers can send and receive text messages and even e-mail.

Be careful how you return calls after you're paged. If you use the office phone system to return calls, you leave yourself open to be monitored again!

✔ **A Palm or other PDA:** A variety of wireless devices and cell phones make it possible for you to receive e-mail and to do some limited Web surfing on your own personal handheld device.

✔ **Web based e-mail:** Free e-mail accounts from Yahoo! or Hotmail enable you to send and receive personal e-mail without using the company's e-mail server. However, be warned that using one of these Web-based systems doesn't guarantee that your employer isn't reading these e-mails, anyway. After all, Web-based e-mail is just like all other Internet content: In other words, your company can easily monitor it if it chooses to do so. However, if you use a free, encrypted, Web-based e-mail system like the one offered by ZipLip (www.ziplip.com), you can send and receive e-mail that may be monitored but cannot be deciphered by your employer. You can read more about Web-based e-mail in Chapter 10.

✔ **Anonymous Web surfing:** Using online products like Anonymizer (www.anonymizer.com), you can surf the Web without revealing to your employer where you have been. (See Chapter 9 for more information about anonymous browsing.) Be aware however, that some companies don't allow you to download the software necessary to use these privacy tools and even if you can use one of these tools at work, it may create other problems for you. After all, even though your employer can't see where you're surfing, he can still see that you're surfing somewhere using anonymizing software, which may raise additional red flags about your Internet use.

Watch your back

Even if you're doing everything you can to faithfully follow the company's privacy rules, the following tips can help you avoid potential misunderstandings.

Beware of spam in your e-mailbox. In Chapters 11 and 22, we teach you how to fight back against spammers by tracking down spam and filing complaints. But lots of spam contains pornographic images and mysterious Web links that lead to all sorts of unsavory things. As you deal with spam at work, ask yourself how the contents of the spam you receive would reflect on you if your employer were monitoring your e-mail and Web usage. If the spam you're getting gives you cause for concern, alert both your company's network administrator and your human resources office to the fact that you're receiving the offensive e-mail and get it on the record that this inappropriate material is being delivered to your mailbox through no effort or fault of your own. By doing this, you're creating a paper trail that may be more of a lifeline at some point down the road, and you may also be encouraging them to put antispam systems in place on the company network.

Several excellent spam-blocking services are free or low-cost for businesses and Internet Service Providers. One service that John and Ray are familiar with is MAPS, the Mail Abuse Prevention System. (MAPS also happens to be *spam* spelled backward!) Your systems administrator can find out more information about MAPS' spam-blocking services at www.mail-abuse.org.

Think twice before clicking Send. As you may have read in Chapter 10 (about e-mail privacy) and Chapter 11 (about tracing spam), anything you send via e-mail may be archived and easily traced, so it can easily come back to haunt you later. If you wouldn't be comfortable posting an e-mail message on the bulletin board in the lunch room for everyone to read, don't send it through your company's e-mail. If you do have to send an e-mail message from work that you wouldn't want the whole world to see, consider using one of the free e-mail services — with or without encryption — that we discuss in Chapter 10.

Think twice before you dial. As we say elsewhere in this chapter, you have plenty of alternatives to carrying out personal business on your company's phone. Emergencies not withstanding, use a cell phone or a pay phone or wait until you get home.

Erase the Redial button. If you've just made a call from your work phone that you wouldn't want anyone else to know about, make sure that you clear the phone number from your phone's Last Number Redial memory by hanging up the phone at the end of the call and then picking it up again and dialing a single digit. This technique erases the sensitive number from the phone's Redial memory and puts the single digit into memory instead.

Wipe your Web slate clean. If you've been doing some Web surfing at work that isn't strictly work-related, you've left a trail of information in your Web browser's History file. Although your company still has several ways track your Web surfing without even touching your computer, why not make things a little harder for it by cleaning out your History file?

- ✔ In most versions of Microsoft Internet Explorer, choose Tools⇨Internet Options from the menu bar. Click on the General tab. Click on both the Delete Files and Clear History buttons.

- ✔ For recent versions of Netscape Navigator, choose Edit⇨Preferences from the menu bar. From the Category menu, double-click on Advanced to display the subcategory list. Choose Cache; in the window to the right, click both Clear Memory Cache and Clear Disk Cache.

For additional instructions on using your browser's privacy settings, see Chapter 9.

The essence of workplace privacy

Think of the advice in this section as the ultimate, universal, one-size-fits-all, always-works-in-a-pinch, can't-go-wrong rules for protecting your privacy at work. Of course, no set of guidelines can replace good old-fashioned common sense.

When in doubt, remember that your personal business is your personal business — and that you have the right to keep it personal, if you choose. With that in mind, always remember that your best bet is to save your personal business for home, your lunch break, a coffee break, or any other time that the company can't claim as its own.

However, if you do choose to handle personal business at work, keep these two rules of thumb in mind at all times:

- ✔ You'll never be surprised by unexpected consequences if you always proceed by expecting the worst and praying for the best.

- ✔ Always assume that someone is peering over your shoulder, even if he has clearly and unequivocally said that he isn't and he wouldn't.

Chapter 17

The Government Is Here to Help — or Not

*L*ots of people think that they have privacy rights that simply don't exist in law the way they think they do. And when those same people find out what the law *really* says about the ways in which it really protects them — or not — they're stunned.

That's why we have agreed to indulge Ray (he's the one with the law degree, remember?) and let him have an entire chapter devoted to privacy, the laws, and the government.

> *If I had a nickel for every time somebody said "That's a violation of the Privacy Act," I could have retired by now.*

— Ray Everett-Church, big shot privacy lawyer and newly famous author

Disclaimer: You can spend years in law school and only scratch the surface of privacy issues, so please don't rely on this chapter for definitive legal advice. Privacy laws change all the time and vary from state to state, so the only one who can really give you precise advice for your particular set of circumstances is a qualified attorney. If you think that your legal rights have been infringed, contact your local bar association and ask for a list of attorneys in your area who specialize in privacy law.

From Bearskins to Brandeis to Browsers

For most of the time in which humans have been on this planet, we have lived in small communities where everybody knows everybody else, and it has been difficult to keep any secrets. We lived that way for thousands of years, perfecting inventions that have become integral to our concept of what it means to be civilized, including

- ✔ Clothes
- ✔ Walls
- ✔ Fences
- ✔ Doors with locks
- ✔ Windows with curtains

These items may have been invented for practical reasons, like clothes that kept our prehistoric ancestors from freezing or getting scratched by brambles while chasing after their dinner, walls that kept out bitter winds, and locked gates that kept barbarian hordes out of the front parlor.

We don't tend to think of these elements as amazing technologies any more. For example, how many times each day do you contemplate the sheer genius of the door? It isn't as exciting as the Internet, that's for sure. But if you stop and think about it, some of those technologies have been so important to humanity that they have shaped the very way we live and think about ourselves and others.

A by-product of all these clothes, walls, and locks is a fairly fundamental idea shared by most of our species, and it just so happens to be the central principle of this book: Some things are just none of your neighbor's business!

It's a concept that your ancient ancestor Og probably never had in mind when he first covered up the family jewels with a bearskin. Practical guy that he was, Og was probably just trying to stay warm, but his action set into motion a chain of events that would inevitably lead three goofy computer guys to write a little yellow book about a concept that was born in the harsh practicality of Og's cave many thousands of years ago.

Privacy: Not Such a New Idea

Thanks to Og and the rest of our ancestors, most of us think that it's a good idea not to have all our body parts, our most personal of personal activities, and our possessions available for inspection by the world. In fact, we have thought this way for so long that, at least in the past few centuries, some of us have come to think of privacy as more than an interesting by-product of civilization; we have come to demand privacy as a fundamental human right that is linked to our very existence.

Unfortunately for us, a few of today's newer technologies seem to be running headlong into conflict with the privacy that saw its birth from some of those older technologies, like walls and doors. If there's good news in this situation, though, it's that these conflicts aren't exactly something new. To prove our point, we offer the following quote from an academic journal, in which two really smart guys recognized the impact of new technologies on privacy:

> *The intensity and complexity of life, attendant upon advancing civilization, have rendered necessary some retreat from the world, and man, under the refining influence of culture, has become more sensitive to publicity, so that solitude and privacy have become more essential to the individual; but modern enterprise and invention have, through invasions upon his privacy, subjected him to mental pain and distress, far greater than could be inflicted by mere bodily injury.*

— Samuel D. Warren and Louis D. Brandeis, *Harvard Law Review* (1890)

What do you mean, 1890? If those learned scholars thought that things were bad in 1890, can you imagine what kind of panic they would be in today?

Fortunately for us, they were forward-thinking dudes. Many years later, that Brandeis fellow would write some of the most important words about privacy since America's founding fathers sat down to write a constitution. Unfortunately, our founding fathers (you know — Thomas Jefferson and Ben Franklin and all those other heavy thinkers from the 1700s) didn't appear to have privacy on their minds when they put quill to parchment, but as you see shortly, some folks think that they did.

Interestingly enough, in the same year that Warren and Brandeis wrote their article, an amazing and revolutionary new communications technology was patented by George Parker: the fountain pen!

Rude awakenings

It's a funny thing about human beings. Many people, in many places and cultures around the world, seem to think that we have a "right" to privacy as though it were a universal irrevocable law of nature, like gravity.

In America, the land of the free and the home of the brave, we don't just think that we have fundamental rights — we know it! Just travel down to Washington, D.C., crack open a glass case at the National Archives, and see the big piece of paper called the Bill of Rights. It guarantees that you can

- ✔ Say what you want.
- ✔ Hang out with whomever you want.

✔ Keep soldiers from sleeping on your couch.

✔ Tote your gun.

✔ Attend the church of your choice.

✔ Cuss at the tax man.

✔ Return to the privacy of your home.

✔ Do whatever you, as a consenting adult, feel like doing behind closed doors.

The problem is that when it comes to our privacy, it's not nearly that cut-and-dried. Surprisingly, when it comes to a constitutional right to privacy, the word *privacy* doesn't even appear in the U.S. Constitution.

Privacy and the U.S. Constitution

Even though you don't find the word *privacy* in the Constitution, that hasn't stopped the Supreme Court from saying that, like the spaghetti sauce ad, "It's in there!"

Here are some of the things that point to the fact that privacy is there, at least in spirit, if not in exact words:

✔ The First Amendment of the Constitution contains the right of free speech, which has been read to include the right to speak anonymously. The free-speech right has also been interpreted in reverse: You have the right to not be forced to say certain things.

✔ The First Amendment also contains the right of free association, which means that you can join clubs and affiliate yourself with anyone you choose (as long as you're not doing so for purposes of breaking the law). Inherent in that right, according to the court, is the right not to say whom you're associating with. If you have a club, you don't have to turn over a membership list to the government.

✔ The Fourth Amendment prohibits the government from searching your home and property and from seizing your papers or possessions, except under very specific circumstances. The Fourth Amendment has also been read to give certain rights against government wiretaps and surveillance.

✔ The Fifth Amendment includes various rights of *due process,* which means that if the government is interested in depriving you of any of your rights — throwing you in jail, for example — it must first follow strict procedures designed to protect your rights. Among those is the right against being forced to incriminate yourself.

> ✔ The equal protection clause of the Fourteenth Amendment requires that everyone of both sexes, all races, and all religions be given equal protection under all the laws of the United States and all the laws of every state. This protection includes amendments that may otherwise allow you to exclude certain classes of people under claims of privacy rights.

It was from these kinds of ideas that, when faced with the question of whether the Constitution gave citizens an expectation of privacy, our old friend Mr. Brandeis — who became a Supreme Court Justice in 1916 — penned some of the most important words ever written about the way Americans look at privacy:

> *The makers of our Constitution undertook to secure conditions favorable to the pursuit of happiness. They recognized the significance of man's spiritual nature, of his feelings and of his intellect. They knew that only a part of the pain, pleasure and satisfactions of life are to be found in material things. They sought to protect Americans in their beliefs, their thoughts, their emotions, and their sensations. They conferred, as against the Government, the right to be let alone — the most comprehensive of rights and the right most valued by civilized men.*
>
> — Brandeis dissent in *Olmstead v. United States*, 277 U.S. 438, 478 (1928)

The case of *Olmstead v. United States* involved the government prosecution of liquor smugglers during the time of Prohibition. The government tapped the phone lines of the smugglers, who were subsequently arrested. The court held that tapping the phone lines wasn't a search or seizure as contemplated by the Fourth Amendment and therefore didn't need a warrant. The message of Justice Brandeis's powerful dissent took nearly 40 years to sink in, but in the 1967 wiretapping case *Katz v. United States*, the court finally rejected the theory from *Olmstead* and gave Americans greater privacy protections by requiring the government to show cause and obtain a warrant before installing a wiretap.

The following links lead you to two court cases that show the evolution of wiretap privacy:

- ✔ **Olmstead v. United States:** In 1928, it ain't a "search and seizure" unless they walk through your door (`laws.findlaw.com/us/277/438.html`).
- ✔ **Katz v. United States:** In 1967, tapping the wires of a phone booth requires a judge-issued warrant (`laws.findlaw.com/us/389/347.html`).

Brandeis's phrase, "the right to be let alone," is one of the most often-repeated ideas in privacy, even by people who have never heard of Justice Brandeis. More importantly, those words drove courts to start looking beyond the plain words of the Bill of Rights to find other privacy rights that are logical extensions of what's written in the original document. Those rights include

- Special privacy privileges for statements made to your spouse, your doctor, and your priest

- The right to control your own body without undue interference from the government, including the right to obtain and use birth control, the right (for now) to an abortion, and the right to refuse medical treatment for yourself

- The right to keep obscene materials in your home

But these rights aren't absolute, for these reasons:

- The government can still set up wiretaps and surveillance and do searches and seizures if they have the reasonable belief *(probable cause)* that a crime has been committed and if given permission (a *warrant*) by a judge. In Chapter 10, we talk about Carnivore, the FBI's tool for wire-tapping e-mail and other digital data.

- The government can do secret wiretaps and surveillance, and even secretly search your home and car, without a normal judge's warrant, if you're suspected of being an "agent of a foreign power" (or a spy or even a friend of a suspected spy!). In Chapter 10, we also talk about how the global conspiracy named Echelon is hard at work looking for spies by listening to every phone call you make, every letter you fax, and every e-mail you send!

- You don't have a right to engage in certain sexual activities, even if they're between consenting adults in the privacy of your own bedroom.

- You don't have a right to keep certain illegal materials in your home, such as drugs or child pornography.

- If you're being chased by the police and run into your house, they can enter without a warrant.

- Certain public organizations (like the Jaycees, which was the subject of a lawsuit that established this precedent) can't use their First Amendment right of free association to exclude protected classes of people, such as women or certain minorities. On the other hand, at the time this book was written, the Boy Scouts could still discriminate against gay people.

- After you set foot on the street, your movements can be monitored and your face can be photographed for comparison to databases of known felons.

But the Constitution covers only privacy issues involving the government. What are your rights against people who aren't part of the government, such as individuals and corporations? That's where a patchwork of common-law rights comes into play, as we describe in the next section.

Common law privacy

The *common law* is nothing more than a set of rights and obligations first recognized by courts rather than by legislatures.

Perhaps you have never thought about the difference between law mandated by courts and law mandated by legislatures. This section describes the difference between the two.

Legislatures in nearly every country write, rewrite, debate, and occasionally get into fistfights over laws. In the United States, we call our national legislative body the Congress, which is made up of the Senate and the House of Representatives. When a legislative body creates a new law (using whatever procedures are required by its governmental system), that law goes into a big shelf full of books that contains all the laws of that government. After it goes into the book, Congress' involvement ends, unless, of course, they decide to rewrite it later.

Courts are then called on to interpret the laws. As you may imagine, sometimes legislators don't foresee every possible consequence of the laws they write. In the United States, the job of the courts is to say what the law really means. This task often requires the courts to look back at what the legislators argued about, to see what their *intent* was in drafting a certain provision in a certain way. Sometimes, if the answer isn't clear, the court must make an educated guess. In the United States, laws can get interpreted and reinterpreted by one higher court after another, but the buck stops after a law reaches the United States Supreme Court and it hands down an opinion — unless the legislature disagrees with the court's interpretation. If Congress doesn't like the decision, it can usually go back and rewrite the law to make its position more clear. Until then, what a court says that the law means is what gets enforced.

Common law is more than a patchwork — it's a massive quilt made up of tons of legal ideas that have been the product of literally hundreds of years of courts trying to settle disputes between people. Much of it is a product of the English court system, and common law has the most influence in courts in the United States, Canada, Australia, and other nations where the British Empire once ruled or had influence. (Other countries use a different system, which we get to in a moment.)

Just because its "judge-made" law, though, don't discount the common law as being less useful. In fact, many common-law rights have been enforced for centuries and are some of the most powerful precedents in our legal system. They're rarely overturned by legislatures, and many state and federal laws are simply codifications of common-law ideas that have been around for hundreds of years.

Practically on a daily basis, modern courts hand down decisions that cite common-law precedents from sometimes as far back as the Middle Ages. Back in the medieval times, all "official" documents were written by the only people who knew how to write — monks and priests — who wrote everything in Latin. That's why so many legal terms are in Latin. And you thought that lawyers just liked to talk in code!

When you violate something in the common law, it's not called a crime; it's called a tort. *Tort* comes from the medieval Latin word *tortum,* which means to twist or to break, as in breaking a law. (Look at how this Latin stuff works its way into everything!) Much of the common law has analogues in criminal laws, such as assault, battery, and trespass. But you can't be thrown in jail for committing a tort. You can, however, be punished by being ordered to pay money in compensation.

O.J. Simpson was acquitted of criminal murder, but was later sued under the common-law equivalent of *wrongful death.* As we all know, he lost big-time.

Slicing up the privacy torts

When Ray was in law school, he studied with a noted privacy law scholar, Professor Robert Park. Professor Park had a novel way of organizing the patchwork of privacy laws into four broad categories, under which a whole bunch of specific legal actions could fall. Many of these actions are closely related, although they put a slightly different spin on similar situations. Putting them into this framework is an excellent way of seeing how similar ideas about privacy affect people in different ways:

Respect for your personal space and physical security

- ✔ **Assault:** Threatening to cause physical harm

- ✔ **Battery:** Causing physical harm

- ✔ **Intentional infliction of emotional distress:** Doing something that you know will be found disturbing, such as stalking or harassing someone or showing autopsy photos of a loved one to the grieving family

Respect for your private places

> ✔ **Trespass:** Invading private property
>
> ✔ **Nuisance:** Causing disturbances

Respect for your dignity

> ✔ **Intrusion:** Invading someone's privacy through snooping, eavesdropping, peeping, or secret cameras, for example
>
> ✔ **Appropriation:** Using someone's name or picture for something not authorized, including using a lookalike to endorse a product
>
> ✔ **False light:** Publicizing information that — whether it's true or false — causes wrong conclusions to be made; for example, posing for artistic nude photos that are later published in a trashy magazine that describes them as being scenes of incest

Respect for your personal potential

> ✔ **Defamation:** Harming someone's reputation by telling lies about that person
>
> ✔ **Disclosure of private facts:** Disclosing information that may be true, but that you have no right to publicize; for example, sneaking a peek at somebody's medical file when you have no right to be looking and then calling that person's employer or the news media to blab to the world about the medical condition
>
> ✔ **Interference with business relations:** Trying to smear someone's reputation with current or future employers, for example, even if the embarrassing facts are true; such as calling someone's employer and relating that the person engages in kinky sex acts in the privacy of their own bedroom

Under today's common law system, when you feel that your privacy has been invaded by another private party, you can bring a lawsuit. But it had better fit, more or less, into one of these categories if you expect to win — unless you can find on the books a law that gives you something better to pin your hopes on. That's where the common law ends and laws written by legislatures come into play.

Privacy laws around the world

The alternative to common law is *civil law,* a concept that grew out of the Napoleonic code in France. Many countries, including much of continental

Europe, are called *civil law* countries, where everything is written into legislature-approved laws. In civil law countries, if it ain't in the book, it ain't law.

In many parts of the world, privacy has been written into law for many years. Many countries have strict laws protecting medical records, financial information, and even court proceedings. In Europe, a person's right to privacy even extends to any records gathered by private companies containing information about

- ✔ Race
- ✔ Religious affiliation
- ✔ Membership in political parties and trade unions
- ✔ Criminal records

These topics are of particular concern to Europeans, in part because of how records containing information about race, religion, and trade union memberships were gathered and used by the Nazi regime in Germany and its occupied countries to decide who should be shipped off to concentration camps. For Europeans, the threat of private information being misused is more than a test of wills between smarmy marketers and tired consumers, but meant the difference between life and death for the parents and grandparents of many of today's European lawmakers.

These concerns have resulted in European countries having some of the strictest data privacy laws in the world. They include a data privacy directive that mandates the following minimum standards in all countries that are members of the European Union:

- ✔ Companies can collect only the information needed to complete transactions and must delete it after the transactions are over, unless they have explicit permission from the consumers to retain it.
- ✔ Consumers' personal information must be kept up-to-date or deleted.
- ✔ The purpose for collecting data must be clearly stated at the time the data is collected.
- ✔ Consumers' personal information cannot be used for any other purpose (such as mailing catalogs or coupons) unless explicit permission is granted.
- ✔ Companies must have appropriate security safeguards in place to guarantee the privacy of any data in their possession. In other words, companies are required to keep their security measures up with the state-of-the-art.

✔ Companies must keep consumers advised in a clear and open manner about their data practices and how the consumers' privacy will be affected by any changes.

✔ Consumers must be permitted to see any information companies have on file about them, must be permitted to correct any errors, and must be allowed to delete data unless the companies have a legally mandated reason for keeping it.

✔ Companies that keep consumer information must have someone in the company accountable for ensuring that the privacy laws are being adhered to.

In the United States, more and more companies are appointing chief privacy officers to fulfill this function, even though no law yet requires them to do so. (Ray is often called "the dean of chief privacy officers" because he was the first person ever to be appointed to that position by a business in the United States.)

Keep in mind that these standards are minimums; individual member countries can — and have — enacted laws that are even more strict.

The European Union's Data Directive is based in large part on privacy principles created by the Organization for Economic Cooperation and Development (OECD). More than a dozen countries, including the United States, are members of the OECD; although their recommendations aren't binding, they have influenced most of the efforts to draft privacy legislation around the globe.

Check out the OECD's "Guidelines on the Protection of Privacy and Transborder Flows of Personal Data":

```
www.oecd.org/dsti/sti/it/secur/prod/PRIV-EN.HIM
```

Canada too has fairly sweeping privacy laws, enacted in response to European privacy legislation. In 2000, the Personal Information Protection and Electronic Documents Act, known by its legislative tracking number, Bill C-6, incorporated many of the same principles embodied in the European Data Directive.

Meanwhile, back in the States

In the United States, privacy laws tend to focus more narrowly on particular types of information, on particular business sectors, or on the ways in which governments gather and use data. Here are some types of federal laws that address aspects of privacy:

✔ **Credit reports:** The Fair Credit Reporting Act (FCRA), passed in the 1970s and amended in 1996, requires that credit bureaus handle your data in certain ways. In Chapter 14, we tell you about what rights you have to review and correct the information they gather and how to make sure that your data isn't being abused.

✔ **Government records:** The Privacy Act of 1974 places some minor and very technical limitations on the ability of government agencies to allow data gathered by an agency for one purpose to be used for another "incompatible" purpose. (Of course, "incompatible" isn't defined.) The Freedom of Information Act, also enacted in 1974, gives citizens access to certain government records about them as well as general information about government operations. But the government is also required to take precautions not to breach the privacy of government employees or other citizens whose information may be included with data that is being made public. Neither of these laws limits the use of data by private parties, like a business or charitable organization — only the government.

✔ **Banking records:** The Right to Financial Privacy Act of 1978 limits the ability of the government to arbitrarily request copies of your financial records, although it places no limits on banks disclosing those records to marketers. A more recent law, the Financial Services Modernization Act (also known by the names of its authors, the Gramm-Leach-Bliley [GLB] Act), limits the ability of financial-services firms to disclose (or sell) your personal information to third parties, such as a business or marketing company or charity. We tell you in Chapter 14 a little more about how to take advantage of GLB and how to protect yourself in cases where the law doesn't help.

✔ **Cable TV:** The Cable Communications Policy Act of 1984 requires that cable providers give notice to its customers about what kind of personally identifiable information they gather and how that data is used. The monitoring of your viewing habits can be done only with your permission, although your name and address can be freely sold to third parties unless you specifically say No.

✔ **Electronic communications:** The Electronic Communications Privacy Act of 1986 prohibits the government wiretapping of telephones and Internet connections except under specific circumstances. The act also prohibits private parties (hackers) from intercepting and tampering with stored communications, such as e-mail that's sitting on your ISP's server, waiting for you to retrieve it.

✔ **Video rentals:** The Video Privacy Protection Act of 1988 was passed in response to the disclosure of the video rental records of Supreme Court nominee Robert Bork. If your video rental records are disclosed without authorization, you can sue for $2,500 plus punitive damages and attorney fees.

- **Telemarketing:** The Telephone Consumer Protection Act of 1991 places limits on the activities of telemarketers, restricting their calling hours, requiring them to maintain do-not-call lists, prohibiting certain types of prerecorded calls and automated dialers, and banning unsolicited advertisements by fax. In Chapter 19, we tell you some specifics about the law and how to fight back against telemarketers.

- **Driver's licenses:** The Driver's Privacy Protection Act of 1994 originally permitted states to sell driver's license records to marketers, with the only requirement that citizens had to be permitted to opt out of such sales. Congress then amended the law in 1999 so that citizens would have to specifically opt in to letting their records be sold. Several states challenged the law, arguing that if you don't want your data sold, you don't have to get a driver's license, but the Supreme Court disagreed and upheld its constitutionality.

- **Children:** The Children's Online Privacy Protection Act of 1999 requires Web sites to obtain verifiable parental permission before collecting, using, and disclosing to third parties the personally identifiable information of children 13 and younger.

- **Health care:** The Health Insurance Portability and Accountability Act (HIPAA) of 1996 contains a section dealing with the privacy of medical records. Specifically, the law prohibits, without the patient's permission, the release of patient data for any purpose other than the minimum amount of information needed for treatment and payment. The law also guarantees a patient's right to access her own medical records (something that wasn't legally guaranteed before) and establishes standards for the security of stored records. It even carries criminal penalties for breaches of patient privacy. The regulations related to the privacy provisions of HIPAA don't go into effect until April 2003, and even now the regulations are being continually rewritten and revised, so it's hard to say how it will change the way your doctor, hospital, and insurance company do business. It's safe to say, though, that the sweeping effects of this law are making everybody scramble to comply.

Your Privacy Is Ultimately Your Responsibility

Blanche Dubois may have depended on the kindness of strangers, but in the battle against privacy invaders, the only person you can count on to look out for your best interest is *you*. What we urge you to do is to take charge of your privacy. Here's how:

- **Fight back!** As you may have already discovered, many tools are available that can help you protect your privacy in cyberspace. Now that you know what you know, it's time for you to put those tools to work.

- **Speak out!** We tell you in this chapter about lots of ways your privacy is invaded that you may never have heard of. Part of the reason these invasions continue is that most people don't know. Tell others what you read here, and tell the invaders that you won't stand for it.

- **Demand action!** The only way the invaders will be stopped is if invading your privacy is less profitable or more cumbersome than just coming straight out and asking your permission. Tell your elected officials that they had better start helping us fight back or you will cast your votes for others who will.

Part V
The Part of Tens

The 5th Wave   By Rich Tennant

"I'm sure there will be a good job market when I graduate. I created a virus that will go off that year."

In this part . . .

The last part of this book contains handy lists of useful facts and handy tips, conveniently organized into groups of ten. These tips didn't fit elsewhere in the book, but they're all important and interesting, we think, so we collected them here in a part so dense with information that you can feel that the pages are slightly heavier.

(Hmm. The last chapter lists 11 books rather than 10. We consider the 11th one to be a spare in case of emergency.)

Chapter 18

Ten Privacy Freedom Fighters Who Fight for You

In This Chapter
▶ A list of fearless freedom fighters
▶ Other groups that fight for you

Make no mistake: A battle is going on out there. While forces for good continue to fight to protect the privacy and dignity of all, other forces (some evil, others just ignorant or short-sighted) continue to chip away at any barriers that stand in their way.

It's now time to pay tribute to ten noble warriors who thanklessly and tirelessly continue to fight this battle for the protection of privacy.

Duncan Campbell

Talk about a conspiracy! Duncan is the British journalist who was the first to start digging to get to the bottom of a shadowy electronic communications spy network that international governments designed to gain access to phone calls, faxes, and e-mail, and he is now the world's foremost expert on the still-rumored but generally believed-to-be true global project that goes by the code name Echelon.

You can read more and about Echelon in Chapter 10 and at www.aclu.org/echelonwatch. You can find out more about Duncan at duncan.gn.apc.org/.

Jason Catlett, Ph.D.

Jason is the president of Junkbusters and a tireless one-man campaign against corporations that try to rob you of your privacy. When you visit his

Junkbusters Web site, you find a wealth of resources that an help you plan and execute a full-frontal assault against unlawful or unscrupulous telemarketers, junk mailers, Web advertisers, and other forces that junk up your life.

You can find out more about Jason and take advantage of all the tools at Junkbusters by visiting www.junkbusters.com.

Ann Cavoukian, Ph.D.

She is not only the information and privacy commissioner for the Canadian province of Ontario, but she is also the author of *Who Knows: Safeguarding Your Privacy in a Networked World* (McGraw Hill, 1996). She was part of the team that founded Ontario's Information and Privacy Commission in 1987, and she served as its first director of compliance. Since then, she has built a distinguished career as a leading expert on balancing the reasonable needs of businesses around the world with the rights of Canada's citizens. For fans of the children's songwriter and performer Raffi: Ann is his sister!

You can read more about Ann and her job as Ontario's information and privacy commissioner at www.ipc.on.ca.

Simon Davies

As the founder of Privacy International, Simon gathers privacy advocates from all over to fight for strong privacy protections. Privacy International also sponsors the annual Orwell award, given every year to organizations that have gone to new lengths to abuse the privacy of citizens the world over.

To find out more about Simon, the Orwell award, and Privacy International, browser to www.privacy.org.

Whitfield Diffie, Ph.D.

The father of public key cryptography, Whit Diffie serves as a distinguished engineer and chief security officer at Sun Microsystems, where he continues groundbreaking research into better ways of keeping secrets secret. Recognized as a quirky genius since he was a small child, he didn't learn to read until age 10, when he spontaneously picked up a science fiction book and didn't put it down until he had taught himself to read it. The Diffie-Hellman encryption system is one of the most popular systems in use and is at the heart of current versions of PGP. (We talk about PGP and Diffie-Hellman encryption in Chapter 10.)

For more information about Whit, browse to `www.sun.com/tech/features/encryption/` or read a wonderful profile of him by *Wired* magazine at `www.wired.com/wired/archive/2.11/diffie.html`.

Beth Givens

As the founder of the Privacy Rights Clearinghouse, Beth is a leading expert in issues like identity theft. Trained as a librarian, she is also a vigilant warrior for the cause of keeping the Web surfing records of library patrons free from the prying eyes of the government. She leads the PRC's efforts to provide tools to countless citizens for fighting back against crooks and other privacy invaders. In 2000, Beth received the Brandeis Award from Privacy International for outstanding privacy advocacy.

For more information about Beth and the Privacy Rights Clearinghouse, point your browser at `www.privacyrights.org`.

Evan Hendricks

As the publisher of *Privacy Times,* which recently celebrated its 20th year of publication, Evan is a pioneer in the field of privacy. *Privacy Times* is a biweekly journal of privacy developments across all areas of industry and government, including excellent tracking of legal developments under the Freedom of Information Act. Evan is a vigorous privacy advocate at heart, and if your company is doing something naughty, you should have a bottle of antacid in your hand as you read his coverage of your transgressions. His coverage is always fair, though, and the major players in the privacy field read his newsletter religiously.

Read *Privacy Times* at `www.privacytimes.com`.

Marc Rotenberg, Esq.

If you ever make a point of reading stories in the newspaper about privacy, you're probably familiar with the tireless work and strong opinions of Marc Rotenberg. As the founder of the Electronic Privacy Information Center

(EPIC), he is an author, lecturer, and advocate for privacy rights who has led major campaigns against such well-known privacy invaders as the Clipper chip, Carnivore and the Intel plan to put a unique identifier on every processor it produced. In 2000, Marc was awarded the Norbert Weiner Award by the organization Computer Professionals for Social Responsibility. During his acceptance speech, he pulled out a hammer and smashed a Cue:Cat bar code scanner into about a hundred pieces. (The Cue:Cat scanner, a product of the now defunct Digital Convergence, allowed magazine subscribers to scan bar codes printed on ads in magazines in order to get more information about the products, but failed to tell users that their personal information and usage were being tracked as they did so.)

For more information about Marc and the Electronic Privacy Information Center, go to www.epic.org.

Richard Smith

Richard is a private consultant in security and privacy, but came to many people's attention as the first chief technology officer of the nonprofit Privacy Foundation. Richard is a ruthless investigator of technology that betrays your privacy. He is continually in the news with new discoveries of technology doing bad things to people's privacy. Richard is responsible for many discoveries of new viruses and spyware, which we talk about in Chapter 8.

You can find out more about Richard and the Privacy Foundation at www.privacyfoundation.org.

Phil Zimmerman

Phil is the author of PGP (www.pgp.com) who risked going to jail to bring free and easy public-key cryptography to the masses. He wanted to make it easy for the average person to make use of public-key cryptography, so he wrote a program named Pretty Good Privacy, or PGP, which we talk about in Chapter 10. PGP lets you quickly encode and decode e-mail messages using a form of cryptography that is *very* difficult to crack. Unfortunately, at the time he wrote the program, the use of "strong" cryptography was closely regulated by the U.S. government, and when somebody posted a copy of the software on the Internet, the Feds came knocking on Phil's door. After years of investigations, the government decided that, rather than prosecute Phil, they should relax restrictions on citizens' use of cryptography.

More Privacy Organizations That Fight for You

Lots of organizations work to preserve your privacy. Many of them even have Web sites so that you can find out more about who they are and what they offer. Some of our favorites are shown in this section.

American Civil Liberties Union

www.aclu.org/privacy

A tireless fighter for civil liberties, the ACLU keeps tabs on all the latest developments in law and policy affecting privacy.

Center for Democracy and Technology

www.cdt.org

Funded by a number of technology-oriented foundations (like the Benton Foundation and the Markle Foundation) and major corporations (like AT&T and IBM), the Center for Democracy and Technology takes a fairly pragmatic (which means a slightly corporate-leaning) view of many privacy issues, but still does good work on issues like encryption.

Center for Media Education

www.cme.org

The CME tracks many technology issues facing consumers, including the slow pace at which many popular Web sites are implementing the Children's Online Privacy Protection Act (COPPA).

Consumer Project on Technology

www.cptech.org

CPT was founded by Ralph Nader. The organization tracks developments in electronic commerce and the health-care industry that affect the storage and use of your personal information.

Electronic Frontier Foundation

www.eff.org

One of the original cyber civil liberties organizations, EFF used to be an influential advocate in the policy arena in Washington, D.C., but left there many years ago and now focuses on grass-roots activism and occasional legal challenges. It was founded by Mitchell Kapor, the founder of Lotus (which made the 1-2-3 spreadsheet program), and John Perry Barlow, a songwriter and lyricist for the Grateful Dead.

Ten Great Privacy Web Sites

The next time you're out Web surfing, check out some of these fact-filled sites:

- ✔ **The American Civil Liberties Union Defend Your Data Web site:** www.aclu.org/privacy/
- ✔ **The Electronic Frontier Foundation:** www.eff.org
- ✔ **The Electronic Privacy Information Center:** www.epic.org
- ✔ **U.S. Federal Trade Commission's Privacy Initiatives:** www.ftc.gov/privacy/
- ✔ **The Health Privacy Project at Georgetown University:** www.healthprivacy.org
- ✔ **InfoWar: Security and Cybercrime Information:** www.infowar.com
- ✔ **Junkbusters: Bust the Junk Out of Your Life!:** www.junkbusters.org
- ✔ **Privacy Rights Clearinghouse — Resources for Consumers:** www.privacyrights.org
- ✔ **SafeKids.com/SafeTeens.com:** www.safekids.com and www.safeteens.com
- ✔ **TCPA Legal Resources Center (fight back against telemarketers!):** www.tcpalaw.com

Chapter 19

Ten Ways to Fight Back for Fun and Profit

1f you have read all the preceding chapters in this book, you may have reached the conclusion that the biggest drag about privacy is that they (you know — them: corporations, businesses, spammers) have everything to gain by invading your privacy while you have everything to lose. To which we must say, "*Au contraire, mon frere!*"

You see, in many ways privacy is a game: A game of skill; a game of knowledge; a game of nerves. In this chapter, we show you how to play to win!

First, a little disclaimer: This chapter is intended to give an overview of how to enforce rights that all consumers have under law. Although we have tried to be thorough and accurate, we always recommend that you check with a lawyer before you rush down to the local courthouse and make a fool of yourself, or worse! Defending your rights in a court of law is your Constitutional right, but a little chat with your friendly neighborhood attorney can save you time, money, and embarrassment and, most importantly, can help keep you from annoying the judge that you're trying to impress!

How to Make Telemarketers Pay You

In the early 1990s, several members of Congress had finally had enough of those annoying calls at all hours of the day and night, so they passed a law named the Telephone Consumer Protection Act (TCPA). Under the TCPA, Congress gave the Federal Communications Commission (FCC) the responsibility of enacting regulations that gave consumers added privacy rights against telemarketers.

Check out the TCPA Legal Resource Center at www.tcpalaw.com.

One of the ways in which the TCPA protects you is by limiting telemarketers' use of automatic telephone dialing systems (sometimes called autodialers, predictive dialers, or demon dialers) and prerecorded voice messages. Unfortunately, when it comes to demon dialers, the devil is in the details, which means that telemarketers have found more than enough loopholes in the law to still be able to annoy you.

Predictive dialers are devices that all self-respecting telemarketers use so that they can dial faster than the speed of light and cram more phone calls into every hour of their working day. They're also the reason that, after you get up from dinner or from reading a good book to answer the phone and say Hello, that telltale pause occurs before Mr. or Ms. Annoying Telemarketer starts rattling off her pitch at you from the other end. What's worse is that sometimes the phones dial so fast that when it connects, the telemarketers are still on another call, so they just hang up on you!

As you have probably noticed in your own run-ins with telemarketers, however, they're a pretty squirrelly bunch that is not by nature prone to respecting others or following the rules. That's good news for you because another way in which the TCPA protects you is by allowing you to sue — for cash! — the pants off telemarketers who disobey the law.

The rules of the game for telemarketers

The TCPA requires all telemarketers to follow some basic rules. When telemarketers get caught violating these rules, they get hauled before the FCC to answer for their misdeeds, and you can sue the sorry so-and-sos for $500 to $1,500 per violation.

Yes, sir or ma'am, just commit the following rules to heart and you may win a barrel full of money or a trip to Disney World for the whole family:

- ✔ Telemarketers can't call you at home before 8 a.m. or after 9 p.m. (your local time).

- ✔ Anyone making a telephone solicitation to your home must provide his own name, the name of the entity on whose behalf he's calling, and the address or phone number where you can contact that entity.

✔ If you clearly ask the telemarketer to never call you again, she must record your request on a do-not-call list, and she can't contact you again for ten years.

✔ Telemarketing staff members must be trained in the do-not-call procedure, and the entity must maintain a written do-not-call policy that it must provide to you on request at no cost to you.

✔ Telemarketers may not make unsolicited calls using a prerecorded message or an artificial (computerized) voice to a home, health-care facility (hospital, doctor's office, nursing home), law enforcement agency, cell phone, pager, or answering service.

The rules of the game for you

We know — it sounds too good to be true. It's almost like a telemarketer's pitch. But trust us on this one: It really works. Between your three faithful authors, we know more than a dozen people who have collected thousands of dollars in legal damages from telemarketers.

Take note: You have to play by some rules yourself in order to be successful at making telemarketers pay for their illegal behavior:

✔ You have to keep detailed written records of your dealings with telemarketers.

✔ You have to ask specific questions and tell the telemarketers specific things in order to catch them breaking the law.

✔ You may have to play along with telemarketers occasionally to get enough information to make your claim against them.

✔ You may have to do some paperwork along the way, such as sending certified letters or even filing a lawsuit in small-claims court.

✔ If a telemarketer gets feisty, you may need to fight him in court.

If you have them dead to rights, though, with evidence to back up your claims, you often don't even have to file suit — because the knees of the lawyers start shaking and their clients just start writing checks. Even if you do have to go so far as to file suit, most get settled in cash (including reimbursement of your court filing fee) before you ever see a judge.

Ironically, many telemarketers know that they're operating illegally, and some even have money in their budgets to cover the cost of these kinds of cases, so who are you to ruin all their careful planning by not suing the pants off them?

How to cash in and make the big bucks

The next time your phone rings with a junk call during dinner, here's what you should do:

1. Keep copies of the Call Logging Form and Script on our Web site (at www.privacyfordummies.com) next to the phone to help you keep accurate and detailed records of telemarketing calls and violations.

2. Every time a telemarketer calls, ask for the caller's name and the name and phone number of the company or entity he's calling on behalf of, and record it all on the Call Logging Form and Script.

3. Keep clear, accurate records of all telemarketing calls — that makes it much easier for you to file complaints and easier to cash in and win because these records demonstrate your diligence and commitment to upholding the law when you use them as evidence in lawsuits.

4. After you have the caller's name and company and contact information, request that he put your number on the do-not-call list. (If the person can't, or won't, make a mental note to begin planning a nice vacation with the money you'll make!)

5. Ask the person to send you a copy of the company's do-not-call policy. If it doesn't have one, ask to speak to a supervisor and record the supervisor's name on your form. (And let your mouth start watering in anticipation of your next stay in the presidential suite at your favorite vacation spot.)

6. If you ask a company or entity to add you to its do-not-call list and someone from there calls again anyway, you should find your notes from the time you asked to be put on the do-not-call list and prepare a letter similar to the draft shown at the end of this list.

7. Notify your local or state consumer-protection office and your state attorney general's office. (You should be able to obtain telephone numbers for these offices from the government section of your telephone directory or from directory assistance.)

8. Send a complaint to the FCC. A sample letter appears in the sidebar "Filing telemarketing complaints with the FCC" later in this chapter.

Here's the sample letter mentioned in Step 6. It's a generic letter, so you have to edit it based on your specific circumstances and insert the correct information in angle brackets, *<like this>*. Be sure to send it as a certified letter with a return receipt requested. (You can also find a downloadable version at the Web site www.privacyfordummies.com.)

Telemarketing Company
ATTN: General Counsel / Legal Department
Whoville, USA
RE: Intent to File Suit for Violations of TCPA (47 USC 227) by your Company

Dear Sir/Madam:

On *<date>*, I received a telephone call from your employee *<name, if known>*, soliciting me on behalf of *<name of organization>*. At that time, your employee:

<Insert all options that apply>

✔ Called my home before 8 a.m. or after 9 p.m.

✔ Refused to provide me with his/her name.

✔ Refused to provide me with your company's name.

✔ Refused to provide me with your company's address.

✔ Refused to provide me with your company's phone number.

✔ Was unaware that your company maintains a do-not-call list.

✔ Was unable to place my phone number on your do-not-call list.

✔ Stated that your company does not maintain a do-not-call list.

✔ Refused to place my phone number on your do-not-call list.

✔ Refused to provide me with a written copy of your do-not-call policy.

✔ Took my request for a copy of your do-not call policy, but even after a second request sent by certified (return receipt requested) mail on *<date>* (copy attached), your company has still not provided me with a copy of that policy.

✔ Claimed to have placed my number on your do-not-call list but then someone from your company called me a second time on *<date>*, *<number of>* days after I requested to be placed on your do-not-call list.

✔ Called me a third *<fourth, fifth, whatever>* time after my original (and repeated) request(s) to be placed on your do-not-call list.

According to the Telephone Consumer Protection Act of 1991 (47 USC 227) and the FCC's implementing regulations (47 CFR 64.1200), telemarketers must adhere to several requirements, including identifying themselves and the entity on whose behalf they're calling; developing a written policy for maintaining do-not-call lists; training their personnel about the existence and use of the do-not-call list; placing consumers that request not to receive further solicitations on the do-not-call list; and, honoring each do-not-call request for 10 years from the time the request is made. Consumers whose rights are violated in these ways may sue to collect $500 to $1,500 per violation.

Because of your company's willful violations of federal law, this letter is to inform you of my intent to file a complaint in small claims court. Based on my personal reading of the applicable law, I believe that I am entitled to statutory damages in the amount of at least $500.

I am sending this letter as a courtesy. If you want to discuss or resolve this matter informally, I encourage you to contact me at the address above within 10 business days of your receipt of this letter.

Sincerely,

<Your name>

A big-game hunter's big moneymaking tips for telemarketing treasure-hunters

If a telemarketer talks too fast while you're asking her questions on the phone, ask her to repeat the information. Sound interested, and she will bend over backward to help you.

Charity registration is required in some states. If someone claims to be calling from a charity, go ahead and ask whether it's registered.

If the call is prerecorded, you may need to listen to the whole message and follow the instructions for contacting the company, as though you were interested, or else you can't get the information you need to pursue a legal claim.

Junkbusters, Inc. (www.junkbusters.com), has created a telemarketing call logging form and script. After you record today's date and time on a piece of paper, ask each question in a courteous but serious manner. Ask each question as written and as clearly as possible because the company may be recording the call to use in its defense. If the person you're speaking to refuses to answer your questions or is confused, ask to speak with that person's supervisor.

Here's the list of questions:

- "I'm sorry, what's your full name again?" (If you're speaking with a supervisor, be sure to get her full name.)

- "You're calling on behalf of?"

- "Do you work for that organization, or did it just hire your company to do the telemarketing?"

  If the person works for a telemarketer, ask this question: "Can you tell me your company's name and mailing address?"

- "In case we get disconnected, can I also get your company's phone number; area code first?"

- "Does your organization keep a list of phone numbers that it has been asked not to call?"

- "I want you to put my number on your do-not-call list. Can you do that now?"

- "Does your company make telemarketing calls for any other organizations?"

  If the answer is Yes, ask this question: "Can you make sure that your company won't call me for any other organization?"

- "Will your company keep my number on its do-not-call list for at least 10 years?"

- "Does your company have a written policy which says that on paper?"

- "Will you please mail me a copy of that written policy?"

- "Have I made it clear to you that I do not want telemarketing calls from anyone — ever?"

Then add "Thank you for your cooperation. Good-bye."

What about Junk Faxes?

Junk faxes are much like telemarketing calls, only worse because you have to pay for the paper they're printed on; meanwhile, they're monopolizing your fax machine with their junk so that you can't use it.

The good news is that unsolicited ads through your fax machine from commercial entities are illegal from the get-go. You don't even have to make a do-not-call request. When someone sends you a junk advertisement by fax, you can head straight to court and collect your $500 to $1,500 dollars!

Filing telemarketing complaints with the FCC

It's the government's job to catch the bad guys. But we're here to tell you that it's much more exciting — not to mention profitable — to make the telemarketers pay you what you're owed under the law for their illegal activities. Remember that the ultimate enforcement authority for the TCPA is the Federal Communications Commission. As a rule, it isn't in a position to force telemarketers to pay you money except under limited circumstances, but it does like to be kept advised of who is being naughty. Reporting the bad guys doesn't affect your right to collect a judgment if you decide to sue for yourself.

If you believe that you have a chronic TCPA violator on your hands, you should send a type-written letter to

Federal Communications Commission
Common Carrier Bureau
Consumer Complaints — TCPA/Telemarketing Violations
Mailstop 1600A2
Washington, DC 20554

In the letter, include the following information:

✔ Your name, address, and a daytime telephone number

✔ The action you're requesting, such as requesting a person or business to stop calling your home telephone number, to add your name to its do-not-call list, or to stop sending unsolicited advertisements to your fax machine

✔ The date you requested to be added to the organization's do-not-call list and the name of the individual you spoke with

✔ The home or business telephone number the solicitor called

✔ The name, address, and telephone number of the organization placing the calls

✔ The dates and times you received calls or fax messages from the organization

✔ The telephone number of the fax machine to which unsolicited advertisements were sent

✔ Copies of any unsolicited advertisements sent to your fax machine

✔ Whether you have filed suit in state court, including the state where any such suit was filed

Remember to say the magic words: "I hereby request that the commission take appropriate action against *<offending company's name>*."

Technically speaking, the TCPA strictly prohibits the sending of unsolicited advertisements to fax machines without your prior express permission or invitation. The FCC has interpreted this statement to mean that if you have an established business relationship with a company, it's permitted to send you a fax, but you can end the relationship (and its right to fax ads to you) by requesting that it never fax you again.

Even if a company does have permission to fax you, under the FCC's regulations that implement the TCPA, all faxes must clearly indicate

- The date and time the transmission was sent
- The identity of the sender
- The telephone number of the sender or of the sending fax machine

Although few people have collected money for the failure to include those pieces of data on a fax, their absence can be used to show a court the faxer's clear disregard for the law.

Collecting from the junk faxer

Collecting from the senders of junk faxes is similar to collecting from outlaw telemarketers:

- Keep the original copy of every unsolicited fax advertisement you receive in a safe place where you can locate it easily.
- If it doesn't say on the fax the date and time it was received, make a note of it.
- Double-check that you don't have an existing business relationship with the sender of the fax.
- Look to see whether the required identifying information is included on the fax.
- Check a site like www.junkfaxes.org to see whether this faxer has ever been sued.

Armed with that information, draft a letter similar to the following example (you must modify this generic letter to suit your particular situation) and send it as a certified letter with a return receipt requested.

Sample letter to avoid junk faxes

Telemarketing Company
ATTN: General Counsel / Legal Department
Whoville, USA
RE: Intent to file suit for violations of TCPA (47 USC 227) by your company

Dear Sir or Madam:

On <date>, I received the enclosed unsolicited facsimile (fax) advertisement. To the best of my knowledge, I do not have any business relationship with your company, nor have I ever given you express permission to send me such solicitations. Because of these facts, and based on my reading of the law, I believe that your advertisement was sent to me in violation of the Telephone Consumer Protection Act of 1991 (47 USC 227) and the Federal Communications Commission's regulations (47 CFR 64.1200).

Because of your company's willful disregard for the law, it's my intent to file suit in small claims court for violations of 47 CFR 64.1200 (a)(3) and to seek statutory damages in the amount of $_____.

[*Note:* *If this is the first fax you have received from the company and it's not on the FCC's list of previously cited companies, insert the amount of $500. If you have sent the company previous complaints and it's still faxing you, if it's on the FCC list of previously cited companies, or if you know that the company has been sued before, change the amount to $1,500.*]

I am sending this letter as a courtesy. If you want to discuss or resolve this matter informally, I encourage you to contact me at the address above within 10 business days of your receipt of this letter.

Sincerely,

<*Your name*>

Enclosure: Copy of fax

CC: Federal Communications Commission — Enforcement Bureau

Filing a complaint against a junk faxer

Although it hasn't done much about telemarketing violations, the FCC has been active in enforcing the junk fax provisions of the TCPA. It issues citations to junk faxers, and if the violators are caught faxing again, the FCC issues fines (some of which have been over a million dollars!).

To file a complaint against a junk faxer, you need to send a letter along with a copy of the fax. In your letter, you must

- ✔ Put near the top, in bold print, "TCPA COMPLAINT — UNSOLICITED FAX"
- ✔ Include your name, address, and daytime telephone number, in case the FCC needs further information.

- State the date the fax was received and the phone number at which it was received.

- Clearly state that you did not invite or give permission for the sender to send you unsolicited faxes.

- Clearly state that you "request that the Commission take appropriate action against the sender." (Otherwise, the complaint is filed, but no action is taken.)

You should then send the letter and a copy of the fax to

Consumer Information Bureau
TCPA COMPLAINT — UNSOLICITED FAX
Federal Communications Commission
445 Twelfth St. SW
Washington, DC 20554

Check the listing of known junk faxers that have been cited by the FCC, kept at www.fcc.gov/eb/tcd/ufax.html. If you know for a fact that your fax came from a company that has been previously cited, you should bypass the Consumer Information Bureau and send a copy of your letter and the fax directly to the folks in charge of whacking scofflaws:

Enforcement Bureau — TCD
ATTN: TCPA Repeat Offenders
Federal Communications Commission
445 Twelfth St. SW
Washington, DC 20554

What the TCPA doesn't do for you

Like most good things, the TCPA has limits:

- These do-not-call rules don't apply to calls placed to business telephone numbers. However, your state may have laws that require telemarketers to keep separate do-not-call lists for calls placed to business numbers.

- Tax-exempt and nonprofit organizations aren't required to keep do-not-call lists.

✔ Some TCPA rules don't apply if you already have an "established business relationship" with a business or entity. If you have ever made an inquiry, application, purchase, or transaction with a telemarketer's company, when they call you it isn't considered unsolicited. However, you can end this relationship by telling the caller that you don't want the business or entity to ever call you again.

✔ The FCC's rules don't prohibit placing artificial and prerecorded voice message telephone calls to businesses.

✔ Most of the rules don't apply to charitable organizations (which explains why Gregg couldn't cash in big when he got prerecorded political calls from Bill Clinton, Barbra Streisand, and Susan Sarandon during the last Presidential election — and he was sorely disappointed about it, too!) or people who aren't soliciting, such as pollsters.

✔ The TCPA doesn't apply to junk e-mail. Yet. (But we have our fingers crossed.)

A word about e-mail spam

BOMBSHELL

Many people who hate spam have taken to responding to e-mail spammers with claims that the spammer has violated the TCPA (sometimes referred to as "47 USC 227"; which translates into Title 47 of the U.S. Code at section 227).

The TCPA was passed in 1991, so it clearly predates widespread Internet usage. Therefore, there's no mention of e-mail anywhere in the law. But a provision of the TCPA describes computers with modems attached to phone lines — essentially describing early computer-based faxing systems — which sounds suspiciously like how most people connect to the Internet to get their e-mail.

"If it sounds like it covers e-mail, can I assume that it does?"

That would have been nice, but no dice, says the noted scholar (and staunch antispam advocate) Professor David Sorkin, of the John Marshall Law School. To quell any doubt, Professor Sorkin has written the definitive analysis of the TCPA's applicability to spam at www.spamlaws.com/articles/buffalo.html.

All this legal gobbledygook doesn't mean that you can't have some fun fighting back against spammers! If you can't wait, turn to Chapter 20 for instructions on how to 'rassle them to the mat.

From TCPA to TPS

Sorry, no cash to be won on this one, but it's still lots of fun to make a predawn preemptive strike against telemarketers to make it even harder for them to call you.

To whack away a little more of telemarketers' access to you, register yourself with the Direct Marketing Association's (DMA's) national do-not-call list, the Telephone Preference Service (TPS). The DMA makes this list available to DMA members who agree to remove everyone on it from their calling lists. Okay, it's true that telemarketers don't have to use the list — but look at it this way: After you register with the DMA, you feel even more justified in being rude to telemarketers because you know that they didn't have the common courtesy to check the DMA list before calling you.

To register yourself with the DMA Telephone Preference Service, send your name, telephone number (including area code) and address (including zip code) to

Telephone Preference Service
Direct Marketing Association
P.O. Box 9014
Farmingdale, NY 11735-9014

In addition to TPS, some states maintain statewide do-not-call lists that in some cases must be consulted by telemarketers before they begin calling. You can find out whether your state has a mandatory do-not-call list and how to get on it by visiting www.the-dma.org/government/donotcalllists.shtml.

Stopping postal junk mail with MPS

Unfortunately, postal junk mail in your mailbox is a much more difficult problem. No laws prohibit junk mail. Indeed, the irony of it all is that bulk mail is reputed to subsidize regular mail for the rest of us. Just think: It may just be the case that, if it weren't for all the postage fees paid by bulk mailers, a stamp for a letter to your Mom might cost something closer to what a FedEx package costs!

If you really want to try to make a dent in the flood of paper that clogs your mailbox, those thoughtful folks at the Direct Marketing Association also operate a Mail Preference Service (MPS), similar to the TPS we discuss in the preceding section. Bear in mind that, like the TPS, junk mailers aren't required by any law to use the MPS list.

In a fit of spite worthy of any 2-year old, many companies that do use the MPS use it without a concern for whether you *asked* to be on their lists. If you call up a company and ask someone to send you a catalog, she may not do it if you have already signed up for the MPS. Call it a load of bellyaching, or call it cutting off their noses to spite their faces, but marketers say that sorting their lists and honoring the MPS is too difficult, even in this day of superpowerful databases that let them keep track of all the other details of your life. If you find it hard to believe that marketers somehow can't figure out how to bypass the names of those who have made a special request for their company's mailings, you aren't alone. They offer a simple solution, of course: Don't put your name on the MPS in the first place!

Others Who Care about All Those Nasty People Who Call You

A few federal agencies stand ready to help (at least somewhat) in your fight to be rid of telemarketers.

Federal Trade Commission (FTC)

The FTC polices false or deceptive telephone solicitation sales practices. You can contact it at

Federal Trade Commission
Consumer Response Center
Drop H 285
6th Street and Pennsylvania Avenue, N.W.
Washington, DC 20580

You can also write to the Federal Trade Commission at the following address to request information about its Telemarketing Sales Rule, which protects consumers from deceptive and abusive telemarketing practices:

Federal Trade Commission
Public Reference Branch
Drop H 240
6th Street and Pennsylvania Avenue, N.W.
Washington, DC 20580

Information about the FTC's Telemarketing Sales Rule is also available on the Internet at www.ftc.gov/.

Federal Bureau of Investigation (FBI)

You should direct complaints about fraudulent telephone solicitation practices to the Federal Bureau of Investigation (FBI) or your state attorney general's office. You should be able to obtain telephone numbers for these offices from the government section of your telephone directory or from directory assistance.

Gee, we feel so unusual

In case you feel that we are being a little harsh on telemarketers, we suggest that you visit the Web site of the DMA (www.the-dma.org) — which is to telemarketers what the major-league players baseball union is to pro ballplayers — and see what they think of *you*.

It was at the DMA site that we learned that we (John, Ray, and Gregg) are unusual. We had thought that the fact that we hate getting calls from telemarketers made us pretty normal, but, according to the DMA:

"Many people enjoy receiving information about products or services in their homes over the telephone."

Just to make sure that we weren't losing our minds, we looked up the word *many* in the closest dictionary and it told us: "Many: constituting or forming a large number."

Please, dear reader, if you're one of the "many people who enjoys receiving information about products or services in their homes over the telephone," especially at dinnertime, would you please drop us a note to let us know that you exist? We will frame it and put it right next to our autographed picture of the Loch Ness monster.

Meanwhile, for the record, you will want to know that the folks at the DMA think you enjoy receiving junk mail even more than you enjoy receiving all those calls from telemarketers. That's why their Web site also told us this:

"Most people enjoy receiving information in the mail about subjects that interest them or products and services they may need or want. "

We could go to the trouble of looking up *most* in the dictionary, too, but we think that it's more fun to just let the DMA's absurd statements stand on their own.

Postal Service Chief Postal Inspector

Complaints regarding information or products received through the United States Postal Service in connection with fraudulent telephone solicitation practices should be addressed to

Mail Fraud
Chief Postal Inspector
475 L'Enfant Plaza, S.W.
Washington, DC 20260-2181

Chapter 20

Ten Easy Tricks for Cutting Down on Spam

*B*e vewy, vewy qwiet! We're hunting spammers!

Ask Elmer Fudd, and he'll tell you that hunting spammers is much like hunting wabbits. Wid a wabbit, the first place you look is in his hole, even though you know that you'll never find him there. With a spammer, the first place you look is at the From line of his spam. Just like wid a wabbit, though, you know that you'll never find him there.

Indeed, 99.99 percent of the time, the From line in a spam message is fabricated and has nothing to do with the spam's source. This trick is just one that spammers use to try to keep you off their trail. After you learn the ropes, however, hunting down a spammer's base of operations and getting him booted off the Web is usually a cinch.

With all due respect to our good friend Bugs Bunny, wouldn't it be nice if Elmer could come out ahead for a change? Therefore, we humbly present ten twicks for twacking tweacherous twicksters. Try these tricks in order on some of your spam to thwack the spammer who sent it.

Step 1: Look at the E-Mail Headers

Like a piece of luggage on an airline, every e-mail message has attached to it a little tag containing data that tells you where it started, where it was routed through, and what its ultimate destination was. On e-mail messages, this data is contained in a block of text called the *header*, which looks something like this:

```
Return-Path: joe@china.com
Received: from ns.yzw.co.jp ([210.226.145.162]) by
           receiving.my-isp.com (8.9.3/8.9.3) with ESMTP id
           NAA06675; Sun, 23 Dec 2001 13:39:46 -0500
Received: from 3Cust198.tnt12.dfw5.da.uu.net
           ([63.44.238.198]) by ns.yzw.co.jp
           ([210.226.145.162]) (SMTPD32-6.05 EVAL) id
           ABDC6E4021C; Sat, 22 Dec 2001 17:09:48 -0800
Received: from billclinton.whitehouse.gov ([184.325.23.124])
           by 3Cust198.tnt12.dfw5.da.uu.net with ESMTP; Sat,
           22 Dec 2001 02:10:27 +0800
Message-ID:
           <000029513725$00004027$00006fba@billclinton.whiteh
           ouse.gov>
From: joe@china.com
To: <Undisclosed.Recipients>
Subject: Free Satellite Descrambler and Porno Channel Decoder
Date: Sat, 22 Dec 2001 02:10:21 -0800
MIME-Version: 1.0
Reply-To: joe@china.com
Errors-To: joe@arabia.com
```

Because most e-mail software creators think that average users would be terrified by all this gobbledygook, the creators try to hide the headers so that users never have to see them. Headers are the keys to finding spammers, though, so we describe how to ferret out headers from most popular e-mail programs.

Using the Unix programs Elm, Pine, and Mutt

Open the offending message and press **h** to turn on the display of full headers.

Using Eudora

Open the offending e-mail message. Under the title bar are four option buttons. The third one is a box that says Blah, Blah. Click on that box to display the full headers.

Using Hotmail

Open the offending e-mail message. Choose Options⇨Preferences⇨Message headers from the menu bar. Then choose the Full option to display Received headers. Choosing Advanced displays the MIME headers too, but those usually aren't necessary for spam hunting.

Using Lotus Notes 4.6.x

Open the offending e-mail. Choose Actions⇨Delivery information. Cut and paste the text from the bottom box, marked Delivery Information.

Using Netscape WebMail

Open the offending e-mail message. In the yellow field atop the message (where the Subject, Date, From, and To information appears), look for a small yellow down-arrow in the lower-right corner. Click the arrow to open the yellow field and display the full headers.

Using Netscape 4.x Mail

Open the offending e-mail message and choose View⇨Headers⇨All.

Using Outlook Express

Open the offending e-mail message and choose File⇨Properties. Click the Details tab. If you're filing a complaint, save some time by clicking on the Message Source button, which opens a text window with the full headers and full plain-text message body displayed. (Spam investigators benefit from having everything in plain text rather than with colorful fonts and other elements.)

Using Outlook 2000

Open the offending e-mail message and choose View⇨Options. You see the message headers in a box at the bottom of the window. You can copy or paste them from that window.

Using Pegasus Mail

Open the offending e-mail message and choose Reader⇨Show All Headers. (You can choose the same command by pressing Ctrl+H too.)

Step 2: Follow the Flow of Received Headers

Every time an e-mail message passes through a system, that system adds a Received line. Although lots of extraneous data is on these Received lines, they're simple enough to read: The mail was received from one computer by another computer at a certain date and time. Each new Received line gets added to the top of the pile, so the most recent one should be the one that says who delivered it to your ISP.

In this example, the first Received line is the latest one, and relevant pieces of data are shown in bold:

```
Received: from ns.yzw.co.jp ([210.226.145.162]) by
          receiving.my-isp.com (8.9.3/8.9.3) with ESMTP id
          NAA06675; Sun, 23 Dec 2001 13:39:46 -0500 (EST)
```

This message says that the mail was received by the ISP (my-isp.com) from ns.yzw.co.jp, which has the IP address 210.226.145.162. Because you can be confident that your own ISP wouldn't be spamming you, you now have the computer named ns.yzw.co.jp in your sight. Don't stop looking there! You can look at the next Received line to see whether the trail goes any farther:

```
Received: from 3Cust198.tnt12.dfw5.da.uu.net
          ([63.44.238.198]) by ns.yzw.co.jp
          ([210.226.145.162]) (SMTPD32-6.05 EVAL) id
          ABDC6E4021C; Sat, 22 Dec 2001 17:09:48 -0800
```

Sure enough, the trail continues. According to the next Received line, somebody gave this spam to ns.yzw.co.jp — namely, a computer named 3Cust198.tnt12.dfw5.da.uu.net. So 3Cust198.tnt12.dfw5.da.uu.net is now the prime suspect.

On the next Received line, you see

```
Received: from billclinton.whitehouse.gov ([184.325.23.124])
          by 3Cust198.tnt12.dfw5.da.uu.net with ESMTP; Sat,
          22 Dec 2001 02:10:27 +0800
```

TECHNICAL STUFF

An explanation of the 255 rule

You don't need to know this rule to be able to track down spam, but because you're here anyway, we explain it. People, most of whom have ten fingers, prefer to count in base 10, and computers, which have, at most, two fingers, prefer to count in base 2. An IP address is really a 32-digit base 2 number (usually referred to as 32 bits.) So the IP address for our Web site at www.privacyfordummies.com is

11010000000111110010101000101011

Even for us computer weenies, that kind of number is a bit challenging to remember, so we divide the number into four 8-bit chunks:

11010000.00011111.00101010.
00101011

Then we treat each 8-bit chunk as an 8-bit number and translate it into its base 10 equivalent:

208.31.42.43

The smallest value that an 8-bit chunk can contain is 00000000, which is 0 in base 10, and the largest is 11111111, which is 255. A number less than 0 or greater than 255, therefore, can't be translated back into an 8-bit number and can't be part of an IP address.

Spam-hunter trivia

If you do enough spam hunting, you may recognize some of the letters in the names of mail servers. In the example in the "Step 2" section, some people may recognize one of the computer names as belonging to the major Internet backbone provider UUNet. If you do a great deal of flying — versus surfing! — you may realize that UUNet likes to use 3-letter airport codes to designate which region their modem pools are in. In this case, the header shows that this e-mail passed through DFW, the airport code for Dallas-Fort Worth.

If something about this line looks funny to you, you're right. First, you know that Bill gave the White House back to the same family he got it from, and, second, you're pretty sure that the folks at the White House have better things to do than to be sending you spam.

On top of that, it turns out that something is wrong with the IP address. It breaks a rule that we call, for simplicity's sake, *the 255 rule*. What this rule says is that the numbers in IP addresses are never, *never,* outside the range from 0 through 255. (If you want to understand why, see the nearby sidebar "An explanation of the 255 rule.") The fact that the second block of numbers breaks the 255 rule means that this IP address is bogus. Coupling that information with the unlikely computer name, you seem to have reached a dead end. That leaves you with 3Cust198.tnt12.dfw5.da.uu.net as the end of the trail.

But, what happens if the last Received line doesn't have a funny-looking name or has an IP address that doesn't violate the 255 rule? What if you see several more Received lines? Then you keep following the Received lines backward until you find one that doesn't link up with the one before it. For a moment, suppose that you don't know anything about the 255 rule and that you have no reason to doubt the existence of a computer named billclinton. whitehouse.gov. In that case, you move on to the next step.

Step 3: Identify the Owner of the Last Verifiable Mail-Handling Server

Suppose that after reviewing some headers, you have collected the following computer names and IP addresses that you suspect of being involved in sending you spam:

```
ns.yzw.co.jp ([210.226.145.162])
3Cust198.tnt12.dfw5.da.uu.net ([63.44.238.198])
billclinton.whitehouse.gov ([184.325.23.124])
```

TECHNICAL STUFF

Nslookup in a nutshell

All computers connected to the Internet are assigned a unique numerical address, called an *IP address.* In addition, many (but not all) computers are assigned names that are more easily remembered by humans. So rather than remember 192.168.123.45, you have to remember only www.some-crazy-website.com, and the Internet's domain name system translates the names into numbers for you. When you have a number but no name, or a name but no number, the program nslookup (also known as *name system lookup*) does a reverse lookup for you and gets you what you need.

Now is the time to put the power of the Internet to work to start tracking down the spammer. You can use the nslookup tool, which enables you to find out whether these computer names and IP addresses match each other. To use nslookup, go to one of the Web-based nslookup services (in this case, try www.samspade.org/t, find the Address Digger field, and type the name of each computer (for example, **ns.yzw.co.jp**). You see

```
ns.yzw.co.jp resolves to 210.226.145.162
3Cust198.tnt12.dfw5.da.uu.net resolves to 63.44.238.198
Error - billclinton.whitehouse.gov doesn't exist
```

Because nslookup can find those first two IP addresses, and they seem to be the same as the names indicated in the headers, you can be fairly confident that they're accurately represented. If you see a discrepancy, try plugging in the number to see whether nslookup can find a name. This process of putting in a number and getting a name and then putting in a name and getting a number is referred to as *forward* and *reverse* look-ups. When in doubt, we usually trust numbers over names because the same server may sometimes answer to many names.

Because the last address appears to be fake, the trail of verifiable mail handlers ends with the UUNet address at 3Cust198.tnt12.dfw5.da.uu.net.

Step 4: Investigate the Contents of the Spam

You should remember that you don't want to just stop spammers at the source — you also want to shut down the spammer's operation that is being advertised in the spam. Otherwise, the spammer just moves to some other ISP and keeps on spamming. You're aided in this effort by the fact that most ISPs forbid their customers to spam — from anywhere — to advertise activities hosted on their network. Thus, even if a spammer is using a UUNet dial-up to send out spam advertising a Web site being hosted by someone else, both UUNet and the site hosting the Web site may give the spammer the boot. So you should look in the text of the spam message for any identifiable information or clues, such as an e-mail address or a Web address.

Suppose that the spammer's message contains the following text:

```
FREE SATELLITE T.V. SYSTEM!!!
Watch over 500 channels of Digital Broadcast quality
           television on your own FREE satellite television
           system. For a limited time we'll give you this top
           of the line Digital Satellite System for FREE!
We'll even include Free installation and 3 FREE months of all
           the movie channels!

Just e-mail freesat034@yahoo.com, or visit our Web site at
http://3286560814/satellite-tv/specialoffer.html.
```

In this example, the spammer is using a maildrop at Yahoo.com and is hosting a Web site. (A *maildrop* is the e-mail equivalent of a post office box: It's easy to set up and provides a good bit of anonymity if trouble arises.) But the Web page address looks a little strange. The domain name isn't the usual www, and it's not an IP address in the form you would recognize from your research, as just shown. In this case, the spammer is using an obscure trick to mask the IP address. (See the sidebar "An explanation of the 255 rule," earlier in this chapter, if you want to know more.) Luckily, most nslookup tools can see right through the subterfuge: Plugging 3286560814 into the nslookup tool at www.his.com/cgi-bin/nslookup tells you that it translates into

```
Name:     business.matav.hu
Address:  195.228.240.46
```

Step 5: Get Ready to Address Your Complaints

After you've identified all the sites the spam is coming from, it's time to figure out how and where to file complaints. Luckily, if you look carefully on the Web site for many ISPs, you often find information about their *terms of service,* or the rules by which all their subscribers agree to abide. In many cases, ISPs prohibit any form of spam-related activity that they can think of and even give you an address for filing complaints.

TECHNICAL STUFF

Do-it-yourself IP address deciphering

So you want to be a Sherlock Holmes or Mike Hammer and find out how to track down the owner of the spam Web site or IP address yourself? There's really not much to it, thanks to some handy Web-based tools, available for free over the Internet. Here's how to do it:

Browse to www.geektools.com and plug the IP address into the whois tool. (No, we're not kidding about the name, and the tool does exactly as its name implies: It tells you "whois" responsible for the IP address.)

When you plug 3286560814 into whois, you get a long listing, part of which includes this information:

```
Name:      business.matav.hu
Address:   195.228.240.46


inetnum:    195.228.240.0 - 195.228.240.255
netname:    MATAVNET-SER
descr:      MatavNet Ltd.
descr:      Hungarian Telecom
country:    HU
admin-c:    IV32-RIPE
tech-c:     MH4239-RIPE
rev-srv:    ns0.matav.hu
rev-srv:    ns1.matav.hu
status:     ASSIGNED PA
changed:    irina@mail.matav.hu 19990823
source:     RIPE
```

What all this means is that the contact point for that IP address is an administrator at Hungarian Telecom. Although you can send your complaint to that person, you probably should try the abuse and postmaster addresses first. You don't want to send complaints to the administrator's personal mailbox unless you have to.

If the whois doesn't like the spammer-obscured URL, you may need to use the nslookup or traceroute programs to convert the 3286560814 into 195.228.240.46 and then try plugging the regular IP address back into whois.

The most common complaint address is abuse@this-darn-spammers-ISP.com. Indeed, most respectable ISPs maintain an abuse address for their domains. In some cases, however, you may have to use a fallback address:

postmaster. Although not every ISP is bright enough to operate an abuse address, Internet e-mail protocols require that any entity providing mail service for a domain maintain a functioning postmaster account and that the account be read regularly by a human being. Therefore, your default complaint addresses usually are abuse@ or postmaster@ at the domain in question.

This method is really hit-or-miss, though, because the domain names aren't always where mail for those domains is supposed to be sent. For example, the administrators of UUNet like to receive their complaint e-mails not at UUNet.com or UUNet.org or UUNet.net, but rather at uu.net.

In truth, the best way to find the right address to send your spam complaint is to sign up for our very own John Levine's Abuse.net forwarding service. (Don't worry: It's free!) The service forwards along your complaint for you. After you sign up for Abuse.net, you just address your complaint to the domain name shown in the spam (for example, 3CUST198.TNT12.DFW5.DA.UU.NET) and add @abuse.net at the end, and Abuse.net figures out the rest. How does it do that? It tries mixing and matching different parts of the domain and then looks them up in a big database that John maintains when he should be writing books. So your complaint to UUNet is addressed to

```
3CUST198.TNT12.DFW5.DA.UU.NET@abuse.net
```

Alternatively, visit www.abuse.net/lookup.phtml to see what addresses abuse.net recommends for any domain of interest. (No registration needed.)

If you don't use Abuse.net, your complaint addresses are likely to be

```
postmaster@yzw.co.jp or abuse@yzw.co.jp
abuse@uu.net
abuse@yahoo.com
abuse@matav.hu or postmaster@matav.hu
```

If you do use Abuse.net, your complaint addresses are

```
ns.yzw.co.jp@abuse.net
3cust198.tnt12.dfw5.da.uu.net@abuse.net
yahoo.com@abuse.net
business.matav.hu@abuse.net
```

Step 6: Send Your Complaints — Nicely

Don't transfer your anger at a spammer to the ISP. In most cases, it's just as angry about the spammer as you are, and although it's pleased to receive your complaint so that it can justify booting the spammer off the network, the spam really isn't the ISP's fault. Just state your case plainly. Here's a good example:

```
I received a piece of spam that I have attached below. The
         headers appear to have originated at UUNet, been
         relayed via ns.yzw.co.jp, and advertise a mailbox
         at yahoo.com and a Web page at business.matav.hu.
         Please take appropriate action to stop this
         spammer. Thanks.
```

Make sure that you attach a complete copy of the spam, including all the headers just as you received them. The ISP will want to do its own investigation and, without the headers, won't have anything concrete to work with. If you're using e-mail software that allows you to send e-mail using HTML or RTF formatting (bold or colored text or embedded pictures, for example), turn those options off and send your message in plain text because those formatting features can make it difficult to read the headers and contents of the spam.

Step 7: Wait for Responses

If your research is good and you were able to locate the correct addresses for filing complaints, you probably will receive confirmations from some ISPs, stating that they received your mail and that they will take action. Don't be surprised if you don't receive anything more than this initial acknowledgement, however. Most abuse departments are overworked and understaffed; in the time it would take them to send you a personal note to thank you and pat you on the back and let you know what became of your complaint, they could have killed a few more spammer accounts.

Signing up for Abuse.net service

You can use abuse.net in two different ways: Ask it to forward your mail to the appropriate place or ask it what the appropriate place is and mail it yourself.

The second way is easier: Point your browser at www.abuse.net/lookup.phtml, type the domain in the box on that page, and click the Lookup button. You see the list of addresses to use.

To use the mail forwarder, you have to register first. To do that, send a blank message to new@abuse.net. You should shortly get back a confirmation with the abuse.net terms of service. Read the terms, and if you agree to them (mostly, you agree not to use abuse.net to harass people), follow the instructions in that message to send back a message indicating your agreement. After you've done that, you can just send your complaint to addresses like example.com@abuse.net, and it automatically forwards the message as best it can.

Don't fight spam with spam

One of the most common tricks spammers use to hide their whereabouts is to relay their messages off the mail server of an innocent third party. This tactic *doubles* the damages because now both the receiving system and the innocent relay system are flooded with junk e-mail. For any mail that gets through, many times the flood of complaints goes back to the innocent site because it was made to look like the origin of the spam. Another common trick is to forge the headers of messages, making it appear as though the message originated elsewhere, again providing a convenient target on whom the anger of recipients and the flood of complaints will land. This is why we point out this information to you: If an ISP claims innocence, don't fight back with more complaints. It really may be innocent.

Likewise, don't be surprised if some of your complaints bounce back to you as undeliverable. With all due respect to the many fine network administrators around the world, it's not at all uncommon for non-U.S. ISPs and corporations to be completely ill prepared to deal with spammers and to even be poorly informed about basic Internet protocols, such as the one requiring the postmaster@ address. You should give them the benefit of the doubt, but you may need to try some whois inquiries to see whether you can locate additional addresses to which complaints can be sent. Meanwhile, many countries that are relatively new to the Internet are lousy when it comes to cleaning up messes caused by spammers. Unfortunately, spammers know this information, so they like to relay their spam off sites in countries like Japan, China, Korea, and India and in Central Europe.

Step 8: When Complaints Bounce Back, Go Upstream

If your complaints are bouncing back and the spam is still flowing, it's time to play hardball. Sometimes, ISPs aren't as enlightened about the problems created by spammers, but the good news is that the company that sells the ISP its Internet connection is probably a bit more spam-savvy. Suppose that your Hungarian friends in the preceding sections haven't clamped down on the spammers and your complaints are falling on deaf ears. That's okay, though, because when data travels from one computer to another on the Internet, the bits of data follow a path, hopping from computer to computer between the origin and the destination. So you can use another tool in your Internet toolkit, traceroute, to find out where the spammer is getting his Internet connection.

You can use traceroute by surfing to `www.geektools.com`. When you choose traceroute, you're presented with a long list of traceroute sites, which is good because by tracing from different places around the world, you can get a more accurate picture of who a site's upstream provider is. If you use the traceroute site at `www.tracert.com/cgi-bin/trace.pl`, it lets you automatically select several places around the world to trace from. Running a trace on `195.228.240.46` yields variations on the following output:

```
traceroute to business.matav.hu (195.228.240.46): 1-30 hops,
       38 byte packets
 1  main1-main2-eth.sjc1.above.net (207.126.96.189)
       0.502/0.560/0.709 (0.56) ms   10/10 pkts (0% loss)
 2  core5-main.sjc.above.net (209.133.31.153)
       0.521/0.654/0.923 (0.131) ms   10/10 pkts (0% loss)
 3  pao-sjc-oc12-2.pao.above.net (207.126.96.65)
       0.961/1.14/1.61 (0.179) ms   10/10 pkts (0% loss)
 4  teleglobe-above-oc12.pao.teleglobe.net (216.200.0.90)
       0.968/1.5/1.38 (0.119) ms   10/10 pkts (0% loss)
 5  if-9-2.core1.LosAngeles.Teleglobe.net (207.45.222.230)
       9.23/9.40/9.59 (0.109) ms   10/10 pkts (0% loss)
 6  if-10-1.core1.NewYork.Teleglobe.net (207.45.222.137)
       89.4/89.6/89.9 (0.138) ms   10/10 pkts (0% loss)
 7  if-7-2.core1.Montreal.Teleglobe.net (64.86.80.25)
       96.6/96.8/97.1 (0.168) ms   10/10 pkts (0% loss)
 8  if-2-2.core1.PennantPoint.Teleglobe.net (207.45.222.82)
       109/109/110 (0.227) ms   10/10 pkts (0% loss)
 9  if-0-0-0.bb3.PennantPoint.Teleglobe.net (207.45.222.78)
       109/109/110 (0.145) ms   10/10 pkts (0% loss)
10  ix-4-0-1.bb3.PennantPoint.Teleglobe.net (207.45.216.18)
       190/191/192 (0.576) ms   10/10 pkts (0% loss)
11  a8-0-0-7.core1.matav.net (145.236.244.18)   191/192/193
       (0.363) ms   10/10 pkts (0% loss)
12  a2-0-3.phobos.matavnet.hu (145.236.250.238)   193/194/195
       (0.776) ms   10/10 pkts (0% loss)
13  195.228.240.6 (195.228.240.6)  *  *  *  *  *   192/193/194
       (0.479) ms   5/10 pkts (50% loss)
```

Because you're tracing from different places, they all start out differently; but in the end, they all seem to go through the same place: a sequence of machines at Teleglobe.net. This information seems to indicate that matavnet.hu is connected through Teleglobe.net. You have no guarantee, but it's a good bet that a complaint to Teleglobe.net may get to someone who knows how to crack some heads at matavnet.hu.

Step 9: If It's Still Not Working, Send Your Spammer to the Black Hole

If none of the steps in the preceding sections has achieved a satisfactory result, you should gather up copies of the original spam, each complaint you've filed, and any responses received and submit them to the Mail Abuse Prevention System (MAPS) at www.mail-abuse.org. Follow the instructions for submissions for the Realtime Blackhole List (RBL). The MAPS RBL is a listing of sites known to send spam or to give aid and comfort to spammers. The list is used by many ISPs, which automatically block all e-mail coming from those sites. When rogue ISPs realize that every piece of their e-mail is being rejected by those ISPs, they tend to realize that spam isn't as good a thing as they first thought, and they get busy fixing the problem more rapidly.

Step 10: When All Else Fails, Tell It to Your ISP

If nothing else is working, you should send documentation of your efforts to your ISP and ask it to block the spamming sites at their routers. If the ISP isn't responsive, take your business to an ISP that is prepared to give you the service you deserve.

Chapter 21

Ten Reliable Sources for Computer Virus Information

In This Chapter

▶ Where to get current virus news
▶ How to debunk virus hoaxes
▶ Where to buy reliable antivirus software

---

*T*he mere fact that you are reading this chapter tells us that you probably already have a problem — a virus problem.

Before you read on, memorize a few simple rules that are bound to be helpful — as preventive medicine *before it happens again*.

Always use antivirus software, and always keep it updated. The McAfee and Norton sites mentioned in this chapter will help.

Be wary of attachments. At the time this book was written, it was impossible to get a virus unless you opened the attachment, so don't open attachments from strangers. Make sure that your antivirus software scans all attachments before you open them — even ones from friends.

Be wary of mass hysteria. Virus warnings that show up as chain letters ("Forward this to all your friends") are almost always hoaxes. If you react to a warning e-mail as the person before you did — you send the e-mail to 250 of your closest friends — you're contributing to a massive misinformation campaign that causes panic and slows the Internet down for everyone.

What's the right thing to do? Go back to the first two points.

Viruses target mostly Microsoft software, particularly Outlook and Outlook Express. If you use a different e-mail program in Windows, such as Eudora or Pegasus, most e-mail viruses don't bother you. If you run a Mac, you're even safer because few Mac viruses circulate these days. If you run Unix or Linux, you're almost completely safe because almost no Linux viruses exist, and the design of Unix and Linux limits the damage a virus can do even if one should ever show up in your e-mail.

General Information about Viruses

These are some of our favorite sources of virus information.

About.com antivirus information

```
antivirus.about.com
```

This excellent collection of information from many sources is a good one-stop shop for antivirus information, although it's not as quickly updated as some of the software vendor sites.

F-Secure Security Information Center

```
www.f-secure.com/virus-info
```

One of many antivirus and security-oriented software manufacturers, F-Secure also has one of the best publicly accessible databases of virus information. If you're curious about how the nasty critters do their dirty work, this is one of the best places to go to find out.

TechTV cybercrime news

```
www.techtv.com/cybercrime
```

TechTV, shown on many digital cable networks, has a show as well as an extensive Web site, chronicling events in information security, privacy, and cybercrime.

The TrendMicro top ten virus alerts

```
www.antivirus.com/vinfo
```

Another manufacturer of antivirus software, Trend Micro has a popular listing of the top ten threats to computer users. You may be surprised to see what old viruses are still rearing their ugly heads!

Computer Incident Advisory Center (CIAC)

```
www.ciac.org/ciac
```

Part of the U.S. Department of Energy (the people who try to keep America's nuclear secrets), these are the guys and gals who stay on top of security threats to the U.S. government's computers. If a security threat is real, they know the solution probably before you even know that a problem is out there. When CIAC issues an alert, the computing world sits up and takes notice.

"How Do I Know Whether This Virus Warning Is a Hoax?"

Unfortunately, the world has at least as many virus hoaxes as real viruses. Here are some sources to check so that you can know the difference.

The About.com virus hoax encyclopedia

```
antivirus.about.com/library/blenhoax.htm
```

If it's a hoax, urban legend, or a tall tale of cyberspace, you can find it listed — and debunked — here.

The CIAC HoaxBusters

```
hoaxbusters.ciac.org/
```

To help keep people focused on real threats, the people at CIAC also keep tabs on bogus threats.

Where to Buy or Update Your Antivirus Software

Many brands of antivirus software are on the market. This section describes the two most popular and reliable.

McAfee.com Dispatch

```
dispatch.mcafee.com
```

Users of the popular McAfee VirusScan software can keep tabs on new viruses and get updates to their software from the Dispatch Web site.

Symantec Norton AntiVirus Center

```
www.sarc.com
```

Users of the popular Norton AntiVirus software can keep up-to-date with the latest virus news and software updates for the whole suite of Norton security products.

Chapter 22

Ten Great Privacy Books (Other than This One!)

In This Chapter

▶ Great books for finding out more about privacy issues

▶ A great privacy newsletter

o paraphrase William Shatner's ads for Priceline.com, "Privacy is big — really big."

Privacy is so big, in fact, that, try as we might, we couldn't fit into this book everything you need to know about it. So, until we write *More Internet Privacy For Dummies*, (hey, publisher, are you reading this?), here are ten — plus a few more — books that can help you find out all you can about taking control of your privacy.

The Privacy Rights Handbook: How to Take Control of Your Personal Information

(Written by Beth Givens and the Privacy Rights Clearinghouse; Avon Books; ISBN: 0380786842.) This book is a true handbook indeed, chock-full of everything you ever wanted or needed to know about how to protect your privacy. The handbook includes information about your personal security and your rights against telemarketers, credit card companies, and government agencies. It's hard to find, but it's worth the search.

Ben Franklin's Web Site: Privacy and Curiosity from Plymouth Rock to the Internet

(Written by Robert Ellis Smith; *Privacy Journal;* ISBN: 0930072146.) If you thought that privacy is a new issue, Robert Ellis Smith shows that it has been a topic of heated, and sometimes hilarious, debate since before America was founded. Smith, the publisher of the highly respected publication *Privacy Journal,* clearly loves the topic of privacy and has assembled a truly amazing collection of real-life privacy tales.

The Unwanted Gaze: The Destruction of Privacy in America

(Written by Jeffrey Rosen; Random House; ISBN: 0679445463.) The journalist, author, and law professor Jeffrey Rosen looks at recent events through the skeptical eye of a privacy advocate and finds much that is troubling. He spends a great deal of time looking at how laws relating to sexual harassment are being used to pry into the personal lives of both victims and the accused, including a famous President of the United States, and why we should all be concerned about the consequences.

How to Be Invisible: A Step-By-Step Guide to Protecting Your Assets, Your Identity, and Your Life

(Written by J. J. Luna; St. Martin's Press; ISBN: 0312252501.) This book is for the seriously privacy-minded. Some suggestions sound like they border on the illegal, but the author (that's not his real name, of course), points out that you have lots of compelling — and completely legal — reasons for vigorously protecting your privacy. In fact, his step-by-step instructions for setting up ghost mailing addresses, owning property through shell corporations, and always avoiding using your Social Security number won't help you if you're trying to do things that are illegal. Rather, they're designed for protecting your privacy from those who don't have a legal right to know, such as stalkers or private investigators. Alas, some recommendations require a serious commitment to your personal privacy and may require changes in your lifestyle (such as moving to a new home to confuse junk mailers and telemarketers), but his methods are solid and legal, and many of them can be integrated into your life without a great deal of difficulty.

Protect Your Digital Privacy: Survival Skills for the Information Age

(Written by Glee Harrah Cady and Pat McGregor; Que; ISBN: 0789726041.) Few people are more widely respected in the technology policy arena than Glee Cady, and her co-author is a leading expert on computer security. This book has collected articles about privacy issues and includes instructions on how to keep the privacy invaders at bay. The book includes useful tips for parents on how to protect children online, including some good ways to teach your kids to value their privacy. It also has lots of detailed information about the current state of privacy laws and regulations.

Your Secrets Are My Business

(Written by Kevin McKeown with Dave Stern; Longstreet Press; ISBN: 1563525771.) As entertaining as it is frightening, this book (subtitled *A Security Expert Reveals How Your Trash, License Plate, Credit Cards, Computer, and Even Your Mail Make You an Easy Target for Today's Information Thieves*) uses stories from the author's own work as a security expert to both educate and amuse, and we guarantee that you will never look at your garbage can, your telephone, or the backseat of your car in the same way again!

The Right to Privacy

(Written by Ellen Alderman and Caroline Kennedy; Vintage Books; ISBN: 0679744347.) Few people are more qualified than members of the Kennedy family to talk about the toll that having little privacy takes on your life. Several landmark court cases about protecting personal privacy from the prying eyes of the paparazzi involved Caroline Kennedy's mother, Jacqueline Kennedy Onassis. This book presents the history of privacy rights through a readable, interesting, and sometimes shocking retelling of important stories in privacy.

Database Nation: The Death of Privacy in the 21st Century

(Written by Simson Garfinkel and Deborah Russell; O'Reilly & Associates; ISBN: 0596001053.) The computer security expert and prolific author Simson Garfinkel has collected his own list of threats to personal privacy. Central to each one is the ability of governments and privacy corporations to gather more and more data about citizens and to use it for purposes both legitimate and illegitimate. He casts a critical eye over technologies like biometrics (using your body for identification, like fingerprints and retinal scans), pervasive video monitoring, and traditional techniques, like data mining. Although the book is short on solutions, Garfinkel details the threats using examples that make some complex technologies easily understood by the lay reader.

Technology and Privacy: The New Landscape

(Edited by Philip E. Agre and Marc Rotenberg; MIT Press; ISBN: 0262511010.) In this scholarly collection of articles and essays about the interaction of privacy and technology, Agre and Rotenberg, noted scholars of privacy and technology, have drawn on many sources to give readers a sampling of the state-of-the-art in technologies that invade and enhance privacy.

Privacy for Sale: How Big Brother and Others Are Selling Your Private Secrets for Profit

(Written by Michael Chesbro; Paladin Press; ISBN: 158160033X.) The author, who claims to be a former intelligence agent (which we can neither confirm nor deny), has assembled an impressive, if sometimes a bit scary, collection of stories and examples of the ways in which your private information is being used for fun and profit by almost anyone. He provides many good suggestions on protecting yourself from data thieves, but you may not want to read this book when you're home alone, lest you spend the rest of the night peering out the windows and looking for data thieves crawling around in your bushes!

Privacy in the Information Age

(Written by Fred H. Cate and Michael H. Armacost; Brookings Institute; ISBN: 0815713150.) This book takes a procorporate view of privacy. Professor Cate is well known as an advocate for the wider use of personal information by companies. This book, as well as many scholarly studies by Cate, point out that stronger privacy laws can have negative consequences for consumers by driving up marketing costs and increasing prices. Moreover, if advertisers don't know more about you, he suggests, you will have to sit through more irrelevant advertisements than you would if they could target only ads that are of interest to you. Many of the claims in this book send privacy advocates into a tizzy, but they're an important part of the debate.

The Transparent Society: Will Technology Force You to Choose Between Privacy and Freedom?

(Written by David Brin; Perseus Press; ISBN: 0738201448.) Brin is an award-winning science fiction author who has turned his creative mind to the question of whether a society with absolutely no privacy would really be as bad as you might think. Brin argues that no privacy for anyone means that everyone will have to think about themselves and everyone else in very different ways. His legal and policy analysis is a bit weak, but the scenes of life in this type of world make this book a fascinating read that will keep you thinking about these issues long after you've put the book down.

The monthly news

Robert Ellis Smith's *Privacy Journal* (www. privacyjournal.com), now in its 28th year, is a monthly newsletter of developments in privacy law and policy. Both Smith and the *Journal* have cut a formidable presence in the privacy policy community, and Smith is also the author of several books detailing privacy laws in the United States. *Privacy Journal* is required reading for anyone who regularly deals with privacy issues.

Index

Notes

Notes

Notes